Charleston and the Great Depression

Charleston and the Great Depression

A Documentary History, 1929–1941

EDITED BY
Kieran W. Taylor

© 2018 University of South Carolina

Published by the University of South Carolina Press
Columbia, South Carolina 29208

www.sc.edu/uscpress

Manufactured in the United States of America

27 26 25 24 23 22 21 20 19 18
10 9 8 7 6 5 4 3 2 1

Library of Congress Cataloging-in-Publication Data
can be found at http://catalog.loc.gov/.

ISBN 978-1-61117-864-7 (cloth)
ISBN 978-1-61117-865-4 (ebook)

Contents

Acknowledgments *ix*
Editorial Principles and Practices *xi*
Chronology *xiii*
Introduction *xix*

1930

Fong Lee Wong to Laura Bragg, 4 March 1930 *1*
Eleanor Loeb Halsey, "Narrative Report,"
Charleston County Tuberculosis Association, August 1930 *3*

1931

The State of South Carolina v. Ray Laurens, 12 October 1931 *9*
Burnet R. Maybank, Inaugural Address, 14 December 1931 *13*

1932

The City Council of Charleston, Minutes, 26 January 1932 *29*
Ella L. Smyrl to Cordella A. Winn, 26 January 1932 *33*
William McKinley Bowman to Franklin D. Roosevelt,
25 November 1932 *36*

1933–1934

Burnet R. Maybank to John L. M. Irby, 25 September 1933 *39*
John L. M. Irby to Burnet R. Maybank, 25 September 1933 *40*
Lorena A. Hickok to Harry L. Hopkins, 10 February 1934 *41*

1935

Norma Mazo, *Payday*, 1935 47

Benjamin F. Cox, Avery Institute, Annual Report, August 1935 48

Franklin D. Roosevelt to Clergy, 24 September 1935 50

A. D. Prentiss to Franklin D. Roosevelt, 27 September 1935 51

DuBose Heyward, "Porgy and Bess Return on Wings of Song," October 1935 52

Elijah J. Curry to Franklin D. Roosevelt, 5 October 1935 58

Franklin D. Roosevelt, Remarks at the Citadel: The Military College of South Carolina, 23 October 1935 59

1936

H. P. Lovecraft to Herman Charles Koenig, 12 January 1936 63

Walker Evans, *19th Century Shop-Front, Charleston, S.C.*, March 1936 85

Allen Jones Jr., Diary, 6 March 1936 86

The State v. Benjamin J. Rivers, 25 September 1936 89

1937

John L. M. Irby to William Watts Ball, 26 May 1937 119

Susan Calder Hamilton, Interview by Augustus Ladson, May–June 1937 121

Susan Calder Hamilton, Interview by Jessie A. Butler, 6 July 1937 125

Susan Calder Hamilton, Interview by Jessie A. Butler, November 1937 129

Program, *The Recruiting Officer*, Dock Street Theatre Dedication, 26 November 1937 131

1938–1940

Photographs from the Charleston Tornadoes, September 1938 135

Marion Post Wolcott, *Negro Home near Charleston, South Carolina*, December 1938 138

Marion Post Wolcott, *The Cook on a Fishing Boat in Charleston, South Carolina, Peeling Potatoes for Christmas Dinner*, 25 December 1938 139

Ruby and John Lomax, Field Notes, 6–8 June 1939 140

Box Score, Columbus Red Birds vs. Charleston Rebels, 24 July 1940 142

1941

Leon Banov to Burnet R. Maybank, 15 November 1941 *147*

Elizabeth Maybank to Joseph Maybank, 14 December 1941 *150*

Memories of the Great Depression, 1996–2012

Gordan B. Stine, Interview by Dale Rosengarten, 19 February 1996 *153*

Abe Dumas, Interview by Michael Grossman, 14 December 1996 *154*

Shera Lee Ellison Berlin, Interview by Dale Rosengarten and Michael Grossman, 16 April 1997 *156*

William F. Ladson, Interview by Kieran W. Taylor, 13 May 2009 *158*

Anne Marie Gilliard, Interview by Clarissa D. Brown, 2 October 2011 *158*

Virginia Bonnette, Interview by Virginia Ellison and Kieran W. Taylor, 15 March 2012 *160*

Henry W. Fleming, Interview by Danielle Lightner, 17 March 2012 *161*

Herman Stramm, Interview by Luke Yoder, 19 March 2012 *162*

Index *165*

Acknowledgments

This volume is the product of a collaborative research project that began in two sections of "Introduction to the Discipline of History," an undergraduate class that I taught at the Citadel in the fall of 2014. I designed the course assignments to provide students with the opportunity to work on a large, publishable historical research project. After selecting primary materials for the collection, I assigned each student one or two documents, which they transcribed, researched, and annotated. The course required both group work and intensive one-on-one tutorials, during which we discussed standard transcription practices, editorial principles, research methods, and historical writing. I wanted the students to learn the discipline of history through the practice of history. I chose "Charleston and Great Depression" as the project theme because of the lack of historical writing on the period and the easy accessibilty of local source material. I also did so as a political intervention. My idea was to expose my students to a period in U.S. history that would be both familiar and unfamiliar to them. The students have ideas about the Great Depression that are a part of our shared national memory. They may have even heard firsthand stories of the 1930s from grandparents or great-grandparents. Like their grandparents and great-grandparents, my students have lived through a period of tremendous economic upheaval and considerable hardship—the recession of 2008–2009 and its aftermath—and they continue to face an uncertain job market and troubling economic trends that include an unsustainable gap between the rich and poor. Unlike their elders, however, they live in a period of widespread cynicism regarding government and the political system. Despite their many differences and disagreements, the vast majority of Americans subscribed to Franklin D. Roosevelt's New Deal. They believed in the idea that government power could and should be used to improve people's lives. I wanted to immerse my students in those more hopeful politics of the 1930s, a period in which Americans believed that politics should serve as an expression of the commonweal. How successful was my intervention? I do not know. It will be up to them to draw their own lessons from the Great Depression. I do know that the following women and men were excellent colleagues—hard working, cooperative, and patient: Preston Abernathy, Ryan Abts, Tjark Aldeborgh, Michael Bell, Sean Brennan, William Brown, Sophie-Leigh Clark, Gregory Copplin, William Denman, Taylor Evans, Ra'Shaud Graham, Logan Higaki, Thomas Jordan,

Anthony Kniffin, Dillon Luedtke, Derek Massey, William Maxwell, Joshua Park, Frost Parker, Monica Paulk, John Pferdmenges, Colin Poppert, William Richardson, Landon Rohrer, Matthew Russell, Joshua Scaife, Megan Sowell, Daniel Trimnal, Joseph Vicci, Maureen Wilkinson, and Justine Zukowski. They all made significant editorial contributions to this volume.

Additionally, several graduate assistants verified transcriptions and followed up on many vague research leads that I provided them. They include Orianna Baham, John Clark, and Matt Carroll, who also enlisted the help of Amanda Graves Carroll. The smart and unflappable Ariel Washington was a model research assistant in the earliest phases of this project. I look forward to working with her again when she finishes her doctoral studies in Chapel Hill.

The following Charleston-area archivists were very generous in helping me locate relevant documents, providing necessary publication permissions, and responding to my research queries: Barrye Brown, Karen Emmons, Mary Jo Fairchild, David Goble, Kathleen Gray, Harlan Greene, Susan Hoffius, Meg Moughan, Elaine Robbins, Dale Rosengarten, Rebecca Schultz, Aaron Spelbring, and Deborah Turkewitz. We are spoiled to have a group of such knowledgeable and generous archivists here in Charleston. I also relied on the generosity of a number of historians in producing the introduction and annotations. On short notice, Bruce Baker, Stephen Hoffius, and Bo Moore offered valuable feedback on the introduction; and several other scholars drew on their expertise to offer guidance on various aspects of the manuscript. They include Tenisha Armstrong, Clarissa Brown, Rachel Donaldson, Erik Gellman, S. T. Joshi, Keith Knapp, Alex Moore, and John Sacca. The Citadel Foundation has provided excellent research support for this project and all of my research efforts, as has the Department of History.

Finally, personal thanks are in order to colleagues and friends who have overlooked my neglect of various professional and community-organizing responsibilities, especially in this last month or two of manuscript preparation. They include Marina Lopez, Christine Nelson, and Leonard Riley Jr.. Kimberly Clifton has been similarly tolerant on the home front, and for her patience, love, and support I will always be grateful.

Editorial Principles and Practices

Each document selected for publication in this volume provides a window into events and themes related to life in Charleston in the 1930s. Their inclusion is intended to spotlight the rich body of primary source material available to scholars of the region's history and to encourage further study in related subject areas. The documents include correspondence, speech transcripts, photographs, artwork, oral histories, organizational reports, diaries, newspaper items, magazine articles, and court documents. Many of the themes they address will be familiar to students of the Great Depression, including stories of human suffering, public health challenges, and various New Deal initiatives. But there is much here that will be less familiar, even to specialists in local history.

A title, date, and place of origin introduce each document. The existing titles of documents are used when available and are designated by quotation marks or italics. For documents that are untitled in their original form, I have created descriptive titles that reflect their content (for example, "Burnet R. Maybank to John L. M. Irby"). When the date or place was not specified on the document but has been determined through research, it is enclosed in square brackets. In some instances, a date range is given when a specific date was not available.

The annotations are intended to enhance the reader's understanding of the documents. Headnotes provide context for each document's creation; a brief summary may also be included for longer documents. Headnotes and editorial endnotes identify individuals, organizations, events, literary quotations, and other references in the source document. The annotations may also refer the reader to relevant correspondence and other related documents. The source note at the end of each document provides information regarding the characteristics of the original document as well as its provenance. The manuscript or archival collection from which each original document was obtained is also listed.

The transcriptions are intended to reproduce the source document accurately and, with minor exceptions (such as substituting dashes for hyphens where the former were clearly intended), adhere to the exact wording and punctuation of the original. Spelling, punctuation, and grammatical errors are retained. They are not corrected or indicated by *"sic."* Capitalization, boldface, abbreviations, hyphenation, strikeouts, ellipses, and symbols are likewise replicated. Some formatting practices such as outlining, underlining, paragraph indentation, and spacing between words or lines of text have been regularized for readability. The internal address, salutation, and complimentary closing of a letter have been reproduced left-aligned, regardless of the original format. Editorial explanations are provided in italics and enclosed by square brackets. Conjectural renderings of text are followed by a question mark and placed within brackets: for example, "[There's?]." Illegible text is indicated by such notations as "[strikeout illegible]" or "[word illegible]."

Chronology

1929

24–29 October	The Wall Street stock market crash signals the start of a ten-year economic depression.

1930

1 January	Mayor Thomas P. Stoney predicts a prosperous year. The annual Emancipation Day parade features five black veterans of the world war.
16 February	President Herbert Hoover, en route to Washington, greets motorists from his train car in North Charleston.
8 May	WCSC, Charleston's first radio station, begins broadcasting.
2 July	Charleston police collect more than $29,000 in fines for the first six months of the year, the bulk of which are related to Prohibition violations.
22 August	The announcement of the probable closing of the Navy Yard prompts a response from Congressman Thomas S. McMillan and other area officials.
9 September	The U.S. Census Bureau reports that the number of farms in Charleston County decreased by 49 percent over the past decade.
5 December	A ten-member mosquito-fleet fishing crew is rescued after being missing for four days.

1931

5 February	Nineteen Charleston women's organizations pass a resolution condemning lynching.
28 February	A riot follows the basketball game between the Citadel and the College of Charleston.
24 May	Eleven-year-old Thomas Joseph Carner is killed by a passing train while riding his pony near Chicora Place.
6 October	Burnet Rhett Maybank wins the Democratic Party nomination for mayor over Lawrence M. Pinckney. He faces no challenger in the general election two months later.

15 October	In U.S. District Court, O. B. Limehouse and A. R. Johnston of Dorchester County are acquitted of charges of peonage.
1 November	The City of Charleston fails to meet its payroll.
17 November	Aviator Amelia Earhart visits Charleston.
22 December	The city council offers taxpayers a discount for paying taxes in advance.
31 December	Coroner John P. DeVeaux attributes a spike in sudden or questionable deaths to the Depression.

1932

1 January	People's State Bank fails and closes its doors permanently.
22 January	Six hundred fifty employees at the Navy Yard donate $6,500 toward unemployment relief.
10 March	Braving severe cold, seven hundred people stand in line to register for work relief as the city opens an employment bureau.
23 April	Charleston teachers' pay is cut 12.5 percent as a cost-cutting measure.
16 June	Three thousand African American women stand in line for donations of flour from the Red Cross.
2 July	On the final day of the Democratic National Convention at Chicago Stadium, Franklin D. Roosevelt accepts the nomination for president.
28 July	The U.S. Army clears the "Bonus Army" protest camps in Washington, D.C.
8 November	Charleston celebrates as Roosevelt defeats Herbert Hoover by a landslide to become the thirty-seventh president.
30 November	Smoke covers the city as air pressure prevents the escape of vapors from chimneys.

1933

12 February	Homeless people seeking shelter set thirteen Southern Railway boxcars on fire at the Gulf Refining Company.
4 March	Roosevelt is inaugurated as president of the United States of America.
6 March	Four thousand relief workers are laid off following the president's announcement of a bank moratorium. Maybank pledges that no one will starve.
7 April	The U.S. Congress repeals Prohibition.
7 August	Public safety officials restrain an angry crowd of two thousand job seekers who gather at 149 East Bay Street to

	apply for relief work. A socialist organizer, who is allegedly agitating the crowd, is asked to leave the vicinity.
30 August	Charleston holds the largest parade and mass demonstration in its history in support of the National Recovery Administration's "Blue Eagle" campaign.
19 October	Two carloads of pork provided by the federal government arrive for distribution to the poor.
1 December	Police place seals on thirty automobiles as part of a drive targeting four thousand delinquent taxpayers.
2 December	The city announces the construction of a yacht basin to be built under the authority of the Civil Works Administration.
8 December	The Navy Yard is awarded construction contracts for three coast guard tugs.

1934

16 March	A parade down King Street opens Charleston's first annual Azalea Festival.
6 September	During the three-week national strike of textile workers, guards at Chiquola Mill in Honea Path kill seven strikers as they flee from a picket line.
16 October	Evangelist Jimmy Hamill declares war on the devil at Chicora.
12 November	"Human fly" Johnny Wood climbs the Francis Marion Hotel.
29 November	Federal Emergency Relief Administration director Harry L. Hopkins visits Charleston to inspect relief work.
11 December	A Federal Emergency Relief Administration–sponsored cannery to put the unemployed to work opens in Charleston.

1935

7 January	Charleston's municipal incinerator begins operations.
12 February	Ground is broken for the Planters Hotel and Dock Street Theatre restoration project.
16 July	Pete, the Hampton Park swan, dies after thirty years on the pond.
12 August	The Public Works Administration grants Charleston $94,400 for a waterworks project.
26 September	Charleston receives a $1.1 million federal grant for the clearance of African American neighborhoods.
10 October	DuBose Heyward and George Gershwin's *Porgy and Bess* opens on Broadway at New York's Alvin Theatre.

23 October	Franklin D. Roosevelt visits Charleston, addressing large gatherings at the Navy Yard and at the Citadel.

1936

25 February	The largest ship ever built in South Carolina, the USS *Charleston*, is launched at the Navy Yard.
1 March	Nearly four hundred people preview "non-objective" art from the Solomon R. Guggenheim Collection on exhibit at the Gibbes Art Gallery.
20 July	Police apprehend Benjamin J. Rivers in connection with the murder of Detective Purse A. Wansley. Rivers is later convicted of the murder and executed.
25 August	In the Democratic Party primary, Senator James F. Byrnes beats back Thomas P. Stoney's challenge to his reelection.
14 September	The Clyde-Mallory Line's Pier 3 is lost in a massive blaze as thousands look on.
18 November	Roosevelt is greeted by cheering crowds as he drives through the city before boarding the USS *Indianapolis* for a goodwill tour of South America.

1937

9 January	A four-day strike at the Century Wood Preserving plant is settled.
14 April	First Lady Eleanor Roosevelt arrives for a brief stay.
24 April	Caddies at the Charleston Country Club go on strike.
29 May	Financier and presidential adviser Bernard Baruch delivers the commencement address at the Citadel.
3 July	The West Virginia Pulp and Paper mill is completed and begins operations in North Charleston.
30 July	Daniel J. Jenkins, founder of the Jenkins Orphanage, dies.
16 October	Piles of cotton grow on the waterfront as longshoremen begin a ten-day strike.
26 November	The Dock Street Theatre, built with more than $350,000 from the Works Progress Administration, is dedicated at the corner of Queen and Church Streets.
31 December	The Works Progress Administration occupies the former site of the Citadel on Marion Square.

1938

13 March	A wave of bicycle thefts is reported.

8 April	African American educator, lawyer, and politician Thomas E. Miller dies. He served South Carolina in the U.S. House of Representatives in 1890–91.
10 April	The chapel at the Citadel, built with New Deal funds, is dedicated.
22 April	The "Congressional Special" train from Washington, D.C., arrives in Charleston with a large delegation to attend the Azalea Festival.
29 September	Tornadoes strike Charleston, killing thirty-two people and causing more than two million dollars' worth of damage. Recovery is aided by the Works Progress Administration.
27 December	Henry W. Lockwood becomes mayor, succeeding Maybank, who was elected governor.

1939

3 January	Traps are placed across the city as part of a rat-eradication program.
28 January	The Riviera moving picture theater opens at King and Market Streets.
15 June	WTMA begins broadcasting from Wagener Terrace.
21 June	The USS *Roe* is launched at the Navy Yard.
1 September	Germany invades Poland.

1940

1 June	Governor Maybank tells the Citadel's largest graduating class (152) to prepare to defend democracy.
25 June	Former mayor John P. Grace dies.
11 August	Charleston County is struck by a hurricane that causes more than two million dollars' worth of damage to farmland, automobiles, and beach cottages at Edisto and Folly.
29 October	Draft-age men in Charleston County learn their order numbers.
19 December	A large fire causes great damage to six buildings on Meeting Street between Horlbeck Alley and Market Street.

1941

21 March	The U.S. Navy awards an $8.1 million contract to Charleston Drydock and Shipbuilding Company.
22 May	Complaining of intolerable working conditions and pay violations, construction workers employed by C. M. Guest and Son go on strike at the Navy Yard ordnance depot.

8 July	After serving South Carolina in the U.S. Senate for ten years, James F. Byrnes is sworn in as a U.S. Supreme Court justice.
19 October	From the pulpit, local ministers denounce the growing threat of vice.
5 November	Maybank is inaugurated as a U.S. senator.
7 December	Japan attacks American bases at Pearl Harbor, Hawaii. Two days later, during an extraordinary session of Congress, Roosevelt declares war on Japan.
18 December	Roosevelt nominates Charleston lawyer J. Waties Waring to the federal bench.

Introduction

Writing from his King Street apartment on the eve of the 1932 election, J. C. Driggers penciled a single, unpunctuated line to New York governor and presidential hopeful Franklin D. Roosevelt. "This is 9 votes I have for you hope you will be our next President we are out of work," Driggers wrote. He scrawled that simple message at the bottom of a typed note containing a dark parody of the 23rd Psalm: "Hoover is my shepherd, I am in want, He maketh me to lie down on park benches.... My expenses runneth over, surely my unemployment and poverty will follow me all the days of my life And I will dwell in the house of poverty forever. Amen." Roosevelt was apparently amused by the letter. He replied to Driggers promptly, expressing his appreciation for the pledge of votes along with the psalm parody, adding that "everyone here at the office that I showed it to had a good laugh over it."[1]

At the time of Roosevelt's election on 8 November 1932, many Charleston-area residents shared the sentiments of the Driggers family. They identified intimately with their struggles with joblessness and poverty. Three years had passed since the stock market plunges of October 1929 marked the onset of what would be the nation's deepest and most prolonged economic crisis. Charleston's economy had already been struggling for the better part of the decade under the weight of a statewide agricultural depression caused by a steep drop in the prices for tobacco and cotton. With the European economies in shambles, foreign demand for both commodities had plummeted following the world war. The boll weevil's appetite for cotton, however, showed no signs of diminishing. Infestations of the beetle-legged pests ruined the livelihoods of hundreds of coastal Carolina cotton growers and devastated the lives of many more sharecroppers and landless farm laborers. A severe

---

[1] J. C. Driggers to Roosevelt, October 1932, and Roosevelt to Driggers, 29 October 1932, Democratic Party National Committee Papers, Franklin D. Roosevelt Library and Archives, Hyde Park, N.Y.: South Carolina, Before Election, (subsequent citations of this source are abbreviated as DPNC Papers, followed by file name). The poem is a version of a popular parody that was disseminated during the Bonus March, a 1932 protest of World War I veterans, whose forced expulsion from the capital became a major issue in the presidential campaign. For a published version of the psalm, see E. J. Sullivan, "The 1932nd Psalm," *Seaman's Journal*, October 1932, 259.

slowdown at the Charleston Navy Yard added to the region's economic woes. On the repair docks and in the machine shops where over five thousand civilian workers had recently toiled, a skeleton crew of a few hundred laborers maintained the odd minesweeper or tugboat. It was becoming increasingly difficult to justify keeping the yard open as the war receded into the past and Congress pressed for military-spending cuts and base closures.[2]

After decades of neglect, city officials authorized much-needed improvements to Charleston's sidewalks, streets, and sewers, but the region's political and business elites rejected more costly proposals to improve crumbling wharves, bridges, and rail lines. They were similarly cool to the need for economic diversification, fearing that industrial expansion would drive up area labor rates, especially for African American farmhands and domestic servants. Largely disenfranchised by the 1895 state constitution, African Americans were subordinated politically, economically, and socially. They made up nearly half of the city's sixty-two thousand residents, but few enjoyed the opportunity to rise above the lowest-paying and most physically demanding jobs. Often the best option for the lowcountry's black and white poor, as well as the aspiring professional, was to leave. Many did just that. Charleston County's population dropped by seventy-four hundred residents during the 1920s.

Local people also shared the Driggers family's scorn for President Herbert Hoover, who seemed so terribly out of touch with the daily suffering of millions of Americans. Hoover opposed direct aid to the poor and unemployed for fear that it would sap their self-initiative and make them reliant on government support, but his dim view of the American people did not extend to businessmen and bankers. His administration provided subsidies for shipbuilders and farmers' associations and increased spending for the stabilization of banks and the construction of federal buildings and public-works projects. These measures—unprecedented during peacetime—were designed to revive the economy from the top down, but they did little to spur sustained economic growth and conditions only worsened. Hoover's initiatives were no match for the Great Depression.

At the time of the election, one of every four workers nationally was out of work, including as many as sixty-five hundred Charleston residents, or 20 percent of the local workforce.[3] Many more suffered from underemployment. Working hours and hourly wages that were already low by national standards were cut in response to slow demand and tightened budgets. The lost income translated into human suffering. Children in one Charleston family reportedly ate donated potatoes "as others would eat ice cream cones," while another family was "kept alive principally on a quart of milk furnished by a dairy and two quarts of skimmed milk furnished from

---

[2] "Work Sought for Discharged Men," *Charleston Evening Post*, 12 August 1919.

[3] City Council of Charleston, Minutes, 26 January 1932 (see pp. 29–33, this volume). See also Marvin Leigh Cann, "Burnet Rhett Maybank and the New Deal in South Carolina, 1931–1941," Ph.D. diss. (University of North Carolina at Chapel Hill, 1967), 72.

other sources," according to one public official.⁴ Like the Driggers family, many of those who were struggling shared their concerns directly with Roosevelt beginning soon after he was named the Democratic Party nominee and continuing through the twelve-year run of his presidency. Lottie Smith, a single mother of three school-age children living at 34 Mary Street, informed the newly elected president that her six-year-old daughter's "ear drums are both gone and she is growing deaf and . . . has got to wear glasses." Her doctor had recently concluded that "she is almost blind." Smith added that the family was surviving on $6.40 a week and lamented, "we will have a Blue Xmas for we have nothing to get nothing."⁵ W. C. Bond from nearby Georgetown was even more direct in his appeal. The self-described "old white man 65 and half-blind" asked Roosevelt for a "black suit of close" and included his measurements. He admitted to the president that "this depression has broken me up."⁶ A disabled shipyard worker and active member of the Emanuel AME Church in Charleston, Henry Brown looked to Roosevelt for assistance with his unanswered disability claim. "I got hurt building the gun boat Asheville" during the world war, Brown explained, "and I couldn't get no consideration."⁷

Relief was hard to come by for Charleston's growing number of poor and unemployed. Most relied on the kindnesses of their employers, friends, and strangers. There was little organized assistance for poor people in the 1920s. A limited number of people—particularly those who suffered from blindness or a disability that prevented them from working—might secure a handout from one of several private charities in Charleston, and the formation of the Community Chest in 1925 brought about better coordination of charitable giving and service provision. However, until it was amended in 1937, the South Carolina constitution prohibited state assistance, with the exception of the pensions provided for veterans of the Confederacy, their widows, and formerly enslaved men and women who had remained faithful to their owners during the Civil War. South Carolina and Georgia long held the distinction of being the only states in the union that provided no aid to the blind, the aged, or dependent children. With so little charity to be had, there was humor at least. "Wasn't the depression terrible?" local people asked one another upon meeting.⁸

For lowcountry residents living outside of Charleston, the situation was too grim even for sarcasm. From Beaufort and the surrounding Sea Islands came reports of deaths by starvation and malnutrition. An African American child had died "because she had gone too long without sufficient food to nourish her body." Nurses were also too late to assist an aged and starving black woman. Countless others suffered from

---

⁴City Council of Charleston, Minutes, 26 January 1932 (see pp. 29–33, this volume).
⁵Smith to Roosevelt, 13 December 1932, DPNC Papers: South Carolina, After Election.
⁶Bond to Roosevelt, 12 December 1932, DPNC Papers: South Carolina, After Election.
⁷Brown to Roosevelt, 30 November 1932, DPNC Papers: South Carolina, After Election.
⁸Frank B. Gilbreth, "Depression Saw Crazy Era Here," *Charleston News and Courier*, 30 September 1935.

nutrition-related diseases like pellagra that proved especially perilous for children and the aged.[9] The isolation of sea islanders limited their access to healthcare, as well as opportunities for wage earning. For residents of Coosaw Island, the thirty-five-mile round trip to Parris Island, home of the U.S. Marine Corps Recruit Depot, offered one of their few employment options beyond subsistence farming. But the "costs to get to the work is more than we can get out of it or at least make clear to feed our families," according to Joseph Holmes of Coosaw. A bateau provided their only means of leaving the island and "at times this is taken away because of some trouble with the ferryman." A full six years after the market crash, a nagging sense of dread continued to trouble the minds of Americans from Coosaw to Cleveland. "I don't know what we are going to do this winter," wrote a frightened Holmes.[10]

Through countless works of art, literature, and scholarship, stories of the Great Depression have been woven into the fabric of our nation's history. The documents in this volume add depth and nuance to our understanding of the Great Depression by focusing attention on the diverse experiences of local people from a single region. To be sure, the documents reflect familiar Depression-era themes of suffering, resilience and ingenuity, shared sacrifice, and collective struggle. More precisely, this theme runs through many of the documents, and it is worthy of our attention: In the face of tremendous adversity, lowcountry residents, many of whom lived at the margins of Charleston's notoriously hierarchical and insular social structure, found their voices, and in doing so they transformed local and national politics by making them more democratic and more responsive to human needs. White and black farm laborers, longshoremen, nurses, civil servants, ministers, educators, and students discovered new ways to articulate their visions for a fairer and more just world. They discussed politics with their neighbors and coworkers. They penned editorials and delivered sermons. They brought their concerns to the attention of public officials—those in charge at City Hall and the White House alike. A few lowcountry residents even had the opportunity to share their stories, memories, and songs with curious folklorists who were sent out from Washington to discover just where the nation had been and where it was headed. The resulting conversations were rich.

In the wee hours of the morning in the late winter of 1936, Citadel cadets debated Roosevelt's domestic policies, racial equality, and the Civil War. Sophomore Allen Jones Jr. recorded the conversation in his diary the following day. His roommate Thomas Daniel had argued against the Confederacy and slavery "from the moral stand point while I tried to defend it from a practical stand point—not that slavery

---

[9]"Beaufort Gets Flour; Two Starvation Deaths Reported," *Charleston News and Courier*, 28 September 1932.

[10]Holmes to Roosevelt, 15 October 1935, President's Personal Files, Franklin D. Roosevelt Library and Archives, Hyde Park, N.Y.: Clergy Letters, South Carolina–Tennessee (abbreviated below as FDR Personal Files).

is right and lawful of course, but that it would have been highly impractical to free them." The verbal sparring grew heated—"sarcasm and irony playing no small part"—but their friendship survived, their tensions eased by the demands of homework and inspections and romantic pursuits.[11] Some fifty miles away from the Citadel, an African American student, roughly the same age as the cadets were, directed his concerns to the president just two weeks after his first election. "Find the colored voters a place in your cabinet," pleaded William McKinley Bowman of St. George. Bowman offered Roosevelt the names of a few qualified candidates and also urged him to sponsor an antilynching bill "to help blot it out in the South, for it is a shame on the Southerners and the United States at large."[12]

Channeling the prophets, the pastor of a white Baptist church near Beaufort implored Roosevelt to relieve the suffering of his congregants and their neighbors. "In the name of God and human fairness how can these people live, with advancing food prices, common white meat 25 cents per pound, with no time of their own to help themselves," asked the Reverend A. D. Prentiss in a letter he wrote in the fall of 1935. "How can you or any one lead out to better times if living conditions remain like the above named?"[13]

In an even more startlingly fierce act of truth telling, Susan Calder Hamilton, a woman who had been enslaved for roughly one quarter of her life, revealed painful secrets about Charleston's past to an African American government worker who had asked about her life's experiences. "W'en any slave wus whipped all de other slaves wus made to watch," Hamilton remembered. "I see women hung frum de ceilin' of buildin's an' whipped with only supin tied 'round her lower part of de body, until w'en day wus taken down, dere wusn't breath in de body. I had some terribly bad experiences."[14] Hamilton's dangerous memories alarmed the white South Carolina–based supervisors of the Federal Writers' Project who had authorized the interview. Perhaps it was her faulty memory, lingering racial bitterness, or the interviewer's biased questions that had caused her to say such outlandish things, they surmised. They arranged for Hamilton to be reinterrogated by a white interviewer, and the results of this second interview were more satisfying to them. "Mr. Fuller was a good man and his wife's people been grand people, all good to their slaves," Hamilton said, recalling the family who had owned her family. "Seem like Mr. Fuller just git his slaves so he could be good to dem," she added.[15] Freed from guilt, the bosses were relieved, even elated to read the second interview. "It is a remarkable story . . . doubly remarkable because it flatly contradicts almost all of the statements in the

---

[11]Jones, diary, 6 March 1936 (see pp. 86–89, this volume).
[12]Bowman to Roosevelt, 25 November 1932 (see pp. 36–37, this volume).
[13]Prentiss to Roosevelt, 27 September 1935 (see p. 57, this volume).
[14]Hamilton, interview by Augustus Ladson, June 1937 (see pp. 121–125, this volume).
[15]Hamilton, interview by Jessie A. Butler, 6 July 1937 (see pp. 125–129, this volume).

article filed by the negro worker," cheered the Charleston-based project director. "I only wish that all interviewers were as careful . . . about these ex-slave stories."[16]

How one experienced the Great Depression in Charleston (and how one viewed the region's history) depended on a limitless combination of factors that included one's wealth, race, age, gender, occupation and employment status, and whether one lived in the city, the sea islands, or inland. Reflecting the experiences of those insulated from the worst ravages of the Depression, a handful of the documents in this volume suggest a level of normalcy that the reader might find surprising. Eighty years later, Virginia Bonnette recalled a relatively happy Depression-era childhood in Charleston. Her father maintained his job with the city even though he was sometimes paid in scrip—vouchers that were honored by some local vendors as cash and redeemable for taxes and utility bills. Bonnette's mother earned extra money from her dry-cleaning business—a makeshift operation she set up in a shed in the yard. What Bonnette mostly remembered of the 1930s, however, were basketball and softball games on the Mitchell School playground and spending Saturdays at the Palace Theater watching cowboy movies.[17] Her childhood may have shielded Bonnette from the worst of the hardships that her parents endured, and the healing distance of time may also have mellowed her memories. But what do we make of the curious silences in tourist H. P. Lovecraft's extensive travelogue from Charleston in the 1930s? A horror writer from Providence, Rhode Island, who toiled in obscurity in that genre until his premature death in 1937, Lovecraft made no mention of Charleston's economic crisis, though his first of several visits to the city took place just weeks after the stock market crash. Lovecraft instead marveled at the grand homes, historic sites, and the elite white families of Charleston, whom he imagined to be of superior moral character and ability. "Today Charleston is probably the most civilized spot in the United States," he gushed. "The place where genuine values most amply survive, and where the false glitter and confusion of mechanized barbarism are least to be found."[18] Countless visitors to Charleston following in Lovecraft's footsteps and, equally beguiled by its historic district and southern charms, have reached the same baseless conclusions.

In the main, this collection spotlights solitary voices of dissent, but Charleston-area residents also joined together to give collective expression to their desires for change. On 30 August 1933, in what was likely the largest mass gathering in the city's history, more than eight thousand women and men marched in a parade to promote

---

[16]Chalmers S. Murray to Mabel Montgomery, 8 July 1937, Federal Writers Project, Records of the Works Progress Administration, Record Group 69, National Archives and Records Administration, College Park, Md.: Correspondence Pertaining to Ex-Slave Studies, 1936–1940, Box 1.

[17]Bonnette, interview by Virginia Ellison and Kieran W. Taylor, 15 March 2012 (see pp. 160–161, this volume).

[18]Lovecraft to Herman Charles Koenig, 12 January 1936 (see pp. 63–85, this volume).

the work of the National Recovery Administration—the Roosevelt administration's initial effort at economic revitalization and an early expression of his New Deal domestic programs and policies. Many thousands more lined both sides of the street from the parade's start at King and Line Streets all the way to the finish at Marion Square. A contingent of nineteen hundred American Tobacco Company workers, most of whom were women, walked alongside two floats, one of which featured a cigar-making machine. Condon's "House of Better Values" department store, the Charleston Florists Association, and the South Carolina Power Company were among hundreds of other area businesses and organizations represented in the procession. The martial feel to the parade reflected the leadership provided by military officials, including Lieutenant Colonel George C. Marshall, the newly appointed commander of Fort Moultrie, and General Charles P. Summerall, the president of the Citadel.

The Charleston parade, along with many similar demonstrations across the country, was a top-down and hierarchical affair orchestrated and financed from Washington. An army of between fifteen hundred and two thousand canvassers, working under Summerall's direction, visited every business in the city to encourage employers to abide by the National Recovery Administration's price, production, and wage codes. The names of compliant businesses were posted to a fifty-foot-by-twelve-foot bulletin board constructed on Marion Square and a smaller board at the post office. Summerall's canvasser army also visited homes to urge consumers to patronize only those businesses displaying the "Blue Eagle" signs that indicated their compliance with the codes.[19] The mobilization nevertheless relied on the enthusiasm and activism of thousands of local volunteers and the support of dozens of popular organizations.

At the conclusion of the parade, the Catholic bishop of Charleston, the Reverend Emmet M. Walsh, praised the NRA campaign as "the greatest effort ever made in the history of social service." He urged the gathered crowd to embrace "a spirit of unity and sacrifice . . . and a commitment to work for the common good of the whole," reminding them that "it must come before the selfishness of the individual."[20] The broad-based campaign for the NRA represented an awesome and elaborate performance of civic pride for which Charleston was becoming nationally notable, but real recovery would require more than compelling speeches and spectacles. The

---

[19]"Sweeping N.R.A. Drive Is Shaped," *Charleston News and Courier*, 24 August 1933.
[20]"Parade 20 Miles Long Is Feature of N.R.A.'s Drive," *Charleston News and Courier*, 31 August 1933. In a unanimous decision, the U.S. Supreme Court struck down the legislation that had created the National Recovery Administration as an unconstitutional abuse of executive authority on 27 May 1935.

wounds that the people of the lowcountry had endured needed healing, but healing demanded material relief and substantive changes.

A more organic mobilization three years later led to the establishment of an institution that continues as the region's most significant expression of black economic and political power. Since long before Emancipation, enslaved African and African American longshoremen had been responsible for literally carrying Charleston's wealth in and out of the city. Their centrality to the region's economy made them both the most loathed and respected segment of Charleston's African American population.

In the fall of 1936, following an escalating series of wage disputes with the shipping and stevedoring companies, the longshoremen went on strike. They demanded better wages and safer working conditions, as well as recognition for their union. On 19 September, Charleston police—armed with the city's machine gun, a pump rifle, and nightsticks—dispersed a crowd of three hundred dockworkers who had gathered at the office of the A. E. Holleman Stevedoring Company on the corner of Hasell and Concord Streets. The men accused Holleman of shorting their pay. The work stoppages and street conflicts continued for several months until, by the end of the year, their employers recognized the International Longshoremen's Association, Local 1422, as the official bargaining agent for the dock men.

What unleashed tongues that had long been tied? What unlocked their imaginations? How did the private needs of so many working people translate into an animating sense of hope, demands for change, and political action? For the longshoremen, collective struggle was an extension of their work. They worked in small groups known as "gangs," and their success and their safety depended upon the gang's ability to work together. Other lowcountry residents were motivated to speak out and take action by their shared desperation and a realization that they had little to lose. The United Workingmen's Society formed in the fall of 1933 to protect the rights of the unemployed by guarding against abuses in the distribution of relief and business violations of the NRA codes. The twenty founding members pledged "that they will not sell their votes, for favors nor profit, to political or religious organizations."[21] Earlier in the year, several hundred African American women working at the Charleston Bagging Company engaged in a work stoppage and refused to leave the plant on John Street after learning that other area workers had received pay raises under the NRA codes. As police entered the plant to restore order, they were greeted by black women wielding bobbins and chopping knives. "Strip 'em!" the women cried, but the atmosphere was as festive as it was menacing. "The floor was vibrating as massive negro women danced in a circle and sang in unison everything from 'I

---

[21]"Unemployed Organize Protective Society," *Charleston News and Courier*, 15 October 1933.

Ain't Gonna Work No More' to spirituals," according to the acting police chief. The plant was idled for ten days before reopening under the terms of new NRA codes for the bagging industry.[22]

President Roosevelt was also a powerful symbol of hope. Lowcountry residents were certain that the White House was occupied by a president who understood their pain and was doing all in his power to relieve their suffering. "I, and thousands like me, look to you as our modern Moses sent by a kind Providence to deliver us from the present economic bondage," wrote Rabbi Jacob S. Raisin of Kahal Kadosh Beth Elohim, among the oldest synagogues in the country.[23] What Raisin and other supporters in Charleston likely missed, however, is that Roosevelt and his advisers were being guided as well—by their cries for help and the grassroots activism emerging from every neighborhood, factory, and farm community. Roosevelt's New Deal—an idea he had discussed only in broad terms during the 1932 presidential campaign—was taking shape around poor people's persistent demands for help and for change.

Still others were moved to express themselves and to take action as they realized that the region's established institutions, business leaders, and constituted authorities had clearly failed them, as had their values. "The greed of the predatory interests that control the government" was fueling social unrest, warned one Mt. Pleasant farmer who was facing foreclosure. "The people have lost respect for the government, and faith in those elected to administer it."[24]

Those failures created opportunities for the emergence of new ideas and reforms. Otherwise moderate professionals such as social workers, healthcare professionals, and teachers began asserting themselves more aggressively. To varying degrees the leaders of the County Tuberculosis Association, the YWCA on Coming Street, and the Avery Institute—a private school for African Americans—took advantage of the crisis to demand more resources and autonomy for their work.[25] They became surer of their commitments and bolder in their pronouncements. "In the city and county there are 100,000 people who are looking to me, as a Government official, to protect their interests," observed a Charleston-area relief administrator. "And I'll be damned

---

[22]See "Bagging Mill Shut as Women Strike for Wage of $12," *Charleston News and Courier*, 27 August 1933; and "Work is Resumed at Bagging Mill," *Charleston News and Courier*, 6 September 1933.
[23]Raisin to Roosevelt, 10 October 1935, FDR Personal Files.
[24]H. R. Hale to Roosevelt, 1 October 1932, DPNC Papers: South Carolina, Before Election.
[25]See Eleanor Loeb Halsey, "Narrative Report," Charleston County Tuberculosis Association, August 1930 (see pp. 3–8, this volume); Ella L. Smyrl to Cordella A. Winn, 26 January 1932, (see pp. 33–36, this volume); and Benjamin F. Cox, Avery Institute, Annual Report, August 1935 (see pp. 48–49, this volume).

if I'm going to be pushed by a dozen [conservative farmers] no matter how many letters they write into Columbia or how many of them go running up to Washington."[26]

The crisis also gave rise to new leaders—especially elected leaders who succeeded in breaking from the strictures of lowcountry conservatism to embrace the New Deal idea that government power should be used to make people's lives better. Foremost among them were Senator James F. Byrnes and Mayor Burnet R. Maybank. Attuned to the urgent need for change, Byrnes and Maybank—both of whom developed close ties to the president and influential New Dealers, including Harry L. Hopkins, who directed the Works Progress Administration—proved adept at harnessing grassroots political power to deliver significant resources and reforms to the lowcountry.

Jimmy Byrnes's reputation as a political power broker stretched back before the war. He had represented Charleston in the U.S. House of Representatives from 1911 to 1925 and was an ally of President Woodrow Wilson. He relocated his law practice to Spartanburg in 1925, making money and extending his political base across the upstate, before being elected as South Carolina's junior senator in 1930. Byrnes was one of Roosevelt's earliest and most reliable southern supporters. In a 28 October 1928 letter, Byrnes reminded Roosevelt that he had supported his vice presidential nomination at the 1920 Democratic National Convention, adding that he was "now only anxious to have the opportunity to urge your nomination for the presidency."[27] Byrnes carefully cultivated his relationship with Roosevelt by providing him with advice and political intelligence that he gathered from Senate colleagues and his many contacts within the state. Advising candidate Roosevelt on his support in South Carolina in the fall of 1931, Byrnes reported that "if the Convention should be held at this time there is no doubt of your receiving the votes of this State." He recommended, however, that "no effort from without the state . . . do any organizing here" and that Roosevelt rely instead on his South Carolina–based supporters: "If we can do this and let your friends devote themselves to other states, it should promote the cause."[28] On the Senate floor Byrnes became Roosevelt's mouthpiece, guiding dozens of key New Deal programs to passage.

Byrnes's political protégé, Charleston mayor Burnet R. Maybank, was the most important locally based New Dealer. Maybank, just thirty-two at the time of his election, was a first-term alderman, College of Charleston graduate, cotton broker, and the descendant of several of South Carolina's most powerful families. Initially ambivalent about pursuing a career in politics, Maybank's strength as a mayoral candidate was that he had working relationships with the various factions that vied for control of Charleston's Democratic Party. In the spring of 1931, Maybank's candidacy was anointed by a group of business and political leaders who hoped

---

[26]Lorena A. Hickok to Harry L. Hopkins, 10 February 1934 (see pp. 41–46, this volume).
[27]Byrnes to Roosevelt, 12 November 1928, DPNC Papers: South Carolina, Pre-Convention.
[28]Byrnes to Roosevelt, 15 October 1931, DPNC Papers: South Carolina, Pre-Convention.

to avoid the violence and occasional bloodshed that had marred past elections in Charleston. They also sought a mayoral candidate and slate of aldermen who would "apply sound business methods toward a solution of the critical financial problems that confront the community."²⁹ To be more precise, they were looking for a mayor to cut spending and lower their taxes. The business leaders joined forces with their political nemesis, former mayor John P. Grace, to deliver his white working-class base for Maybank as the consensus candidate.

The truce lasted just a few weeks because they were unable to satisfactorily divvy up seats on the city council and the executive committee of the county Democratic Party. The election devolved into nasty accusations and counteraccusations of the sort that all had pledged to avoid. Maybank nevertheless beat his opponent in the Democratic Party primary, Lawrence M. Pinckney, by a wide margin. There was no Republican opposition in the general election and the entire slate won unanimously. Maybank quickly proved himself to be politically independent and highly capable. In keeping with his campaign platform, Maybank signaled his commitment to fiscal conservatism in an ominous 14 December 1931 inaugural address. After declaring that "retrenchment is absolutely necessary," he explained to the citizenry that their demands for services and improvements over the previous decade had buried the city in debt. He promised spending cuts coupled with an aggressive tax-collection campaign that he acknowledged would be painful. "The city of Charleston is broke, flat broke," Maybank said. "And unless one and all cooperate, the best thing for us to do is auction off our community right now and get the agony over with."³⁰

Nonetheless, Maybank was pragmatic in his embrace of the New Deal as he realized that it was the vehicle through which he could deliver much-needed improvements to the city while putting people to work and establishing a potent political base. Often working closely with his mentor Byrnes, Maybank succeeded in bringing over $36 million dollars of federal aid to the lowcountry between 1933 and 1936.³¹ Among its many local accomplishments, the New Deal rescued faltering banks, repaired the City Hall and public market damaged by deadly tornadoes in 1938, and upgraded the airport and the Navy Yard. The city's first incinerator and the Dock Street Theatre—the Charleston elite's favorite cut of public pork—were both constructed with New Deal money. Old buildings at the Citadel and the College of Charleston were renovated and new ones were built, including a gymnasium for the college and a chapel for the Citadel. Poor students on both campuses received tuition assistance that allowed them to remain in college, while thousands of area young men received an education of a different sort—along with food, clothes, housing, medical care, and a small salary—through their participation in

---

²⁹"Geer Seeks Help of Faction Heads," *Charleston News and Courier*, 14 February 1931.
³⁰Maybank, Inaugural Address, 14 December 1931 (see pp. 13–27, this volume).
³¹Walter J. Fraser Jr., *Charleston! Charleston! The History of a Southern City* (Columbia: University of South Carolina Press, 1989), 380.

the Civilian Conservation Corps. The corps, which enrolled fifty thousand men statewide, put them to work combatting soil erosion, planting trees, and establishing sixteen state parks. The New Deal initiative that would have the greatest impact on the state—the Santee-Cooper project—remapped South Carolina by flooding low-lying areas, rerouting waterways, and constructing hydroelectric dams and power plants. Santee-Cooper provided low-cost electricity to thousands of state residents, while powering the region's industrial growth during and after World War II.

Maybank was not a strong public speaker and his regional brogue sometimes proved to be challenging to audiences outside of the area, but he nevertheless projected optimism and vigor. He remained tremendously popular in Charleston during his eight years as mayor, drawing frequent comparisons to the president. He is "just the kind of Mayor that Mr. Roosevelt is President," a small business owner told a New Deal official who was equally enthusiastic about "young Mr. Maybank."[32] By the spring of 1936, a year in which he was reelected without opposition, Maybank felt confident enough in the successes of his first administration to declare victory over the "dreadful depression." In a letter that was placed in a time capsule in Columbia and scheduled to be opened fifty years hence, Maybank wrote that "Charleston looks today into the future with more hopefulness than in any of the past few generations." He credited recent federally supported improvements to the region's infrastructure and transportation systems as reasons for optimism, as well as the anticipated expansion of the paper industry.[33] The early successes of Santee-Cooper—a project with statewide impact and one for which he served as the chairman of its board of directors—allowed Maybank to cultivate support from beyond the lowcountry. Upon the strength of that support, he was elected governor in 1938 and U.S. senator in 1941, a position he held until his death in 1954.

To be certain, not everyone in the lowcountry lined up behind Maybank, Roosevelt, and the New Deal. The most persistent and vocal dissenters were reactionary farm owners whose wealth relied upon their having at their disposal a surplus of African American laborers to work their fields. The farmers feared that unemployment relief, federal jobs, and economic diversification would drive up prevailing wages in the region and undermine their control of the labor market. As one farm demonstration agent observed tartly, "they still think of farming as riding around over their plantations on horseback, superintending their slaves."[34] These farmers were few in number, but they had pull within Charleston's delegation to the South

---

[32]Other leading New Dealers with lowcountry ties included the Charleston-born economist Leon Keyserling, who helped draft the National Industrial Recovery Act, the Social Security Act, and the National Labor Relations Act, and Bernard Baruch, a Wall Street financier from Camden, South Carolina, who owned an estate near Georgetown.

[33]Maybank to His Honor the Mayor, 16 March 1936, Burnet R. Maybank Mayoral Papers, 1931–1986, City of Charleston, Records Management, Charleston, S.C.: Folder 29.

[34]Lorena A. Hickok to Harry L. Hopkins, 10 February 1934 (see pp. 41–46, this volume).

Carolina legislature. Working through those representatives, they lobbied Maybank to request exceptions to the mandated wage rates for federally funded programs. But as one state New Deal official explained to Maybank, lowering the wages for South Carolina to accommodate the farmers would defeat the purpose of federal assistance and that paying a living wage was at "the heart of the whole recovery plan."[35]

The conservative critics of the New Deal found high-profile allies in former mayors Grace and Thomas P. Stoney, and especially W. W. Ball, the editor of the *Charleston News and Courier*. Ball gave prominent news coverage to reports of fraud and waste in New Deal programs. On his editorial page he urged state leaders to reject federal aid and to "stand on our ancient and honorable ground that South Carolina can take care of itself, that she is not, will never be, a dependent and a beggar state."[36] He railed against the growth of federal power and warned that the spending frenzy threatened to bury the state in debt while "undermining the solvency of the commonwealth and its people."[37] Ball shared the concerns of local employers who feared losing control over their employees, but he also viewed the New Deal in broader cultural terms as a threat to the two values that he held most dear—aristocracy and white supremacy. With a degree of prescience that should not be casually dismissed, Ball predicted that industrialization and modernization of the sort facilitated by the New Deal would inevitably lead to class conflict and the eventual extension of voting rights and political power sharing to the black and white working class.

The continuing flow of federal dollars into the lowcountry and enthusiasm for the president guaranteed that Ball's politics remained at the margins in the 1930s. Ball was honest in acknowledging the limits of his appeal and likely even reveled in his unpopularity, finding within rejection further confirmation for his worldview. "Where have our leaders, governors, senators, state officers, college presidents, candidates and learned people been while all this was going on?" he asked in a 1937 editorial decrying overspending. "The News and Courier has been harping on it—but the News and Courier is regarded as unworthy of attention, much less of belief, by the great gentlemen in control of South Carolina."[38]

A more serious threat to Charleston's New Deal—and the cozy relationship between the lowcountry and Washington upon which it was built—emerged in the weeks leading up to the 1936 Democratic primary. On the evening of 20 July, police apprehended Benjamin J. Rivers from underneath a house on Duncan Street, where he had eluded capture for six days. Rivers, a forty-five-year-old African American maritime worker, was wanted in connection with the murder of Purse A. Wansley, a

---

[35]Maybank to John L. M. Irby, and Irby to Maybank, 25 September 1933 (see pp. 39–41, this volume).
[36]"The South Threatened," *Charleston News and Courier*, 25 October 1933.
[37]"50,000 Deeper in Debt," *Charleston News and Courier*, 25 May 1937.
[38]Ibid.

Charleston police detective who had attempted to arrest Rivers and an associate on Montagu Street in the early hours of 14 July.

An angry white mob gathered outside the police station where Rivers was being held until he was removed to the county jail on Magazine Street. There he was threatened by an even larger and angrier crowd of five hundred people "uttering threats of violence." The county sheriff requested backup from the U.S. Marines, but was informed that such a request could only come from the governor. Into the morning a contingent of city and county police, "armed with rifles, shotguns, clubs and tear gas, guarded the massive entrance to the jail, while high police officials parleyed with the apparent leaders of the mob." As negotiations with the crowd continued, police secreted Rivers to Columbia, returning him to Charleston only after the threat of mob action had subsided.[39]

Few white people in Charleston had much sympathy for Rivers, and none expressed any publicly, save for a handful of brave coworkers who spoke as character witnesses at his trial. Local law enforcement officials and political leaders, however, understood that a lynching in Charleston—a city led by a personal friend of the president—could make political problems for the national administration. It would provide ammunition to those of Roosevelt's liberal critics who were demanding that he support passage of the Costigan-Wagner antilynching bill. Roosevelt resisted those calls for fear of alienating his southern white base.

Comprehending these political risks as well as the financial stakes, Charleston and state officials took measures to give Rivers's subsequent trial the appearance of legitimacy. While he received competent legal counsel from two prominent Charleston attorneys, his plea of self-defense, supported by evidence of a wound to his leg and recovered cartridges indicating that Wansley had fired two rounds, was disregarded by the all-white jury. They were similarly unmoved by other facts that emerged during the trial. Wansley had no warrant for Rivers's arrest. He had dressed in street clothes, displayed no badge, and drove an unmarked car to the site of the arrest. The jury deliberated for less than an hour before finding Rivers guilty with no recommendation for mercy. After he had exhausted all of his appeals, Rivers was electrocuted at the state penitentiary in Columbia on 29 April 1938.[40]

The New Deal coalition was expanding but not quickly enough to save Benjamin Rivers. Its democratic impulses—which achieved so much of substance for so many Americans in the 1930s—foundered on the shoals of white supremacy. African Americans in Charleston held the president and the first lady in high regard for signaling a new openness to their concerns, and they welcomed vital public

---

[39]"Two Lodged in Columbia Jail," *Charleston Evening Post*, 21 July 1936. "Mob Outside Jail; Marine Help Asked," *Charleston News and Courier*, 21 July 1936.

[40]For Rivers's trial testimony, see *The State v. Benjamin J. Rivers*, 25 September 1936 (pp. 89–117, this volume).

assistance and the unprecedented employment and educational opportunities that were provided by the New Deal. But they embraced the New Deal without illusions. They remained keenly aware of the ways in which government initiatives were compromised by white political, business, and community leaders who were placed in administrative positions that granted them control over who received government jobs, contracts, and other benefits. "Concerning the Works program I wish to say that the ones who really need the jobs at a living wage do not get it," complained Elijah J. Curry, an African American minister from St. George in a 1935 letter to the president. "It is rather unfortunate," he wrote, for African Americans "that the matter of jobs and wages is handled, in the final stages, by local representatives who in most cases either by coercion or choice, will show favoritism to certain people."[41]

The black critics also understood that the New Deal's race problems were systemic. Presumably race-neutral programs benefited whites and blacks unequally. The NRA codes, for instance, exempted the most common occupations for black South Carolinians—domestic workers, farm laborers, and casual employees—from their protections, as did the Social Security Act of 1935, the most transformative and lasting social legislation to emerge from the New Deal. "Some of those exempted are the very ones that should receive pension in their old age," Elijah Curry explained to the president. "In this, 'The land of the Free' it seems that we would still retain slavery when it comes to a certain group if those clauses were retained."[42]

Neither the African American critics nor the conservative dissenters were ever able to muster a serious electoral challenge to either Maybank's political power or New Deal orthodoxy. African Americans were almost wholly excluded from the Democratic Party, and as late as 1940 fewer than fifteen hundred voted in the general election in South Carolina.[43] White voters of the southern states remained the most reliable members of the New Deal coalition in the 1930s, and no state delivered larger pluralities for Roosevelt than South Carolina. In 1936 almost 99 percent of South Carolina's 115,400 voters in the general election cast votes for Roosevelt, and the same pattern held for each of his four campaigns. Only in 1944 did his vote total drop slightly below 90 percent.

In the late 1930s Charleston's New Deal took on a distinctly military cast as the focus of federal spending—in amounts that dwarfed earlier expenditures—shifted to Fort Moultrie, the Navy Yard, and the construction of housing and schools for war workers and their families. This new weaponized New Deal facilitated a wartime boom in Charleston like nothing the city had ever experienced. The high unemployment rates that had persisted for more than ten years fell to historic lows and enabled

---

[41]Curry to Roosevelt, 5 October 1935 (see pp. 58–59, this volume).

[42]Ibid., 000.

[43]Jack Irby Hayes Jr., *South Carolina and the New Deal* (Columbia: University of South Carolina Press, 2001), 170.

the lowcountry to make significant contributions to the "Arsenal of Democracy." The Navy Yard once again became a center for shipbuilding and a military port of embarkation. The 1938 Azalea Festival—established during Maybank's first term as a way to draw visitors to the city—provided an early indication of the growing linkages between recovery and the economic engines of Charleston's future: defense spending and tourism. Aboard the "Congressional Special" train from Washington, D.C., Vice President John Nance Garner, two cabinet officials, and more than eighty members of the U.S. Senate and House of Representatives arrived in Charleston on 22 April. Their trip offered the group, which included Senators Richard B. Russell and Harry S. Truman, House Majority Leader Sam Rayburn, and Representative Lyndon B. Johnson, the opportunity to see historic plantations and Fort Sumter, as well as the results of New Deal spending with an emphasis on military projects. At the Navy Yard, Senators Byrnes and Ellison D. "Cotton Ed" Smith drove the first rivet in the keel of the destroyer *Roe*, while congressmen spoke with reporters regarding the need to expand the dry dock and improve housing at Fort Moultrie. "With all this talk of slums, we should look to the slums in our own army," said Representative A. J. May of Kentucky, the chair of the House Committee On Military Affairs. "A good portion of the funds which the president has recommended for public works should be devoted to the betterment of army housing."[44]

A Charleston newspaperman in 1935 warned future critics against evaluating the New Deal solely on the basis of financial criteria. Frank B. Gilbreth wrote that a reasonable person might review the dollar amounts and conclude "that the Roosevelt administration went raving mad." He reminded those imaginary critics, however, to "take into consideration that a national crisis existed: that children were without food and that men who wanted to work could not find it." The New Deal met those real human needs of millions of Americans, while restoring their confidence in the nation's political system and major institutions. A nation teetering at the edge of chaos stabilized over the course of about two years through bold and decisive federal action. As Gilbreth put it, "The United States, in orderly fashion, passed through a bloodless revolution."[45] The people of the lowcountry passed through that bloodless revolution: they lined up for relief and enrolled their sons in the Civilian Conservation Corps. They supported their families on the jobs created by massive public expenditures for new buildings, roads, and other infrastructural improvements. They sent their children to newly constructed modern schools and took advantage

---

[44]W. D. Workman Jr., "Bigger Dry Dock for Yard, Housing for Fort Promised," *Charleston News and Courier*, 24 April 1938.

[45]Gilbreth, "Dollar-Alphabet Grows During '34," *Charleston News and Courier*, 21 October 1935.

of federally backed loans to avoid defaulting on their mortgages. But the people of the lowcountry were not merely passive recipients of government largesse. They also helped make the bloodless revolution. Their willingness to express pain and dissent, to articulate political demands, and to engage in collective action provided momentum and structure to Charleston's New Deal.

Charleston and the Great Depression

1930

Fong Lee Wong to Laura Bragg

4 March 1930
Charleston, S.C.
Beginning in 1926, the Citadel, the Military College of South Carolina, accepted a small number of transfer students from Chinese colleges to "familiarize them with American military tactics."[1] Charleston Museum director Laura Bragg helped acclimate the students to the United States. She founded the Ta T'ung Club to promote cultural exchange between the students and local residents.[2] Bragg also arranged for the students to attend various off-campus social and educational functions.

In the following letter to Bragg, who was traveling at the time, Cadet Fong Lee Wong reported being punished by the Citadel commandant for "having not borne my sorrow in a military manner" after receiving news of his father's death in China.[3] "I do not care his punishment which means nothing to me," wrote Wong. "What I do not approve is that the

---

[1]"More Chinese for Citadel," *Charleston Evening Post*, 17 March 1927. From 1904 until the outbreak of World War II, at least ninety Chinese students studied at the Citadel and other U.S. military colleges, including the Virginia Military Institute, Norwich University, and the United States Military Academy.

[2]Laura M. Bragg (1881–1978) graduated from Simmons College in Boston in 1906 and became curator for the Charleston Museum three years later. From 1920 to 1931 she served as the museum's director. During her tenure at the museum, she undertook an aggressive educational outreach program while maintaining a strong scholarly interest in the history and culture of local Native Americans and African Americans. After retiring from the Berkshire Museum in Pittsfield, Massachusetts, Bragg returned to Charleston in 1940. Many of the Chinese students Bragg befriended continued to correspond with her long after they returned to China.

[3]Fong Lee Wong was born in 1908 in Beijing and attended Quinghua College before graduating from the Citadel in 1930. His senior yearbook entry indicated that "'Fongy' seems to be thoroughly agreed with the theory that two-thirds of the value of a college education lies in the friends one makes. Though a native of a far-off land, of peculiar customs and traditions, he has

military training in time of peace should aim at an entire elimination of human emotion and feeling."[4]

Dear Miss Bragg:

By this time you probably are about to leave New Orleans for Texas and I hope this letter will wait for you at Brooks Field, San Antonio before your arrival at this place.

Now, week end is setting in and I begin to feel the difference of your being at home and your going away. To-morrow or day after to-morrow I will pay a visit to Miss Richardson and Mrs. House. I-men probably will go with me.[5]

After you left, we have had only two raining days, but the weather has been beautifully warm and an amiable spring has at last come. But I am sorry that we cannot enjoy such a fine season.

In school everything goes on as usual except that I just recently received a reward, from the Commandant, of five demerits and ten confinements because of my taking a day to bemoan my late father.[6] This is a bygone matter and I can never think he will take it up again. He censures me for my having not borne my sorrow in a military manner. This, I believe, I can do easily in war but not in peace time. I do not care his punishment which means nothing to me. What I do not approve is that the military training in time of peace should aim at an entire elimination of human emotion and feeling. Such kind of military education is bound to produce war since the military class of a country, nurtured by their training, always welcomes war and even is quite willing to create war. The present London Naval Conference, I think, must receive a centralized keen interest of all the military classes of the big three or five powers. Whatever result, whether a failure or a success, that conference will produce, another world war may be effected in one way or another. But I hope it may not.[7]

---

particularly well adapted himself to American modes of living, and at the Citadel has made a great record, but a greater number of friends" (Citadel, *The Sphinx*, 1930, 83). Major General Wong later served as commander of the chemical warfare branch of the Chinese army before joining the People's Liberation Army in 1949.

[4]In a 7 March 1930 letter to Bragg, Wong expressed his continuing sorrow over the loss of his father and his frustrations with the Citadel: "As you were driving me back, my heart weighed down within, and a kind of deep, strong emotion mixed with consolation, thankfulness, and sorrow occurred in my mind. I was, and still am, so absorbed in this peculiar state of mind that I did not know what I should say to you when you let me off at the gate of this unpleasant barracks" (Laura Bragg Papers, Citadel Archives and Museum, Charleston, S.C.: Box 6).

[5]Emma B. Richardson served as Bragg's assistant at the Charleston Museum. She lived with Eva C. House at the historic Heyward-Washington House at 87 Church Street. I-men was one of Wong's Chinese classmates.

[6]William C. Miller served as Citadel commandant from 1926 to 1931.

[7]Representatives of the United States, Japan, France, Italy, and Great Britain met in London in the spring of 1930 and agreed to limits on their naval capacity.

Yesterday I did something for myself: that is a definite decision to go to Harvard University this summer. I believe, I will not change my mind and nothing can make me change. I feel I have had enough military training, and what I am yearning for is knowledge. Too much being military seems to me a sheer ignorance. This case is especially true of China, and I dare not allow myself to be a mere military man as our Commandant tries to train me to be.

Hoping you enjoy an exceedingly fine trip.

Yours affectionately,
[signed]
Fong Lee

P.S. With my kindliest regards to Chai Mei[8]
F.L.W

Autographed Letter Signed. Laura Bragg Papers, Citadel Archives and Museum, Charleston, S.C.: Box 6.

Eleanor Loeb Halsey, "Narrative Report," Charleston County Tuberculosis Association

August 1930
[Charleston, S.C.]

The Charleston County Tuberculosis Association opened Pinehaven sanatorium in 1924 to treat patients suffering from tuberculosis and to limit its spread through health education and testing programs. Located seven miles north of downtown Charleston, the sanatorium included separate facilities for black and white patients, who were further separated by sex.[9] This monthly report prepared by Eleanor Halsey, the executive secretary of the association, indicates the enormous scope of the problem in Charleston.[10] Fighting tuberculosis

---

[8]Chia-Mei Hu graduated from the Citadel in 1928. He was killed in an airplane accident at the Chinese Central Flying School in June 1934.

[9]Pinehaven was built with surplus building materials from World War I. The lean-to buildings offered patients little shelter from the inclement weather.

[10]Eleanor Rose Loeb Halsey (1883–1968) was born in Charleston and was active in civic affairs and public health. She served as chair of the Charleston Chapter of the American Red Cross during World War I and was active in the Charleston section of the National Council of Jewish Women. She served as the Tuberculosis Association's executive from 1926 until 1956.

and other infectious diseases during the 1930s was complicated by poverty and malnourishment. Subsequent reports by Halsey indicated that the problem only worsened over the next several years.[11]

Since the last meeting of the Executive Board, the annual Survey of Deaths from tuberculosis in Charleston County in 1929 has been made. This shows the death rate for 1929 was 98.1 per 100,000, whereas the average in the United States Registration Area for 1927, the last figures available, was 80.8 per 100,000. It is thus seen that Charleston still has a big piece of work to do along the lines of tuberculosis if it is to approach the National Average. The total number of deaths for the year was 119; 86 being in the city and 33 in the county; 27 being white people and 92 being negroes. Of the total 119 deaths, 49 were between the ages of infancy and 25 years. A report in full is here for the inspection of the Board.

The extended clinic service planned by the Board has started. According to schedule, Dr. Huggin, after a month's study, returned to the city August 1, 1930.[12]

Two morning clinics have been held on successive Fridays at Roper Hospital with an attendance of 13 and 4 respectively, rain having interfered with the second clinic.

Through the courtesy of Mr. [Frederick G.] Davies, the Tuxbury Lumber Co. has assigned one of the houses at its Logging Camp to the Association to serve as a clinic station for the people from Mt. Pleasant to McClellanville. At present bi-monthly chest clinics will be held here, the first of them being held today. The Association is certainly indebted to the Tuxbury Lumber Company for the trouble it has taken. The building has been repaired and repainted and made ready for the Association's work. A stationary metal washstand and curtains for the examining room represent the equipment purchased by the Association for this clinic up to the present time.

Through Mrs. Lloyd [Louise Rhodes] Ellison, a member of the Advisory Committee, the Montague Lumber Company has agreed to allow the Association the use of a building for the clinic station at North Charleston. A meeting is scheduled for Thursday evening, Sept. 11, at 8 P. M. at the Baptist Church at North Charleston in order to arouse local interest and cooperation in this clinic.

---

[11] In her March 1936 report, Halsey indicated that "the work of the sanatorium is heavier than ever before in the history and there seems to be no indication of any let up in the need for it." She also recommended expanding the staff and limiting new admissions (Halsey, "Report of the Executive Secretary," Pinehaven Sanatorium Records, Waring Historical Library, Medical University of South Carolina, Charleston: Box 2).

[12] Perry McKown Huggin, a graduate of the Medical College of the State of South Carolina, had recently joined the association staff after studying at tuberculosis clinics in Philadelphia and New York ("Will Increase Chest Clinics," *Charleston Evening Post*, 7 August 1930).

On Tuesday, September 23, at 10 A. M. the first of these periodic county clinics at Adams Run will be held in the Harmon Health Center, the Association being granted permission to use this place through the courtesy of Dr. Banov.[13]

The committee at Wadmalaw and Johns Islands has been unable to secure a building for a permanent use as a clinic station. The Secretary wrote Mrs. Hills, Chairman of the Committee, asking if a place could be lent for the use of the Association once every two months, even if not given over entirely to this purpose. She has not heard from Mrs. Hills in answer to this.

New clinic records have been worked out and printed in connection with the clinic extension as per samples enclosed.

The school clinics held in the spring are revealing some interesting results. One family, where several children showed a high tuberculin reaction, after a further study, has revealed the mother to have an active case of tuberculosis. She is now on the waiting list for Pinehaven. In another case a little girl showed a negative tuberculin reaction but was 25 pounds underweight. The mother of this child was admitted to Pinehaven last week. A young colored boy discovered at one of the spring clinics has been diagnosed as a positive case of hilum or childhood tuberculosis. This case will be further studied in an effort to find the source of infection.

The annual follow up of all patients discharged from Pinehaven is now in progress. The Secretary being assisted in this by the Clinician and Field Nurse.

Seal Sale preparations are progressing slowly. Additions to the list are being made according to the telephone directory, the work having progressed as far as the letter O. Mrs. Rhett, Chairman, and Mr. Alfred Huger, Treasurer, have accepted these offices to which they were elected by the Board at its last meeting.[14] Letters were sent to all member of the Advisory Committee asking them to serve again as the Seal Sale Committee for 1930. Answers have been received from all but _____. The Seal Sale Contract has been signed and returned to the State Association.

The Annual dues of $5.00 have been paid the South Carolina Tuberculosis Association. In this connection the following extracts from a letter of Mrs. [Roberta Chauncey Blackburn] McDonald's are pertinent:

"You have the privilege of naming a representative director on our Board of Directors who will be voted on at the Annual Meeting. We have not had Charleston on our Executive Committee recently because we have been trying to have a group who could rally quickly and at small cost as the members have been paying for their trips up to the meetings. Charleston is certainly entitled to representation on the

---

[13] Leon Banov was the longtime director of the Charleston County Health Department; for more on Banov, see pp. 147–150, this volume.

[14] Blanche Salley Rhett led the association's annual fundraising drive for several years. Her husband was the former mayor of Charleston. Huger was a prominent lawyer.

Executive Committee, however and if you think that someone from your Association could meet with us quarterly I shall be glad to see that the name is brought up at our Annual Meeting on the 4th of November."

A contract has been signed with the Texas Oil Company whereby this Association is to be given the privilege of buying gasoline at 2 ¢ less than service station prices. This arrangement was entered into with the National Tuberculosis Association. The secretary wrote Mr. Thornhill of the Charleston Oil Company asking him if he would make a similar offer. Mr. Thornhill finds himself unable to do this.[15] As a matter of policy, the Secretary is having the field nurse continue to purchase gas and oil from the Charleston Oil Company, the clinician's car being supplied by the Texas Company. For sometime she has meant to ask the Health Officer if it will be possible for the Association to secure its oil from the service station in the yard, which would effect a considerable saving.

Thirteen children, all of them tuberculosis contacts, enjoyed a stay at the Holiday House; two remaining for the entire period six weeks. The Secretary has advanced the idea and hopes that some day it may be possible to run the Holiday House as a summer camp and later as a year around preventorium, instead of the policy being followed at present, as a vacation home for underprivileged children. A questionnaire asking for information about the Holiday House has been filed with the Association by the State Tuberculosis Association and information is being procured for it now.

At the suggestion of the Secretary, Dr. Smith wrote the Mayor calling attention to the fact that the report of health work in the city of Charleston did not include any reference to preventive measures in tuberculosis, as this work is being conducted by the Association.[16] In view of this fact and because the Association is in reality the tuberculosis bureau of the Health Department, a brief outline of the work for 1929 was given with Dr. Smith's suggestion that it be used in the Year Book so that the public might know that Charleston is not indifferent to this menace. A copy of the Annual Report of the Executive Secretary was sent the Mayor for his personal information. The Secretary has heard, unofficially, that this report is not to be appended to the Year Book.

Some of the money given to Pinehaven through Dr. Smith has been used to purchase two sections of a bookcase for the medical library at Pinehaven. Dr. Smith is anxious to present to Pinehaven a file of the Review of Tuberculosis dating back for several years, if the Association will have them bound. The Secretary recommends that this be done and that the few missing copies be supplied.

---

[15] Theodore Wilbur Thornhill was the longtime president of the Charleston Oil Company.
[16] William Atmar Smith was Pinehaven's medical director.

Mrs. S. G. [Susan] Smith, who was employed temporarily as night attendant, has decided that she would like to keep the position permanently and as her work is highly satisfactory Miss Woosley has decided to retain her.[17] Miss Evelyn Damewood has been supply nurse during the vacation period.

Pinehaven has a waiting list on all wards save the white female. The desire of the colored people to receive treatment there and the length of their waiting list speaks well for the educational work done by the Association, as it will be remembered that for fully two years it was difficult to get the colored people to make use of the sanatorium.

The frigidaire at Pinehaven has been giving considerable trouble and causing expense this summer.

The question of the rural power rate for Pinehaven is still in status quo. This is due to the failure of the A. C. L. [Atlantic Coast Line Railroad] to sign the petition which to become effective must be signed by all consumers on the circuit. The Secretary wrote the purchasing agent of the A. C. L. last week asking him please to sign or give her some definite information as the delay of the A. C. L. has cost the Association to date approximately $330.00.

Upon two recent visits to Columbia the Secretary conferred with Mrs. McDonald. There is no new development in the Duke affair. Mrs. McDonald is in touch with Dr. Rankin and is doing her best to avert the threatened disaster.[18]

The Secretary suggested that it would be well if Miss [Nell] Whaley, the director of Health Education, would use Charleston as a demonstration of her work. The time spent by the Association and the interest aroused in health education make this desireable. Mrs. McDonald promised to confer with Miss Whaley about this but nothing has been heard. The expense of the extended clinic servicemand the staff at the disposal of the Association will make it impossible to continue the intensive health education program carried on for the past three years. It is planned to keep in touch with the schools and so in a measure keep this work alive in the minds of the children through the method of special school clinics. The Secretary has conferred with a member of the County Board of Education and a conference is planned with them during the present week so as to outline the work to be done in the county schools this year and to get their approval.

The piano given to Pinehaven was obviously second-hand but upon the advice of Mr. Jordan, who said that it was a far better instrument than a new one at the price

---

[17] Ola M. Woosley served as superintendent of Pinehaven.

[18] Watson Smith Rankin was director of the Hospital and Orphans section of the Duke Endowment, which provided funding to cover the cost of nonpaying patients at Pinehaven until discontinuing support in 1931.

within the limit assigned, it was ducoed by the Star Painting Company and now presents a nice appearance.[19]
Respectfully submitted,
Eleanor L. Halsey, Exec. Sec'ty.
RLH/cb

> Typed Document. Pinehaven Sanatorium Records, Waring Historical Library, the Medical University of South Carolina, Charleston: Box 1.

---

[19] Frederick Jordan owned a Charleston music store and was cofounder of WCSC radio station.

1931

The State of South Carolina v. Ray Laurens

12 October 1931
Charleston, S.C.

Prohibition rarely prevented the determined Charleston resident or visitor from obtaining a drink. The city gained a reputation for the widespread availability of liquor, and its production, transportation, and sale became very lucrative in the 1920s. Prohibition also kept local police officers busy. Between 1930 and 1932 the Charleston Police Department carried out nearly four thousand raids for alcohol violations.

 The following court transcript provides insight into one Prohibition-era police raid at the intersection of Wentworth and Coming Streets. Ray Laurens, about whom little is known, was tried for violating prohibition laws. Defense attorney J. C. Long appealed for a directed verdict, arguing that "the evidence is that it is a dwelling house and they had no reason for searching a dwelling at night time. The evidence is entirely unequivocal it was not legally secured."[1] The judge, however, declined Long's motion, asserting that "it is nothing more nor less than a house of prostitution and barroom." The case was continued two days later, but its ultimate outcome is unknown.

---

[1] John Charles Long (1903–1984) was an attorney who served one term in the state senate (1931–35) representing Charleston County. After leaving the senate, he expanded his real estate holdings, eventually becoming one of the largest Federal Housing Authority developers in the country. He was a lifelong Democratic Party activist but clashed often with state and local officials.

STATE VS. RAY LAURENS charged with violation prohibition law.

Chief Detective Healy, Sworn: We had a search warrant for the premises of 116 Wentworth St, on the Northwest corner of Coming & Wentworth. We have two policemen there at the present time taking turns. Objected to.[2]

Mr. Long: He states that at present two policemen are there. If they had 40 there now it has nothing to do with the time this offense was committed. It is put in for nothing but to throw a cloud on this Court. This is not charging the man with a crime. We are interested only up to the time the arrest was made and only to facts that pertain to the offense charged. Objection overruled.

Chief Healy: The policemen were stationed at the door when we made the raid. We went into the premises this young man was there and 5 sailors a̶l̶l̶ sitting at a table with glasses of beer in front of them drinking. I came in thru the garage on Coming Street side the time was in the neighborhood of 8 or 8.15 PM. We continued to search and in the bureau drawer there were 4 pints and 4 half pints and 1 small pint of whiskey. We destroyed a lot of empty beer bottles in the yard. There was a carton of 12 or 14 bottles of beer near the icebox and [Frank T.] McNeill and [Edward P.] Wyndham took the rest of the beer out of the icebox. It looked like a regular barroom to me.

The Court: What is the reputation of 116 Wentworth St.

A: The reputation we had is that they are running a disorderly house. We received information that she has moved from there. This man here "Whitie" I understand he is in partners with. I asked the officer at the door, "did you see that man and woman go inside" and he said No. On the information I received from the officer I went upstairs and found this man in a room with a woman. I asked this woman if she was married to this man and she said No.

The Court: Did you have any talk with the defendant.

A: Yes sir, he said it was his stuff and his place, there were 5 sailors sitting around a table with beer glasses about ½ full of beer. I asked the Provost Guard to order the boys out of the place which he did.

Mr. Long: I believe you stated that there were some bedrooms in the house upstairs occupied by people sleeping in them.

A: Yes sir

Q: Were you present at the raid on Escoffie's place on Saturday.[3]

A: Yes sir

---

[2]John Joseph Healy joined the Charleston police force in 1898 and served as chief of detectives from 1924 to 1937.

[3]In August police arrested Robert W. Escoffier after raiding his home at 64 Butler Street and discovering nearly five hundred bottles of illegal liquor ("Home Brew Is Seized," *Charleston News and Courier*, 21 August 1931).

Q: Were you present at the raid on Live Oak Shriver's place.[4] I think I was, yes sir.
Q: It was dark when you entered this house.
A: Yes sir
Q: You didn't testify of any evidence of sale.
A: I could not say about any money being passed.
Q: From what Magistrate did you secure your search warrant.
A: Magistrate [C. Roessler] Burbage.
Q: Did you swear out the warrant.
A: No sir, Detective [Herman] Berkman swore it out.
Q: Upon information and belief
A: Yes sir (Search warrant offered in evidence)

Detective McNeill, Sworn: I accompanied Chief Detective Healy on this raid Saturday night. I went to the front door the door was locked I knocked on the door and this man let me in, meantime Detective Windham came in behind me we went in the kitchen and there were 5 sailors with glasses in their hands with beer in them. I found some beer in the icebox. Right by the icebox was a carton with beer. In the kitchen closet were 4 pts and 4 half pts and 5 small whiskey glasses in the drawer. All told we got 58 bottles of beer. This man said he bought a ½ gallon and colored it with root beer white whiskey it turned it red. He said it was his stuff. He said there's no use to look I only bought ½ gallon. The sailors were drinking each had a tall glass of beer. He claimed the entire stuff belonged to him. He said somebody brings it to me, I don't make it myself.
Mr. Long: Mr. McNeill have you got any of that stuff. (shown)
Q: There was some home brew also.
A: Yes sir
Q: What time did you go there
A: We went in in the neighborhood of 8 P.M.
Q: Do you know where 8 Beresford St. is.
A: You mean No. 11
Q: Is that a whore house
A: For a fact I don't know
Q: What about 45 Market St.
A: I don't know about 45 Market St.
Q: What about 8 Cumberland St.
A: I could not swear to it
Q: Do you know what the search warrant says.
A: The search warrant says by day or night.
Q: Did you on your oath have one bit of evidence of sale.

---

[4] William Henry "Mr. Live Oaks" Shriver was arrested several times for various liquor-related crimes.

A: Only on information
Q: Do you know John Sack.[5]
A: Yes sir
Q: He says that's its on his information
A: Yes, it reads that way.
Q: Is he the source of your information
A: Yes sir
Q: Do you raid every place you know or have information that they have home brew.
A: Only the ones I am told to, I work under orders.
Q: It was under orders you went to this place.
A: The Chief said go and I went.
Q: Do you know whether the warrant came out of the Detective Office.
A: I don't know
Q: You never saw a warrant like this come from a Magistrates office.
A: It may be a different color.
Q: Did you ever see any other warrants that said search by day or night.
A: I don't think Magistrates have any warrants like this.

Lieutenant [Charles W.] Jenkins, Sworn: This young man was brought in and I asked him about the 58 bottles of beer 4 pints and 4 half pints and one ½ pint containing whiskey. He said the stuff belonged to him. No further conversation.

Detective [Purse Wansley] Wamsley, Sworn:
Q: Where you there Saturday night
A: Yes sir, I followed Chief Healy thru the garage into the house I was in front, he stopped in the garage. I walked to the screen door to get in. This gentleman here put down a beer bottle which from which he was filling a glass of beer. Detective McNeill walked in and he opened the screen door and we went in and I came back on the porch and found 2 bottles in the icebox.
Q: What is the reputation of 116 Wentworth St.
A: Bad reputation, I have been stationed there at night by orders of Chief Healy and Chief Ortmann and I seen men and women come up in cars and some were so drunk they could not get [strikeout illegible] in the cars. I heard bottles popping. I have been on office duty the last 4 months and I have never missed a week of making a call there.[6]
Q: Did you arrest any of these people leaving there drunk.
A: No sir
Q: You all went out in the back yard and went to search.
A: The man was in the house.

---

[5]John W. Sack was a Charleston police detective.
[6]Christian H. Ortmann served as Charleston chief of police from 1924 to 1953.

Q: You could see him thru the house
A: There are two ends to the house, I went thru the garage with Chief Healy. I seen McNeill come in the front door and speak to these men.

Mr. Long: I ask for a directed verdict according to the laws of South Carolina. It has been admitted the search was at night. Upon affidavit of information and belief to the effect that liquor is unlawfully kept or stored in the place. (Law read as to the definition of warrants) I say that being true they had no righ legal right to enter that house in the night, no legal right whatsoever. [words missing] to enter the premises. This is to my mind treading on dangerous grounds. I believe that under the decision rendered by Justice Watts that a man in his dwelling house could have shot these men.[7] They had no more right there than a rank stranger. The evidence they secured is not legal. The evidence is that it is a dwelling house and they had no reason for searching a dwelling at night time. The evidence is entirely unequivocal it was not legally secured.

The Court: Chief Healy stated it was not only a disorderly house but also a barroom. Officer Wamsley testified to the same thing. It is nothing more nor less than a house of prostitution and barroom.

In a matter of this kind when the case has been thrashed out and down in evidence the court thinks best to have it reduced to writing and I will make the bond $50.00, for a continuance until Oct. 14th.

Typed Document. Records of the City Court and Police Court, Case Files, Charleston County Public Library, Charleston, S.C.

Burnet R. Maybank, Inaugural Address

14 December 1931
Charleston, S.C.

On 8 December 1931 Charleston voters elected a thirty-two-year-old cotton exporter, Burnet R. Maybank, to be their new mayor, along with a board of aldermen made up mostly of young businessmen.[8] The newly elected leaders took office the following week "at

---

[7]Judge Richard C. Watts served on the South Carolina Supreme Court from 1912 to 1930.

[8]Burnet Rhett Maybank (1899–1954) was born in Charleston and graduated from the College of Charleston in 1919 after serving in the navy during World War I. A descendant of five governors of South Carolina, Maybank worked as a cotton exporter before being elected to the board of alderman in 1927. As mayor, Maybank led the city during the Great Depression. His close ties to Senator James F. Byrnes and New Deal administrator Harry L. Hopkins ensured that Charleston received a steady stream of New Deal funds. Maybank later served as governor of South Carolina (1939–41) and U.S. senator (1941–54).

a time when the city is faced with what may be the greatest financial crisis in its history," according to the News and Courier.[9] The public's expectations for Maybank ran high, as did their anxieties.[10] Several hundred residents filled the council chamber for this noon address; many more listened to the radio broadcast on WCSC.

Maybank began his remarks with a review of the recent election, which he won following a contentious primary.[11] He blasted the former mayor John P. Grace, who had initially supported his campaign before making "demands on me, which, had I granted, would have been a betrayal of trust on my part to the community."[12] Maybank also outlined his plans for dealing with municipal debt, budget constraints, and delinquent tax payments. He encouraged city residents to unite and persevere during the difficult times, and urged them to pay their taxes.

With regard to the many job requests he had received from voters, Maybank reminded city residents that he was not elected the "President of an Employment Agency" and that it would be unrealistic to assume that he could find jobs for everyone. He concluded

---

[9] "Maybank Advises Drastic Economy in His Inaugural," *Charleston News and Courier*, 15 December 1931.

[10] As the ceremony began, aldermen-elect from the six lower wards entered the chamber through the west door and the aldermen-elect from the upper wards entered through the east door. Maybank took two oaths. In the first oath, he pledged to fulfill "the duties of his office, and to support and defend the constitution of the United States and the 1895 constitution of South Carolina." In the second oath, a ceremonial holdover from the nineteenth century, Maybank swore that he had not engaged in a duel since 1881 nor would he during his term in office. Maybank then accepted the keys to City Hall from the outgoing mayor, Thomas P. Stoney, and he administered the oaths to the aldermen (see "Maybank Will Be Installed Today," *Charleston News and Courier*, 14 December 1931; and "Maybank Advises Drastic Economy in His Inaugural").

[11] Maybank defeated Lawrence M. Pinckney, 9,630–5,030, in the 6 October Democratic Party primary.

[12] John P. Grace (1874–1940) was a lawyer and publisher who served as mayor of Charleston from 1911 to 1915 and 1919 to 1923. His four mayoral campaigns, including two failed runs, were hotly contested by Charleston's "Broad Street Gang," a group of lawyers and merchants who wielded tremendous political power. Each of those elections were close and were marred by political violence as well as a rise in religious animosities among Charleston whites. Grace was a Roman Catholic of Irish descent, and his opponents were mostly Protestants, many of whom descended from South Carolina's powerful slaveholding families. In 1916 Grace began publishing the *Charleston American*, a daily newspaper that was under constant fire for its antiwar and pro-German editorials. Grace remained an important political force in Charleston and South Carolina politics after leaving office. Though as mayor he had championed expanding municipal services and public spending to benefit Charleston's working-class majority, he was antagonistic to President Roosevelt and the New Deal.

on a dire note: *"The city of Charleston is broke, flat broke and unless one and all cooperate, the best thing for us to do is auction off our community right now and get the agony over with."*

At this time, I believe that in justice to my friends who supported me so loyally throughout the longest political campaign the City of Charleston has ever known, and in fairness to myself, a short resume of the political campaign from its incipiency should be given. The public is aware of the movement which got under way early last year looking to a peaceful administration to handle Charleston's affairs. It was also hoped that local factions could agree on a candidate who would go into office unopposed, free of political debts, and in position to do the best for the City of Charleston.

It was in the belief that I would be able to go into office unopposed and head an administration that would be equipped to give Charleston the business-like government it needed, that I announced my candidacy for mayor, stating that I was running as an independent.

The citizens committee, headed by Dr. A. J. Geer, endorsed my candidacy, John P. Grace, a former mayor, organized the peoples committee and at a mass meeting held at the Hibernian hall, he unreservedly endorsed my candidacy and the meeting unanimously voted to support me.[13] Others who had been active in politics here, such as John I. Cosgrove, J. C. Long, A. Russell McGowan and others, likewise endorsed me and pledged their support.[14] Now I gave Grace, Cosgrove, McGowan and Long credit for the same sincerity which governed me. It was not long after these developments, however, that Grace made it evident that he was not interested in Charleston so much as he was in restoring the political futures of himself and others who had been repudiated overwhelmingly by the people of Charleston. Mr. Grace made demands on me, which, had I granted, would have been a betrayal of trust on my part to the community. I refused to become a puppet in his hands, and when he found he could not control me, he started to condemn me.

In the meantime, there was a conference held to decide on the personnel of the city Democratic executive committee. All who were selected were pledged to support me. Even while Grace was agreeing to this, he was contemplating the treachery

---

[13] At the 14 April meeting, Grace spoke for nearly three hours, during which he exclaimed that "the best that my leadership can offer you is to ask you to endorse that splendid native son of Charleston, Burnet R. Maybank" ("Maybank to Get Grace's Support," *Charleston News and Courier*, 15 April 1931). Two months earlier, Andrew Jackson Geer, the founder and president of the Geer Drug Company, had initiated efforts to unify the electorate around a candidate friendly to business leaders ("Geer Seeks Help of Faction Heads," *Charleston News and Courier*, 14 February 1931).

[14] Maybank referred to attorneys John I. Cosgrove, John Charles Long, and Alonzo Russell McGowan.

which came to a head on the floor of the Democratic convention. Grace deferred breaking with me until, under the guise of peace and harmony, he could pack the executive committee and the convention with members and delegates who were ready to do his bidding. My real friends, as I did, went to the convention believing that the Democrats of Charleston were united peacefully and harmoniously for the good of Charleston. It will be recalled that at the convention a resolution was introduced condemning Mayor Stoney and all members and employees of the Stoney administration, and calling into question my sincerity.[15] This resolution was introduced for the sole purpose of precipitating the break which ensued, when I and my friends at the convention refused to support it. Grace had hauled down his flag and shown his true colors. He was still the same old "ruined politician" who had divided Charleston into hostile camps for a period of twenty years or more. Again my friends were in the majority at the convention and John I. Cosgrove, president, twice ruled in my favor when votes were taken. When Grace ordered him to reverse his ruling, he promptly complied. Once again Grace had turned minority into majority. His solemn pledge to support me meant nothing at all to him.

We next found out that thirteen members of the executive committee, who had been elected with the understanding that they would support me, were under Grace's control. It was plain that Grace believed that by tactics such as had been used by him in the past in politics, he would be able to prevent me from becoming elected mayor of Charleston.

Charleston was not to be afforded a peaceful political campaign. In due time J. C. Long and A. Russell McGowan yielded to Grace's dictates and refused to abide by their promises to support me. The Grace regime, augmented by a few new recruits, was making its last desperate effort to obtain control of the city government for their private, personal and selfish ends, as had been the case before when Grace, W. Turner Logan and John I. Cosgrove controlled our city.[16]

Grace was himself again. He was the same John P. Grace who had always sought to stir up religious prejudice, class hatred and bitterness as his stepping stones to

---

[15]For coverage of the Charleston Democratic Party convention, see "City Democratic Meeting Marked by Many Clashes," *Charleston News and Courier*, 6 May 1931. Within a few weeks of the convention, Grace withdrew his endorsement of Maybank, calling it "the greatest mistake of his political career." Grace claimed that he had been misled by Maybank, who promised him the right to select a majority of the board of aldermen and pledged to replace a number of city officeholders ("To Name Man to Run for Mayor," *Charleston News and Courier*, 23 May 1931). Thomas Porcher Stoney (1889–1973) was a Charleston attorney who served as mayor from 1923 to 1931. His victory over John P. Grace in the 1923 mayoral primary signaled the return to power of the Broad Street Ring. Mayor Stoney promoted Charleston as "America's most historic city" in an effort to encourage tourism.

[16]William Turner Logan (1874–1941) served two terms in the U.S. House of Representatives (1921–25). Logan was also a law partner of John P. Grace and held various positions in local government and the Democratic Party.

success. False statements by Grace made in reference to me were put in the local press and obtained circulation throughout the state of South Carolina, but the decent people of Charleston rallied to my cause.

What they could not possibly accomplish in a fair and honest election, the Grace ring sought to achieve by characteristic tactics in the executive committee where they had a majority. They sought to disfranchise many of my supporters by intimidation and by challenging enrollments, but thanks to those devoted friends of mine in the executive committee, headed by Henry W. Lockwood and J. Roy Jones, the rights of all qualified Democrats were protected and a fair and square election was insured.[17] On October 6 people in Charleston swamped the Grace machine by the largest majority ever recorded in the history of municipal politics on Charleston. The votes that I received at the polls were in recognition of the fact that I was an independent candidate, neither dominated by an administration, or controlled by, nor responsible to any group of politicians, clique or ring. The community showed that it resented the efforts of Grace and his associates to regain control of the city, and demonstrated, I feel, a vote of confidence in me and those who were on my aldermanic ticket. They showed they were willing to entrust the administration of the city's affairs to a group of men pledged to give an honest, efficient and businesslike government.

Of course, great numbers of my devoted personal friends, and close friends of my father and family, worked for me untiringly and did most to bring my victory. Our administration is one that goes into office entirely free of any political debts, and it is up to us to give the city the finest administration, which their vote shows it wants.

Throughout the United States today and particularly in the agricultural districts the people are short of funds and general depression exists throughout most of the sections of our country. Most of us are familiar with these conditions and most of us have our own ideas as to why they exist. Through the vain promises of high price cotton and wheat, the farm was directly responsible for the enormous overproduction of cotton in 1930 which led to the ruinous decline last season, and which has been followed this year by a further decline. The politicians promised the farmers 16c cotton and $1.10 wheat. The farmers are getting 5c for their cotton and about 40c for their wheat. The cotton mills in South Carolina, upon the theory that the government would maintain the price of cotton at 16c, bought enormous quantities and they find themselves very much in the same fix as the farmers. They have costly inventories on hand, resulting in heavy losses. The City of Charleston is solely and entirely dependent upon the state of South Carolina and parts of Georgia and North Carolina for their export and import business. The sources of new money in our community are derived almost entirely from waterfront activities, our tourist business and a few manufacturing plants located in or near the city, and the United States

---

[17]In 1938 Henry Whilden Lockwood succeeded Maybank as mayor of Charleston, serving until his death in 1944. J. Roy Jones was active in Charleston Democratic Party politics.

government Agencies especially the Navy Yard, Fort Moultrie and the headquarters for the destroyer squadron. As we all know, Charleston was for years the largest fertilizer center in America.[18] This industry, almost entirely depending on the price of cotton in the interior, was seriously injured last year. With the panicky conditions and the lack of money in South Carolina, the fertilizer business will suffer severely this winter and spring, and business will probably be materially curtailed from last year. The export cargoes depending upon cotton have likewise suffered, due to the collapse in farm products, and as one looks into the near future it is impossible to see many bright spots for Charleston. In fact, before our commerce can revive, it is necessary that agriculture be stabilized on a safe and sound basis. The people of Charleston have endured far more calamities in the past than those with which they are now faced, but together with cooperation, they will weather this storm as well as any community. However, while we are in the midst of such unsettled business conditions, each of us must use every effort to pull Charleston forward and all of us must do our very best to curtail expenditures and meet obligations.

The City of Charleston is an excellent place in which to live, and has many attractions. The tourists in recent years have come here in increasing numbers, due to climatic conditions together with the beautiful back country which surrounds Charleston. Most of us believe that there is no place comparable to Charleston in which to live, but if we are to continue to live here, then we must lend our efforts to solve its present problems.

We all know that the county has been built up materially in the past few years at the expense of the City. Most of those who have built residences in the country are entirely dependent upon their jobs or their business in the City to survive. Most of us who own country property realize that without the City our property would be valueless, and the time has come when the people of the county must not only depend upon the City for their source of income and amusement, but must assist the City of Charleston in financing the projects that are for the good of both the county and city government.

At this particular time the finances of our City are in much the same condition as the finances of other municipalities, counties and states of the United States, and it is a source of great anxiety and distress to me as to how we will be able to raise enough money to finance the City of Charleston. The time has come when our credit has been exhausted. The acceptances of this City are very difficult to negotiate owing to the financial plight of the country and to the lack of cash money on all sides, and I trust that most of the citizens of this community realize the fact, as I do, that from

---

[18] Beginning in the 1870s, fertilizer production grew rapidly as a result of the mining of large phosphate deposits along the area's inland waterways. The mining and the processing of phosphates employed thousands of local freedmen as well as convict laborers. By the turn of the century, the industry had declined from its peak years in the 1880s.

now on we must run a cash business and that taxes must be paid, if we are to operate the City.

It is my purpose to enforce, as far as it is humanly possible to the letter of the law, the collection of all taxes. Public money is a trust and I shall treat the same as such. Early in January I shall request publication in the press of all those in arrears for taxes and there shall be no exception to the rule. Anyone who owes and who has not paid by this time, their names will be advertised in the usual manner.[19] The lack of money will necessarily mean curtailment of expenditures of the city of Charleston. I do not propose to hire people and then be unable to pay them and sincerely hope that the banks of this community will cooperate, endeavoring to arrange a market for paper of the city of Charleston, and will give us enough to operate on and pay our interest requirements. If the banks of this community are unable to do this, then the city will have to resort to scrip. However, I do sincerely hope that we will not have to resort to any such means as this, and in case we do, I shall endeavor to arrange it so that the scrip will be good for the payment of taxes and in this way it will have a market near its value.[20]

It is a source of much regret to me that the financial condition of the City of Charleston is such that retrenchment is absolutely necessary. Doubtless you have heard of the improvements that various administrations at various times have made for the city of Charleston. However, these great improvements were all made on credit and it is going to be the duty of those associated with the government of the city of Charleston for the next ten or twenty years to pay for these improvements.[21]

I am attaching at the end of this address a statement sent to me at my request by R. G. [Robert] White, controller, and shall ask this statement be included with this address.

There is, at the present time, due the City of Charleston in uncollected taxes prior to 1931, $445,696.22. There are deficits in the operating fund amounting to $195,853.64. There are deficits in the bond fund of $217,611.23. There are various deficits amounting to $55,000.00. This makes a total deficit, exclusive of the loss of $120,000.00 in assessment for the year 1931, of $468,464.87.

There is due in the year 1932 bonds and notes amounting to $1,109,265.00. In addition to this, there is a deficit in the bond coupons due January 1, $13,260.40, and the interest on $3,350,000.00 in bonds amounting to $67,000.00 and the Port Utilities commission interest of $56,250.00. In other words, we find the City of Charleston is due on January 1, 1932, interest on bonds outstanding against the city amounting

---

[19] On 2 November 1932, the city impounded 107 vehicles for delinquent taxes; the following year Maybank authorized the seizure of another five thousand automobiles.

[20] To meet expenses, Charleston resorted to paying employees in scrip; however, within two years the city was again able to meet its payroll obligations.

[21] These improvements included new sidewalks and drains, as well as a street-paving program and the construction of the Ashley River Bridge.

to $136,510.40, of which there is on hand, nothing to pay. Again I repeat to you, in order that there be no misunderstanding, that we are due in 1932, $1,109,265.00, and due on the 1st of January, $136,510.40. In addition to this, there will be due the interest for next year on bonds and notes outstanding against our city, and its operating expenses and deficits. We have only uncollected taxes, cash on hand, and next year's levy to pay these accounts with. It is going to be extremely difficult and well-nigh impossible for Charleston to pay its present indebtedness and at the same time maintain the city as a going institution, and I ask that everyone read carefully the statement forwarded to me by Mr. White.

In addition to the deficits, notes that are due and interest that is due the people of Charleston must not forget that they have bonded their city for practically $11,000,000.00. The interest on this account without any sinking fund yearly is about $500,000.00, which is 25 mills. It is true that some of this interest is taken care of by the water department, but the majority of it must be levied for by the city to take care of railroad bonds, street bonds and the Port Utilities commission.

The Street Bonds show assessments in arrears of over $600,000.00, and in addition to this, the City of Charleston is due the street fund $100,000.00 plus $60,000.00 for interest. It is my belief that a large portion of this $600,000.00 will have to be paid for by the general taxpayers, as the abuttment tax on this property is not worth the cost of the street improvements. I am also attaching statement of the Street Bonds as of November 1, 1931.

The people must realize that they have bought $11,000,000.00 worth of property for their city in the way of streets, Port Utilities and other measures. This property has not been paid for, it has been bought on installments and the installments are becoming due, and it is either up to the people of Charleston to pay their taxes in order that these installments can be met, or those who hold mortgages against our city will take the necessary steps. I cannot impress too clearly upon the people of Charleston the debts they owe. These debts are occasioned by their demand for services and improvement, and the indifference of many in paying their share of the cost during the past twenty years. The day has come now to pay, and unfortunate as it may be, it is going to interest everyone. It is useless for me to speak at greater length on the financial condition, because the more I say the darker I would be forced to paint the picture. With this financial outlook it is necessary to collect every cent of revenue in every available manner and therefore, I recommend that all things that are taxable be taxed. I think the financial condition is such that all and every one must be made to pay, and I heartily approve and recommend placing upon the tax books of Charleston between three and four million dollars on personal property, and sincerely trust and feel certain that the board of assessors will make it their business to put every one who should pay on the tax books and distribute the burden fairly and equitably.

Business is now taxed almost to extinction not only by City but by the county, state and United States Government. The present financial plight of the country is due to the wealth of the rich being invested in tax-free securities while the wealth of business is invested in real estate, machinery and other items, upon which are levied high Federal, State, County and City taxes.

The City of Charleston pays about two-thirds of the County taxes. Without the City of Charleston there would be no County. Four years ago Mayor Stoney recommended increasing the city limits. On account of bad conditions existing among the business interests, especially the Fertilizer and Oil Companies, I disapproved of this; however, at this time it is absolutely essential that the County assume an equitable share of some of the burdens that the City has been laboring under. The County has shared in the benefits of the City's expenditures at the Airport, Golf Course, the Health Department, Fire Department and various other projects. At this time there are two institutions, namely the Roper Hospital and the Health Department, that are essential to this community. These institutions are provided for by small donations from the City. I recommend that the people of Charleston request the Delegation to take over these two projects and finance them in their entirety. I believe that if the Charleston county Delegation would finance these two institutions and put the entire responsibility on the County, it would result in more efficiency and less politics. It would reduce the City's taxes some 5 mills and increase the County tax some 3 mills. The taxpayers of the City of Charleston under this plan would, of course, pay a little over two-thirds as their share of the County appropriation. Should the personal property be put on the books, necessarily there would be enough of this to levy against to keep down any increase in County taxes.

I shall endeavor to provide for these institutions as far as it is possible until the proper transfer can be made.

It is the duty of the people of Charleston to afford proper elementary and high schools for the education of all of its citizens. The people of Charleston pay state taxes for the upkeep of colleges and universities of the state, and the people pay city taxes for the upkeep of the college of Charleston. The College of Charleston is just as dear and close to me as the public school system. I received my education at this college and certainly appreciate its worth to the community. The city will continue to support the college, however, with the present financial condition, I recommend that the board of trustees increase the tuition fee of the College of Charleston to a moderate sum and afford free scholarships to those worthy boys and girls who are entirely unable to secure a college education without this assistance. I shall ask the delegation to transfer the collection of the school tax from the city to the county. In all other counties of South Carolina the school tax is collected by the county treasurer, and there is no reason why the Charleston district tax should not be collected by the county treasurer just as are the district taxes of St. Michael's, St. Philip's and the other school districts. I make this request for three reasons: First, the children deserve an education and for them to receive an education it is necessary that taxes be paid. The state law grants certain privileges and gives certain powers through the county sheriff's office that puts the county treasurer in a better position to collect taxes.

Second, I believe that the teachers should be fully protected and their salaries should be paid. There is no doubt but that the county treasurer's office with the sheriff can better collect taxes than the mayor's office with the city treasurer.

Third, the county taxes are moderately low, while the city taxes are very high, and it will be much easier to collect the school tax on low county millage than on high city millage. The people of Charleston pay nearly two-thirds of the upkeep of the county treasurer's office and it appears to me that they certainly should have this service at the treasurer's office rather than to make additional payments for the collection of these taxes.

I am delighted to know that the County Teachers' association is working on the lines suggested by me for a summer school for teachers at the College of Charleston. I have discussed the matter with the president of the College and with several members of the board of trustees. They are all elated, and I assure the teachers of this community of my whole-hearted support if they will assist me in establishing a summer college here in order that they may save expenses, which they are called upon to pay when they are forced to go elsewhere. It is the duty of the teachers and the parent-teachers' associations to make this a reality, and I sincerely believe that if this is done, it will be only a short time before we have a large enrollment of teachers from all parts of South Carolina, because Charleston has unusual summer attractions in the way of golf, beaches and various water sports that should make it more desirable for the teachers to spend their vacations here and combine pleasure and work. This movement will have a far-reaching effect.

It is a source of great regret to me that the last City Council, of which I was a member, found it necessary to reduce the wages of those in the employ of the city who were barely making a living wage. High salaries and moderate salaries must be reduced, but I have no intention of either voting for or recommending anything but a living wage to the members of the various departments and institutions. As soon as I am able to find out how much money we will get, I intend to have a conference with some of my labor friends and do all that I can to see that the wages of the underpaid city employees are reestablished on their old basis.

I wish the people of Charleston to know that I shall change the police force as I stated in the campaign and endeavor to have law and order as far as possible. I realize that there are certain things that must exist in certain places and that this is far better than having them existing throughout the community. I also realize that the police department is an expensive organization set up to preserve law and order and not to chase people around for having half pints in their possessions. Every time the prohibition question has been put before the people of Charleston it has been overwhelmingly repudiated, and it is not my purpose to have the police force arrest poor people for possessing a pint while the rich and well-to-do have what they wish.

The police department will enforce to the letter of the law violation of city ordinances, especially those relating to drunkenness and reckless driving. It is also my purpose not to tolerate any drinking among any city employees. I have nothing to do with what the city employee does in his off hours, provided he conducts himself in proper manner; however during working hours no city employee will be allowed to drink or come to work under the influence of liquor. There is a certain amount of drinking going on in certain departments that I know of at this time, and I mention this fact as a fair warning, because anyone who is found with whiskey or under the influence of whiskey while he is working for the City of Charleston, regardless of his length of service or regardless of what department he belongs to, will be immediately dismissed.

I feel certain that all the aldermen endorse the statement that I will not stand for any graft or corruption on any occasion or in any office. I shall demand that there be no graft in the City.

We are the only city in America that has wonderful beaches in each direction but no way to get to them except by paying toll. Everyone is familiar with the diversion of approximately $30,000.00 State Highway money to build a private road to a private colored beach resort. Things of this sort should not be tolerated by the people of Charleston and they should appeal to the Governor not to permit a recurrence of such a scandal. No new concrete roads have been built in this section in recent year, except Route 40, which was built because Senator [William S.] Legare and the delegation demanded this for their vote for the $65,000,000.00 Highway bond issue.

I believe that the best way to operate the Golf Course is not to make any levy for this activity but to permit the Commissioners to run the golf Course from the receipts, and at the end of each year turn over whatever profits may be derived to the City of Charleston, to apply to the reduction of expenditures that have been made towards this project. I try to have this arranged with the Legislature.

The Port Utilities Commission is composed of a group of gentlemen who have given their time without remuneration in order that the business of Charleston can be developed. No one appreciates their efforts more than I and I will work in harmony with these gentlemen. It will be necessary to reduce the operating expenses and salaries in this organization, for with the financial plight of the city, it is essentially necessary that the Port Utilities Commission earn their requirements. Experience has shown that it was unwise for the city to have gone in the water front business, and all of us know that if it were not for the lease that the city has on the army base, the water front property as purchased by the city would be inadequate and of limited use. Nearly ninety per cent of the city property is either leased or rented, and it seems almost impossible to make any money out of the same. The Port Utilities is really a real estate agency for the leasing of public property.

When the city of Charleston purchased the water front from the railroads it took away all incentive that the railroads had to do business here, with the result that the railroads use their own terminals in Savannah and Norfolk whenever possible. The water front business of Charleston is practically done by independent people. I shall use my every effort to have Senator [Ellison D.] Smith and Senator [James F.] Byrnes request the farm board and the cooperative associations to ship all of their South Carolina cotton through the Port Utilities Commission. It has always been the custom that Georgia cotton be shipped through Savannah, and Alabama cotton through Mobile, and I believe the South Carolina cotton should likewise be shipped through Charleston. I am advised that a vast amount of this cotton has been shipped through Savanna, Georgia, which is manifestly unfair to South Carolina's state port. As far as my private associations with Maybank & Company in the past are concerned, we have been among the largest customers of the Port Utilities Commission, but we do not need any assistance from them to operate our own business. We own extensive docks and properties in this community and the interest which I take in the Port Utilities Commission shall not be governed by any private interests or desires which I may have.

The United States government has never shipped us or any compress or storage plant in which we have interest a single bale of cotton. The cotton which we have at our compresses, ninety per cent was shipped there by Maybank & Company. The other ten per cent by various cotton firms who are friendly disposed towards us. The government has some cotton at our plants which they demanded from us and our friends on New York future contracts, but they have never shipped to us one single bale of cotton.

The water front of the City of Charleston on the Ashley river is ten miles long; on the Cooper river is fifteen miles long, and a large part of this is for sale. There is plenty of room for all the business firms in the southeast to settle here if they wish. The absurdity that one person or any one thousand people could bottle up a port is not only ridiculous but is flase and untrue. If there is any business firm that wishes to come to Charleston, or if anyone can persuade any organization to make this port their headquarters, I will see to it that they got all the facilities as far as Charleston is concerned that they need. There is enough vacant water front property in and around Charleston to build another New York if there were need for it. The City owns West Point Mills and I would be glad to have some large industrial or export firm take over this property for nothing if they would be willing to develop it properly. Therefore, if any man knows of anyone whom he could persuade to come to Charleston, it will only be necessary for him to communicate with me and proper arrangements will certainly be made. At the present time there is a law restricting business from certain sections of the city, but with the financial conditions and lack of business that exist here now, there will be no trouble to have this law changed over night if any large firm or firms would consider our city. I believe that such action will meet with public approval.

The people of Charleston have for generations been led by politicians to believe that all that is necessary for a port is to have a good harbor close to the open sea. This, of course, is utterly ridiculous to anyone familiar with world commerce. A port is solely and entirely dependent upon railroad terminals and its back country. This back country consists either of thickly populated sections that demand considerable importation of goods, or agricultural and manufacturing sections from whence export cargoes are derived. The chief ports of the world are situated far from the open seas and their harbors are of little consequence. Everyone is familiar with New York; where center the enormous railroad terminals of America and which is hours away from the ocean. New Orleans, La., over one hundred miles from the Gulf, represents the terminals of not only railroads but the barge lines of the Mississippi river. London, England, miles away from the ocean, represents thickly populated areas in which large cargoes must be imported. Liverpool, England, a port which can only be entered during certain hours of the day on account of the tide, represents large manufacturing centers of the British Isles. In our own southland, we have Houston, Texas, a model example of railroad terminals. The steamships pass by Galveston's beautiful harbor which is located on the open sea, similar to Charleston's, and go up a canal twenty-five miles to reach the railroad terminals of Houston. A harbor is no good without organization to feed it, and what Charleston has needed for years was not the purchase of the waterfront but the bringing to Charleston of some railroad which would have supplied cargoes. Ships will go anywhere for cargoes, but will go nowhere for empty harbors, except in times of storms. We have placed far too much emphasis on our harbor and not enough upon the business of Charleston as a port.

The Water Commission, as the Port Utilities Commission, is composed of men who are giving their time and thought towards the development of Charleston and I for one appreciate what they are doing. Under present conditions, I believe that profits of our waterworks should be used towards paying the City's obligations. These gentlemen on the Water Commission assured me that they would cooperate along these lines, and they also assured me they would cooperate along the lines of reducing expenses and salaries.

It shall be necessary for me to reduce expenses in the neighborhood of $100,000.00 to $150,000.00 in order that the taxes shall not be increased. In this connection, it will be necessary to cut every department from last year's budget and to eliminate several departments. I regret exceedingly that the City of Charleston has no money at present with which to advertise and no money with which to run a Traffic Bureau; therefore, it is the duty of the private individuals, the hotels and merchants, who benefit from these departments, to raise a subscription among themselves to keep them, if they desire. I will, as an individual, contribute to such a fund.

I trust that the people of Charleston realize that I have been elected Mayor and not President of an Employment Agency. I realize that some ten thousand people voted for me and it is only natural that I must look after their interest. The general widespread unemployment in the City of Charleston makes my position very difficult. A great many requests have been made upon me. In fact, I believe that two thousand of the four thousand unemployed have either telephoned, written or called on me in person with the hope that I would be able to give them a position, but the present financial condition makes it necessary that expenses and positions be curtailed, and at this time and until conditions improve and tax receipts are more favorable, it will be impossible to give but very few jobs and therefore, those out of work will have to be patient. It will be very hard for me to be forced to release some of those in the employ of the City, but the financial conditions are such that it is either a question of some being released or not being paid. It is also my purpose to request that only those living within the corporate limits of the City of Charleston be hired in any municipal project and that Charleston firms be given the preference on all City business. The people of Charleston are called upon to pay taxes to run the City and no one should be employed by the City Government who does not live within the city limits. I shall request Council to enact a law requiring everyone working on the City's or Commission's payroll to be a resident of the City of Charleston, and that everyone desiring a position to show that they have been a resident of Charleston for at least two years. With the present unemployment and bad business conditions existing in our community, it is our duty first to look after our own people and while this may not be advantageous at some future date when business revives, it is certainly essential and necessary at the present time.

And now in closing let me say that the recommendations which I have made have been made as a private citizen and as an individual sees conditions in our community. It is the duty of every individual to advise what he thinks best for the common interest and not for his own individual gain. The recommendations which I have made towards reducing expenditures have been made after mature judgment and without consideration or discussion with anyone else. These recommendations can only be carried out if my aldermanic board backs me up. I do not request them to follow me blindly, but I do insist that they give careful and due consideration to all that I have said and use their own judgment as to what is best for Charleston. All of these things or any small part of them can only be done if public sentiment is with us, and I trust and hope that the public of Charleston will support us. I can only make recommendations to my aldermanic board and can only make recommendations to the legislative body. I have no right and no authority to demand anything. Therefore, it is up to the sixty-two thousand citizens of Charleston to back me up if they want their city relieved of the present debt and tax burdens for the next generation. The city of Charleston is broke, flat broke, and unless one and all cooperate, the best thing for us to do is auction off our community right now and get the agony over with. Under these conditions, I again make one last appeal for assistance from everyone.

The business of this community is suffering from the general depression in the United States and particularly the agricultural conditions of the southeast. I believe that most business firms are using their every effort to keep in their employ as many men as possible. In our business we are employing as many people as possible, although there is little work to do and will not be any large amount of work in my opinion for at least another year. Jobs are very scarce and there is no money in the City Treasury to pay salaries. As far as the clerical forces, the engineering forces, and the professional forces of Charleston are concerned, it is with much regret that I am forced to express an opinion, but it is my belief that not only will there be no help needed along any of these lines, but some of those now in the employ of the city will have to be released.

Therefore, in closing let me say that those who wish their friends retained or their friends given positions, to consider the financial plight of our city before making any requests.

I want again to voice my appreciation of the work done in my behalf and that of the candidates on my ticket by loyal supporters in every ward in the city. We are pledged to and will render the best service of which we are capable. We want the cooperation and the assistance of the business people of Charleston in our efforts to solve the serious financial problems which confront us. We want the support of the community at large in our efforts to give Charleston the kind of government which our city should have. We invite cooperation from all. Conditions in Charleston are such that every man, woman and child must put his or her shoulder to the wheel if we are to advance and prosper.

Published Document. Charleston (S.C.). City Council.
Journal of the City Council of Charleston, 1927–1931.
[Charleston, S.C.: The Council], [1931]

1932

The City Council of Charleston, Minutes

26 January 1932
Charleston, S.C.
This excerpt from the minutes of the first regular meeting since their inauguration reveals members of Charleston's city council discussing the economic crisis and its impact on their constituents. Several committed to shielding low-wage city workers from pay cuts. They also formed a committee to coordinate relief efforts. Portions of the minutes not included below indicate that the aldermen received various departmental reports and unanimously elected J. Waties Waring to serve as corporation counsel under the new administration.[1]

Alderman Wilson declared that there were a couple of things that he wanted to talk about. The first was the salary cut and he recalled the promises made in the campaign last summer to protect the man with moderate salary or wages.[2] He admitted that he did not feel as keenly for the higher priced labor but the men on a wage scale of $100.00 or $125.00 are more severely affected by a 10 or 15 per cent cut than the men who draw the larger salaries. The men on the smaller wage scale have their noses to the grinding stone while the men who have the larger scale have been able not only to have lived better but to have made investments and provided themselves against the period of stress. He favored a sliding scale of salary reductions which

---

[1] Julius Waties Waring (1880–1968) was named a federal judge in 1942 and ruled in favor of proponents of desegregation in key civil rights cases. His minority ruling in *Briggs v. Elliot* 342 U.S. 350 (1952) provided the foundation for the U.S. Supreme Court's historic desegregation decision in *Brown v. Board of Education of Topeka* 347 U.S. 483 (1954).

[2] Isaac Ripon Wilson Sr. (1875–1959) was a pharmacist for a number of years before returning to medical school to become a physician. He served as assistant surgeon of the United States quarantine service.

would make the cuts more equitable. He suggested that the men with a salary of $125.00 per month should suffer no cut and the rate should follow the following form: $150.00, a reduction of 5 per cent; $200.00, 10 per cent; $300.00, 20 per cent; $400.00, 30 per cent; $500.00, 40 per cent and $600.00, 50 per cent.

The other matter that he wanted to speak about was the destitution which is now existing especially in the upper sections of Charleston. Families are in great want because the heads of the families are without work. They are anxious to work to provide for their needs but they are unable to find employment. There were three cases which he said that he had in mind, typical of many others. There is a druggist, with seven or eight children. The oldest at the Memminger School and the youngest nine months old. He has been out of work for sometime and what he brings home is in a paper bag. A gift of a peck of Irish potatoes recently was relished by the children as others would eat ice cream cones. There is another case of a former insurance collector, now out of work, living on what his friends may contribute. The children are kept alive principally on a quart of milk furnished by a dairy and two quarts of skimmed milk furnished from other sources. A third case is that of a former policeman with seven children who are in great need. He said that the Welfare Bureau is of course trying to do all that it can in aiding the distress but he only wanted to emphasize the pressing need of family relief in the community, the necessity of furnishing grits, flour, etc, in homes where there is no food. The Public should be acquainted with these conditions and should not complain when appropriations have to be made to meet such pressing necessity.

Alderman Stehmeyer remarked that he understood that the policeman referred to had quit his job because his salary had been cut but Alderman Wilson replied that this was not entirely the case, although the salary cut might have been a contributing cause.[3]

Alderman Hoppmann was in hearty accord with Alderman Wilson's remarks, adding that he proposed to stick to the campaign promises if possible. He declared further that he was opposed to any employee, directly or indirectly employed by the City, receiving a larger salary than that paid to the Mayor.[4]

Alderman Hilton endorsed the remarks of Aldermen Wilson and Hoppmann.[5] He was opposed to the 17 ½ per cent cut but that was not the measure of this administration. He was hopeful that it will be possible to restore the salaries to the moderately paid employees and prorate the others in accord.

The Mayor said that he was glad that Alderman Wilson had brought up the matter and he was much of his opinion. He recalled the frequent sessions of the

---

[3] Diedrich Stehmeyer (1863–1941) was born in Bremen, Germany, and immigrated to the United States in 1881.

[4] William "Walter" Hoppmann (1888–1951) worked as a machinist at the Charleston Navy Yard.

[5] Archie Smith Hilton (1895–1972) was an insurance agent.

Committee on Ways and Means, at which the two were laboring together. The Committee on Streets has also been lending its hand in attempting to solve the wage scale, to reduce the high salaries and bring up the small salaries. The promises to the small salary men were made in good faith, the Mayor said, and he thought that everybody understands the situation. The banks will not advance the City one dime and the City has to operate without the financial support that it formerly had. He has spent a whole month working on finances and right now, he is endeavoring to establish some medium of exchange. The City is getting in some money by the allowance of a discount on taxes which has netted $30,000.00 to $40,000.00, and unless the people take advantage of this offer, the City will be further handicapped. The plan of issuing the pay warrants was the only resort of the City to keep going and the Mayor expressed confidence in the support of the community in maintaining the value of the script. The Chicago script went down to fifty cents on the dollar but he was sure that nothing like this will happen here. With the reduced salary and wage scale, the City is obligated to pay the rate to be fixed and any depreciation of the script will mean an increased issue so that the city employees will not be subjected to loss. As to high salaries in certain commissions, the Mayor declared that he had only one vote and it is his purpose to fight for a reduction of any excessive salaries. He had insisted upon a cut for himself and it was his purpose to reduce the big salaries and raise the small salaries wherever possible.

Alderman McGowan told of his efforts in interesting the merchants and business people in the acceptance of script and he found a very ready response expressing confidence in the general circulation of the medium.[6]

Alderman Renken declared that in working on the budget of the Public Service Department, the idea was by reduction of salaries to keep as many people as possible on the pay rolls.[7] There is no desire to cut unnecessarily any man's pay but there is an obligation not to turn people out to starve.

Alderman Lewis remarked on the efforts that are being made to adjust a situation that has probably never before confronted a City administration.[8] The Committee on Ways and Means is doing everything in its power. It is not desired to pay an employee for eleven months and then find that is has nothing to pay him for the twelfth month, so, the salary and wage question like the many other phases of the situation, has to be carefully gone over and he asked that the Council would wait until the Committee is ready to submit its report.

Alderman Von Dohlen declared that the employment situation is a serious one and it is growing more serious.[9] As a member of a sub-committee of the Committee

[6]William Oliver McGowan Sr. (1881–1956) worked in the tailoring and dry-cleaning business.
[7]Walter Albert Renken Sr. (1896–1973) worked as an automobile salesman.
[8]David Sloan Lewis (1883–1950) was a sales manager for the Standard Oil Company.
[9]James Albert Von Dohlen (1879–1945) was president of the J. A Von Dohlen Steamship Company and had served on the United States War Industries Board during World War I.

on Ways and Means, he has been looking into the service, given by the Social Welfare Bureau and he commented upon the heavy demands upon this agency. He had been giving study to the subject generally and he has become convinced that the handling of this situation is a community and not a municipal problem. This is the way it is generally viewed. Along the coast, organizations have been effected with a slogan as, "I will share," everybody contributing to the employment and relief fund, and it was his idea that Charleston should fall into line and effect a community organization at once. The charitable activities should be interested at once in the proposition so as to meet the demands of food and clothing. The situation, he insisted, can be handled only as a community proposition.

The Mayor remarked that there are 6,000 to 6,500 people out of work in Charleston. Fourteen truck loads of vegetables had been gotten recently in the county and distributed. The Social Welfare Bureau was caring for over 800 families feeding them at a rate of forty-nine cents per week, per person. The fleet has left Charleston and the loss of this spending agency will be felt in the trade.

Alderman Geer requested Alderman Wilson to furnish him with the name of the druggist who was in distress that he might take up the matter for his relief with the druggists association.

The Mayor said that he understood that Columbia had raised about $110,000.00 for the demands of the employment situation and Alderman Von Dohlen thought that Charlotte had raised $100,000.00. They ventured the opinion that a like amount would be required for Charleston.

Alderman Grice remarked that it is clear that the municipality can not assume the financial burden but the responsibility is with City Council to see that this necessary relief work is undertaken.[10] He suggested that the Mayor appoint a committee of Aldermen, citizens, charitable workers and representatives of the labor organizations, and perhaps some representative of the unemployed to study the situation and make an effort to alleviate the suffering. He alluded to the possible use of the already organized set-up of the City in handling the situation and that plans be made to cover a period of twelve months, if the period of stress continues this long.

The Mayor suggested that a committee be appointed to serve with him in effecting the general plans of the organization and the following were named: Aldermen Grice, Wilson, Geer, Von Dohlen, Lockwood and Connelley.[11]

---

[10]Edmund P. Grice Jr. (1890–1961) served as the director of the Federal Emergency Relief Administration for Charleston County and district administrator for the Works Progress Administration. In 1942 he was named executive secretary of the Charleston County Board of Public Welfare. He worked with the United Nations during World War II and was appointed Charleston postmaster in 1946.

[11]Alexander Chambliss Connelley (1882–1957) was an undertaker and owner of a funeral home.

The Mayor requested the Aldermen to confer with him tomorrow afternoon on the matter

Council then adjourned.

JOSEPH C. BARBOT, Clerk of Council[12]

> Published Document. Charleston (S.C.). City Council.
> *Journal of the City Council of Charleston, 1931–1935.*
> [Charleston, S.C.: The Council], [1935].

Ella L. Smyrl to Cordella A. Winn

26 January 1932
Charleston, S.C.

From 1920 to 1967 the Coming Street YWCA served as an African American branch of the YWCA of Charleston.[13] *In this letter Smyrl, the general secretary of the Coming Street YWCA, requested advice from Winn, a national YWCA staff member, as to how she should respond to a request from Central branch leaders that the "Colored" branch modify its sign to avoid the possibility of white people arriving at Coming Street mistakenly: "This has arisen because they failed to have the address of the Central placed on some highway cafeteria signs that were made recently." Smyrl also indicated that the staff "received 90% of our December salary," despite press reports of bank failures in South Carolina.*[14]

---

[12]Joseph Claude Barbot (1874–1937) worked as a reporter for the *Charleston Evening Post* before serving as clerk for the Charleston City Council for more than twenty years.

[13]In May 1967 the Central YWCA of Charleston disaffiliated from the national YWCA in opposition to their support of desegregation. Coming Street branch activists who were aligned with the national office began meeting to reconstitute the YWCA. It was nationally chartered in 1970 as the YWCA of Greater Charleston.

[14]In a 5 January letter to Smyrl, Winn wrote that she was "terribly distressed about the bank situation," and "wondered whether Charleston was being affected" (Winn to Smyrl, 5 January 1932, Young Women's Christian Association Papers, Avery Research Center for African American History and Culture, College of Charleston, Charleston, S.C.: Box 3 [abbreviated below as YWCA Papers]). Ella Louise Smyrl Jones (1899–1983) served as the general secretary of the Coming Street YWCA from 1928 to 1933. Cordella Arthur Winn (1878–1965) graduated from Columbus Normal School and worked for the YWCA from 1918 to 1938, when she left to teach at Florida A&M.

Mrs. C. A. Winn
600 Lexington Ave.
New York, N.Y.

My dear Mrs. Winn:

Thank you and Miss Bowles for the very nice letters that I received earlier in the month. I have been and still am quite busy as you know we are at this time of year.[15]

First, I want to say that we received 90% of our December salary since I heard from you. We do not know just what will be done. But, we are going on. One Secretary at Central is discontinued and several of the general help. Nothing definite has been given from the Bank, as you have seen, perhaps. We hope that the adjustment will be favorable.

Last week, we were agreeably pleased to begin what we are calling our Leadership Hour at the Branch on Tuesday night. This to be continued each third Tuesday evening for one hour at least. We are using Conference delegates (especially, Branch Conference) as a steering committee for these. We are using Conference findings and other Nat'l news as basic discussional material. We had twenty persons at this first meeting. I am so glad that one of our younger Ministers came, too, because, he can be a good bit of help to us.

I am enclosing copies of the ballot and Who's Who. Some of these persons may be new to you. We have been trying to reach some new gr groups at this time. I hope we succeed. You notice that we have seven vacancies, two of them are for two years filling the unexpired terms of Mrs. Zara Gailliard and Mrs. M. E. Fields. Mrs. Gailliard asked to be released and the committee decided that in view of the six month's unexplained absence, with due notification of meetings, of Mrs. Fields, the vacancy must be filled, so, that explains the extra two vacancies.[16]

Mrs. Winn, I'd like to ask you if it is general to use the name of the particular Branch in the addition to the sign Y.W.C.A. in front of our Branches? A request has come from the Central asking (and now, it seems that they are determined to have the change made, even if they have to bear the expense themselves as we have no money for such, since, in our thinking, especially, it does not seem necessary) that the word Branch be added to our Y.W.C.A. sign in order not to confuse persons wishing to locate the Central. This has arisen because they failed to have the address of the Central placed on some highway cafeteria signs that were made recently.

We explained to them that less than a half dozen white persons had made this mistake and that we could direct any others who may do the same just as we had directed the few who had come in the past years. And that if anything additional

---

[15]Winn's sister Eva D. Bowles was also employed in the YWCA's national office.

[16]Zara Gailliard Hamilton (1900–1991) was a Charleston schoolteacher. Mamie Elizabeth Garvin Fields (1888–1987) was an educator and community activist.

should be added, it should be the entire name of the Branch, not just the word Branch. To persons from cities having more than one branch, that would mean nothing; therefore, nothing would be gained. This is to come to the Committee of Management again on Tuesday night of next week. I hoped to have heard from you on this before, but, other things have been so pressing. However, I'll appreciate it very much if I may have your thoughts of it by that time, or Miss Bowles', if possible. I do not recall observing such arrangement, generally, in the cities where I've visited our Branches.[17]

I'm attempting to present "The Adventures of Ella Cinders" as I've written the most of the speaking parts, using the outline from the Womans Press at our Annual on this Friday night. Will send you a copy later, hope it comes through all right. Haven't had much time. Intended using something else, but, it was out of print. So, I had to use this.[18]

Thursday night, we are having a Modern Movie Star Musical Revue, a Minstrel Farce; which is lots of fun, and dancing afterwards. I haven't heard of any reaction thus far, guess it may come after the affair. However, I think the committee is quite prpared for such. Some of the more hesitant ones have benefited by certain observations made during the past summers where dancing was enjoyed without injuring any of the young people in the Branches where this obtained.

This is my usual period for [strikeout illegible] decision as to future work with the Association. I am not positive in my decision as yet. But, again, I want to say that for many reasons, I am ready to leave this field, naturally, there are reasons why I am not ready to leave. I realize, too, that this is a most critical time for changes. However, I want both you and Miss Bowles to know that whatever I decide, I shall have endeavored to consider all viewpoints. And intend, if possible, with your advice of the past and any that you will please give now, to do the best for the majority group; which is the Association.[19]

---

[17] In her 29 January reply, Winn stated: "I think you have already used wise judgment in your thinking. The only thing that we are very anxious about is that branches have their sign with their name, but no word 'colored.' There is no objection as far as we are concerned to have your sign state 'The Coming Street Branch,' and if it eases the minds of the other group and they are willing to pay for it, it will not hurt, because we will still continue to have people come and to send them on" (Winn to Smyrl, 29 January 1932, YWCA Papers).

[18] "The Adventure of Ella Cinders" was a Cinderella-themed syndicated comic strip that ran from 1925 to 1961. A film based on the comic was released in 1926.

[19] In her subsequent correspondence with Winn, Smyrl continued to express ambivalence regarding her future with the YWCA, mostly because of the association's precarious finances: "Money is certainly not my major interest, but, we carry too much of a load now and with so much irregularity, one has to look ahead, despite the fact that we all know that conditions are bad generally (Winn to Smyrl, 18 March 1932, YWCA Papers).

With best wishes from all of us.

Very sincerely yours,
Ella L. Smyrl Branch Gen'l Sec.

> Typed Letter Copy. Young Women's Christian Association Papers, Avery Research Center for African American History and Culture, College of Charleston, Charleston, S.C.: Box 3.

William McKinley Bowman to Franklin D. Roosevelt

25 November 1932
St. George, S.C.

On 8 November 1932 Franklin D. Roosevelt won the presidential election by a landslide, taking more than 57 percent of the popular vote and winning the electoral votes of all but six states. Of the 104,407 South Carolinians who voted, more than 98 percent cast ballots for the Democratic governor from New York. The incumbent, Herbert Hoover, received fewer than two thousand votes. In the weeks between the election and his 4 March 1933 inauguration, Roosevelt received congratulatory letters from across the country, including this one from an African American teenager in rural Dorchester County.[20]

Hon. Franklin D. Roosevelt,
Governor of New York, President-Elect,
Warm Spring, Georgia.

Dear Mr. Roosevelt:

    I am very glad, as I predicted that you won, and on a clean sweep too. Now I did not canvass very much for you, but every voter I came in contact with I persuaded them to vote for you, and I spoke for you at 3 or 4 meetings in this state. Now Mr. Roosevelt to make my letter brief, and to the point, I want you to remember the colored voters of America, who gave you approximately 6,000,000 (six million) votes,

---

[20] A staff assistant replied that Roosevelt would "keep these matters in mind and give them his most careful consideration" (Secretary to Mr. Roosevelt to William McKinley Bowman, 26 January 1932, DPNC Papers: South Carolina, After Election). William McKinley Bowman (1914–2000) was born in St. George and was injured in a sawmill accident as a teenager. The poor treatment he received instilled within him a lifelong commitment to justice. He was ordained into the ministry in 1938 and served as pastor of Second Nazareth Baptist Church in Columbia (1949–1996), during which he encouraged his congregation members to support the African American freedom movement. Bowman also hosted a radio program on WOIC in Columbia.

and please replace the Republican Colored office holders with Colored Democrats & give find the colored voters a place in your cabinet as (Register of Treasury, Asst. Secretary of Labor). Now Mr. Roosevelt I think if you look over the list of Colored Democrats, you will find no better men fitted for the positions mention than for (Register of Treasury) Seymour Caroll, Columbia, South Carolina, (Asst. Secretary of Labor) Dr. Robert R. Moton of Tuskegee Alabama.[21]

Now Mr. Roosevelt I am very interested in the progress of Negro Race of America, they will make good if white people will give them a chance. One more wish and I am through: I wish in your inauguration speech you will condemn Mob Rule and Lynching of the South and also sponsor a bill nationally to help blot it out in the South, for it is a shame on the Southland and the United States at large.[22]

Hoping you a successful and happy Administration. I am praying for your success every day.

I am, your ardent supporter,
William McKinley Bowman

Autographed Letter Signed. Democratic Party National Committee Papers, Franklin D. Roosevelt Library and Archives, Hyde Park, N.Y.: South Carolina, After Election.

---

[21] Robert Moton succeeded Booker T. Washington as principal of Tuskegee Institute. Seymour Carroll was a Republican Party activist and field secretary for the American Humane Education Society. While Roosevelt did not name an African American to his cabinet, he drew on the expertise of the Federal Council of Negro Affairs, which included several dozen New Deal administrators, scholars, and advisors. The council was informally known as Roosevelt's "black cabinet."

[22] While passage of a federal antilynching bill had long been a priority for African American reformers, Roosevelt refused to champion such legislation for fear of alienating his strong support among southern white voters.

1933–1934

Burnet R. Maybank to John L. M. Irby

25 September 1933
[Charleston, S.C.]
Mayor Maybank wired Irby, the State Director of the Public Works Administration, to inquire whether proposals for construction projects might reflect Charleston wage standards rather than the higher federal rate.[1] The Public Works Administration was established in 1933 as part of the National Industrial Recovery Act. It sought to promote economic recovery through the construction of public works such as schools, hospitals, airports, and dams.

As federal money began rolling into South Carolina, local employers fretted that better-paying government jobs would force them to pay higher wages to their employees, especially African American farmhands and domestic workers.

J L M IRBY
STATE ENGINEER
COLUMBIA, S.C.

IS THERE ANY CHANCE OF SUBMITTING ANY PLANS ON THE BASIS OF LOCAL WAGES AND CONDITIONS STOP COUNTY DELEGATION HERE FIGHTING MANY IMPROVEMENTS ON ACCOUNT DOLLAR AN HOUR WORK STOP I HAVE ADVISED THEM NO

---

[1]John Laurens MacFarlane Irby (1885–1960) graduated from the Citadel in 1906 and served in the 117th Engineer Regiment of the U.S. Army during World War I. He served as South Carolina state engineer and state director of the Public Works Administration before taking a position as a regional director of the Works Progress Administration.

CHANCE REDUCE GOVERNMENT WAGE SCALE STOP PLEASE WIRE ME IF IN YOUR OPINION IF ANY WAY TO ADJUST WAGES.

BURNET R. MAYBANK
GOVERNMENT TELEGRAM

> Typed Wire Copy. Burnet R. Maybank Senatorial Papers, Special Collections, Addlestone Library, College of Charleston, Charleston, S.C.: Box 142.

John L. M. Irby to Burnet R. Maybank

25 September 1933
Columbia, S.C.

Irby wired an immediate response to Maybank's 25 September telegram. He indicated that it would be "impossible" to lower the rates and that the "government grant" would "take care of increased scale."[2] Irby followed up his telegram with this letter, in which he urged Maybank to explain to the county delegation that the higher wages are "the heart of the whole recovery plan." In a 26 September reply to Irby, Maybank wrote, "I explained long ago to the County Delegation this status but I have been unable to do anything."[3]

Burnet Maybank,
Mayor,
Charleston, S.C.

Dear Mr. Maybank:

In further reference to your telegram in regard to change of wage scale, explain to your County Delegation that the wage scale against them amounts to only twenty eight cents and seventy cents, and that they must look on it from the standpoint of thirty hours per week and not per hour basis.

---

[2]Irby to Maybank, 25 September 1933, Burnet R. Maybank Senatorial Papers, Special Collections, Addlestone Library, College of Charleston, Charleston, S.C.: Box 142 (abbreviated below as Maybank Senatorial Papers).

[3]Maybank also promised Irby "that I will continue to do all I can and I hope it will have some effect." In a second letter from the same day, Maybank indicated to Irby that he took "the same attitude as you do" (see Maybank to Irby, 26 September 1933, Maybank Senatorial Papers).

This matter was brought up before Col. Waite by the Mississippi and Alabama delegations and Col. Waite is emphatic on no reduction of the wage scale, as he says this is the heart of the whole recovery plan.[4]

Very truly yours,
[signed]
J. L. M. Irby,
State Engineer, P. W. A.
JLMI:AF

Typed Letter Signed. Burnet R. Maybank Senatorial Papers, Special Collections, Addlestone Library, College of Charleston, Charleston, S.C.: Box 142.

Lorena A. Hickok to Harry L. Hopkins

10 February 1934
Charleston, S.C.

Lorena Hickok, a New Deal investigator, reported on the use of Civil Works Administration funds in the Charleston area.[5] The CWA operated under the Federal Emergency Relief Administration (FERA) and was designed to provide jobs for the unemployed during the winter of 1933–34. To gather information, Hickok interviewed employers, public officials, and New Deal administrators. In this report to Hopkins, the FERA director, she contrasted Charleston-based supporters of the New Deal with area farmers who complained that government jobs had created labor shortages.[6] "I wonder if there are any really disinterested people in this country, in the matter of acquiring and spending

---

[4]Henry Matson Waite was deputy administrator of the Public Works Administration.
[5]Lorena Alice Hickok (1893–1968) worked as a newspaper reporter for the *Minneapolis Tribune, New York Mirror,* and the Associated Press, where she was assigned to cover Eleanor Roosevelt during the 1932 presidential election. They developed a close relationship that lasted until Mrs. Roosevelt's death in 1962. The relationship also drew Hickok into the New Deal. She worked as an investigator for FERA (1933–36) and later with the Democratic National Committee (1940–45), during which time she lived at the White House.
[6]Harry Lloyd Hopkins (1890–1946) was a social worker whose efficient management of public relief funds in New York caught the attention of Governor Roosevelt. Following the 1932 election, Roosevelt asked Hopkins to join his administration. Hopkins supervised the FERA, the CWA, and the Works Progress Administration (WPA). During World War II he served as a key diplomatic advisor to Roosevelt.

Government money," she asked. "I'd lay my money on the social worker. But maybe I'm wrong."

Harry L. Hopkins, Esq
Federal Civil Works Administrator
Washington, D. C.

Dear Mr. Hopkins:

Well, it looks at the moment as though we're not going to be able to quit the relief business down here on the Carolina coast for some time.

They are having here today the worst ice and sleet storm since "befoah de Wah." Somebody said it was the first snow since 1915. The children love it, but their elders are wringing their hands. Just how much damage it's going to do I don't know, but obviously it's not very good for the truck business. Nor for the famous gardens that attract their big tourist crowd here in March and April. The palms are sheathed in ice. Icicles hang from the eaves. The pavements are as slippery as skating rinks. I had intended to drive on toward Raleigh this afternoon, but the Automobile Club told me it was worse north of Charleston, and, still having a cold and being unwilling to match what driving skill I have against the inexperience of these South Carolinians who don't know how to drive on sleety pavements, I decided to wait over until tomorrow. It does look as though the truck gardeners—or farmers—already complaining about the low prices they are getting for their stuff, are going to be hit pretty hard.

Since coming to Charleston, I've been hearing the other side of the story—"other" from that told me by the 15 farmers in Columbia Thursday. The Mayor of Charleston, the county CWA and relief administrator, and the social workers, the county home demonstration agent—all have earnestly warned me not to accept unreservedly the statements of those farmers. They insist there is no farm labor shortage, or wouldn't be, if the farmers were willing to pay a living wage, and that there is very likely to be a surplus of labor. They think we should be able to pull CWA out of the rural areas down here along the coast and possible out of Charleston, but they insist there must be some kind of relief.[7]

These people say the farmers who are doing the kicking are Bourbons—or Tories, as the President might call them—and that they want as big a surplus of labor as possible, so they can keep wages down. The more unemployed there are hanging around begging for work, the lower wages can be.

---

[7]CWA projects in the Charleston area, including the construction of a municipal incinerator and an extensive road-resurfacing program, began winding down in February and March. The program ended nationally on 31 March (see "Work on CWA Projects Ends Here Thursday," *Charleston Evening Post*, 14 February 1934; and "Revision of CWA Program," *Charleston Evening Post*, 2 March 1934).

The farmers, on the other hand, would no doubt point out that Mayors like to have "Guv'ment easy money" puring into their cities, and that CWA and relief administrators and social workers are afraid that, if we pull out, they'll lost their jobs.

I wonder if there are any really disinterested people in this country, in the matter of acquiring and spending Government money. If I had to make a bet on anyone being disinterested, though, I'd lay my money on the social worker. But maybe I'm wrong.

I should add that the townspeople, outside the CWA crowd, seem to side with the farmers. But I wonder if they know what they're talking about. So much of this stuff is hearsay. The switchboard at the hotel has been bothered to death. I have steered clear of it, however, because it results from that damnable publicity—"friend of Mrs. Roosevelt," "confidential investigator for Harry Hopkins," and so on.[8] It just sets all the people who haven't got jobs and think they ought to have them, who have some grudge against some case worker, all the individuals with personal grievances on my trail. I can't see that it has any value, that I'd get from it any true sort of picture. God help the next state administrator who lets out any publicity on me, that's all—In considering the attitude of some of the townspeople whom I've asked about this, one should remember that these truck farmers are of the "leading citizen" type. They're not like Western or Northern farmers, although we used to have in Minneapolis some big wheat growers of the same type somewhat.

"These farmers around here, the big fellows, are all Bourbons," Edmund P. Grice, Jr., the CWA and relief administrator, assured me. Then he added angrily:

"There are probably 500 of them. But in the city and county there are 100,000 people who are looking to me, as a Government official, to protect their interests. And I'll be damned if I'm going to be pushed by a dozen or so of those 500, no matter how many letters they write into Columbia or how many of them go running up to Washington."

"There IS no shortage of farm labor in Charleston county. There IS A shortage of farm labor that is willing to work for 40 cents a day or less, which is what those fellows want to pay."

Mayor Maybank joined in these sentiments—and just as vigorously.

Mrs. [Caroline Alston] Alsop, the county home demonstration agent, who comes from a family of planters and has been a planter herself, was gentle, but firm.[9]

"The trouble with them is," she said, "that they haven't progressed beyond the slave labor idea. They still think of farming as riding around over their plantations on horseback, superintending their slaves.

---

[8] Press reports followed Hickok as she traveled across the South, many of which referred to her as a "friend of Mrs. Roosevelt" and "confidential investigator" for Hopkins (see "CWA Investigator Now at Columbia," *Charleston News and Courier*, 6 February 1934).

[9] Caroline Simonton Alston (1888–1969) worked as a home demonstration agent for Charleston County from 1918 to 1948.

"That idea is what has kept the South down where it is. (Mr. Grice nodding vigorously at this point.) But that kind of farming isn't paying any more.

"Those people are through—all through—whether they realize it or not. I'll wager there aren't more than five of those big planters in the county right now who are solvent. Why, even the seed salesmen have stopped coming down here from the North! They quit a couple of years ago. They know these fellows are through. One of them told me so.

"And I think the Government ought to take this fact into consideration, entirely apart from the social aspects of the case, in making any decision on this relief business."

They agree with the farmers that, if CWA stays in much longer, there should be an adjustment in the wage scale. They even believe that it might be a good idea to take CWA out, if some sort of relief is continued. The farmers, as nearly as I can figure them out, want everything pulled out except during their slack season, and each year they want it pulled out far enough ahead of the beginning of their work "so these niggers will be good and hungry." In effect, they want us to take over the load they say they used to carry—that of keeping their peons alive during the slack seasons on pork and meal—and have everything nice and lovely so they can go on getting all the cheap labor they want when they want it, without any responsibility toward that labor. They'd be perfectly happy, I think, if we'd give their Negroes during the slack seasons a little extra, for clothes, so they could hire them for even less when they want them—say, 20 cents a day, instead of 40! Remember, I'm quoting their own figures on present wages—40 cents a day for a Negro woman, 50 cents a day for a Negro man, and they employ about 75 per cent women, they tell me. They certainly are a fine lot of gentlemen, aren't they?

Mayor Maybank is inclined to boil over whenever he gets started on the subject. He points out the millions the Government has spent down here in the South trying to help the farmers, pumping up the price of cotton, giving them seed loans, helping them to hang onto their farms, and—well, he just boils. He is an interesting chap, the Mayor. He is about 40, I should say, and belongs to one of the state's best known families. He told me his grandfather ran for President of the Confederate States against Jefferson Davis. He is related to most of the aristocracy in Charleston. His family has always been in the cotton business. He is himself in the cotton exporting business—which is certainly on the bum now. Any Government program that effectively reduces cotton acreage and raises the price is going to ruin him permanently, he told me.

"But I reckon some of us have got to fall by the wayside," he added calmly.

He is almost fiercely loyal to the President and the Administration generally. You see, he and several other prominent Southerners I've met feel that Mr. Roosevelt is the first President since the "War between the States" who has recognized the South as a part of the Union. Really, that's the way some of them feel. I've had it said to me over and over again:

"He's the first President who has even tried to help us, down here. He's the first President who has made us feel that we really are a part of the United States."

Mayor Maybank, I'm told, was elected after a very hot campaign in which he represented the younger element bent on wresting control away from some of the old line politicians who had got a bit crooked. I was told that some of the moneyed interests backed him, thinking they could run things after he got in. But they haven't.

"He's just the kind of Mayor that Mr. Roosevelt is President," the proprietor of a hairdressing establishment remarked yesterday.

Another thing that burns Mr. Grice and the Mayor up is that "these farmers beg us to take their Niggers off relief and CWA and turn right around and try to get us to put their own sons on as foremen at a dollar an hour." They both feel that, if CWA should be continued much longer, some of the higher wage rates should be materially lowered.

"That's what's causing us most of our trouble," Mr. Grice said. "The white people keep exerting pressure to grab off those good jobs. And it's bad for the Negroes, too, because they keep hoping that they'll be promoted."

They very earnestly begged me to try to give you the mental makeup of these farmers.

"They are all gamblers," the Mayor assured me. "They think only in terms of big money—$100,000 a year. They're not interested in any ordinary, even income. (They are talking, of course, of the truck farmers, not Southern farmers generally.) And the kind of gambling they do doesn't make for any stable employment. They're up today and down tomorrow. And what they want is plenty of cheap labor, to grab on a moment's notice, whenever they happen to want it."

If you don't already know him—he didn't say whether he had ever met you or not, he isn't the kind who boasts about knowing people in Washington, but I noticed he had an autographed picture of the President in the living room of his home, which is a very beautiful old Southern house, by the way, I think you'd like young Mr. Maybank.

It may interest you to know that Mr. Grice thinks the sewing rooms for women constitute about the best project down here.

"It's doing the women themselves a world of good," he said. "You'd be surprised at the changes in their appearance and their attitudes. And I believe in it, too, because when the money is paid to the wives, you jolly well know it's going into the home, where the whole family will get some benefit."

Mrs. Alston—who confessed that, while she doesn't belong in our show, she has been sneaking into the sewing rooms, carrying the gospel of better cooking and better sanitation—agreed with him as to the value of the sewing room in social work.

They're kicking here, too, about those surplus commodities. Mr. Grice says we're crazy to keep shipping pork down here where every Negro has hogs.

"You don't raise pigs down here," he said. "Pigs just happen. I can't get rid of pork here. They don't want it."

In the meantime, while the truck farmers are kicking about a labor shortage, there are in the city and county of Charleston 6,550 men and women employed on CWA and CWS, 2,821 families on direct relief, and about 15,000 persons registered at the Reemployment office.[10]

One thing I guess we don't need to worry about. Mrs. Alston told me that when the cut in hours came in, many, many people on CWA said to her:

"Well, after all, Mrs. Alston, even if they take it all away from us, it's given us a breathing space."

I give you Good Evening, Suh!
Lorena A. Hickok

P.S. I'm simply appalled at that Senate amendment, placing the appointment of state relief administrators on the same basis as postmasters—and IN AN ELECTION YEAR! But they'll never get away with it, will they?[11] The Mayor remarked that he didn't go around Charleston talking the way he had done—that, socially, these men were his friends. I told him that what he had said would go only to responsible people and would be treated as confidential.
H.

> Typed Letter. Papers of Harry L. Hopkins, Franklin D. Roosevelt Library and Archives, Hyde Park, N.Y.: FERA-WPA Narrative Field Reports, S.C.

---

[10] Civil Works Service (CWS) programs employed mostly women and white-collar workers.

[11] The amendment, which ultimately failed, proposed that presidential appointments of CWA and state relief administrators require U.S. Senate confirmation.

1935

Norma Mazo, *Payday*

[1935]
Charleston, S.C.
In the painting reproduced below, Charleston artist Norma Mazo captured a scene that would have been familiar to waterfront workers and area residents in the 1930s.[1] Mazo's painting depicts African American longshoremen, who had loaded and unloaded ships in Charleston since before the Civil War, lining up to receive their pay at the United Fruit Company dock at the end of Laurens Street on the Cooper River.[2] The artist's perspective may be from a dock to the north of United Fruit. This painting presently hangs in the Special Collections Department of the Addlestone Library at the College of Charleston.

[1] While this painting is undated, the layout of the buildings strongly resemble photographs taken of the United Fruit Company docks shortly after the 1938 tornadoes. Norma Mazo Perlmutter (1917–2001) was a Jewish immigrant from Poland who moved to Charleston with her family in 1922. Living above the family delicatessen at 171 King Street, Mazo discovered her love of art and began painting images of her surroundings. Mazo studied at the Art Students League in New York City, as well as at the University of Minnesota and the Corcoran School of Art in Washington, D.C. She was active in the arts communities of Washington and Pittsburgh.

[2] Mazo's painting captures the workers during a period of transition. The following year they affiliated with the International Longshoremen's Association (ILA), an American Federation of Labor union founded in 1892. Charleston ILA Local 1422 went on strike in 1937 and 1938 to protest proposed wage cuts. The United Fruit Company, which specialized in the harvesting and shipping of bananas from Latin America, established a presence in Charleston shortly after its founding in 1899. The company exerted considerable political influence on the countries in which it had a presence.

Benjamin F. Cox, Avery Institute, Annual Report

[August 1935]
Charleston, S.C.

From its founding in 1865 as a primary and secondary school for African Americans through its closure in 1954, the Avery Institute has educated generations of black Charlestonians. In this annual report, Principal Benjamin F. Cox provided an overview of Avery's activities to its sponsor, the American Missionary Association.³ Cox struck a tone of optimism while acknowledging the financial burden that many families endured to send their children to Avery. Cox resigned the following year to join the faculty at Fisk University, his alma mater.

89th Annual Report, 1934–35
AVERY INSTITUTE, Charleston, South Carolina, Benjamin F. Cox, Principals

Although there is still much unemployment in our group and as a consequence much scarcity of money, our patrons have made great sacrifice and have kept their

---

³Benjamin F. Cox (1874–1952) served as principal of the Avery Institute from 1914 to 1936. Cox was a Charleston NAACP leader and his wife, Jeannette Keeble Cox (1876–1956), was active in the city's African American women's clubs.

children in school. The physical condition of the school has greatly improved, by transferring from Capahosic to Avery, desks, chairs, science equipment and more than a thousand books for our library.[4] For the first time the school has enjoyed the services of a full-time librarian. The Dramatic Club did unusually fine work. It has given various plays and sketches, but its most outstanding presentations were "Daddy Long Legs" and "The Importance of Being Earnest."[5] Our basketball team won the South Carolina State High School basketball championship.

Last year every graduate of our Normal Course who wanted to teach was employed. Our Negro colleges offer our graduates liberal inducements to enter their freshman classes because previous graduates have often proved the ranking group of the class.

This year the Lincoln Fund was the largest in the history of the institution —$869.85 was raised.

Our closing exercises were of a high order and were well attended. On commencement night the diplomas were presented by Mr. W. A. Schiffley, Asst. State Supervisor of Negro Schools. His remarks were very gratifying. He was high in his praise of the work of the Avery graduate as he observes him in the working field over the State. He said without qualification that our Teacher Training Department is the best in the State. He further said that the particular commencement occasion was the "snappiest commencement program I have ever attended."[6]

The Alumni Association in appreciation of 21 years of service here by the principal and his wife, held a testimonial meeting in their honor and presented them with a silver water set.

Enrollment: Total students, 356; senior high, 159; junior high, 74; elementary, 110; specials, 13;
boarding students, 8.
Total graduates: Senior high, 52.
Staff: Total, 17, consisting of: Principal, 1; teachers, 15; one other.

> Typed Document. Avery Normal Institute Papers, Avery Research Center for African American History and Culture, College of Charleston, Charleston, S.C.: Box 1.

---

[4]The Gloucester Agricultural and Industrial School commonly known as Cappahosic Academy was a private high school in Virginia for African Americans founded in 1888. Avery acquired equipment from Cappahosic, which was also sponsored by the American Missionary Association, when it closed in 1933.

[5]*Daddy Long Legs* was a novel published in 1912 by American writer Jean Webster, who later adapted it for the stage. Oscar Wilde's *The Importance of Being Earnest* was first performed in London in 1895.

[6]William Archibald Schiffley served as assistant state supervisor of Negro schools from 1930 to 1954.

Franklin D. Roosevelt to Clergy

24 September 1935
Washington, D.C.

On 14 August 1935, President Roosevelt signed the Social Security Act, which included provisions for retiree pensions and assistance to the unemployed. The following month he sent this letter to more than 120,000 faith leaders, inviting them to describe "conditions in your community." Roosevelt requested that they indicate "where you feel our government can better serve our people." The White House received nearly thirty thousand replies.

Reverend and dear Sir:

Your high calling brings you into intimate daily contact not only with your own parishioners, but with people generally in your community. I am sure you see the problems of your people with wise and sympathetic understanding.

Because of the grave responsibilities of my office, I am turning to representative Clergymen for counsel and advice,—feeling confident that no group can give more accurate or unbiased views.

I am particularly anxious that the new Social Security Legislation just enacted, for which we have worked so long, providing for old age pensions, aid for crippled children and unemployment insurance, shall be carried out in keeping with the high purposes with which this law was enacted. It is also vitally important that the Works Program shall be administered to provide employment at useful work, and that our unemployed as well as the nation as a whole may derive the greatest possible benefits.

I shall deem it a favor if you will write me about conditions in your community. Tell me where you feel our government can better serve our people.

We can solve our many problems, but no one man or single group can do it,—we shall have to work together for the common end of better spiritual and material conditions for the American people.

May I have your counsel and your help? I am leaving on a short vacation but will be back in Washington in a few weeks, and I will deeply appreciate your writing to me.

Very sincerely yours,
[signed]
Franklin D Roosevelt

Typed Letter Signed. President's Personal Files, Franklin D. Roosevelt Library and Archives, Hyde Park, N.Y.: Box 35.

A. D. Prentiss to Franklin D. Roosevelt

27 September 1935
Sheldon, S.C.

A. D. Prentiss, the pastor of a rural congregation near Beaufort, replied to the president's request for guidance in crafting the government's response to the economic crisis.[7] *After describing the needs of local working people, Prentiss urged the President to act boldly "in the name of God and human fairness."*

Honorable Franklin D Rosevelt,
President, United States of America
Washington, D.C.

Honorable and dear Sir:

I have your letter. I am glad that the new Social Security Law will soon be in effect, it did not come to early, I think this is one of the greatest things for our own country's good, also I hope that the Work Program will work for good of all of our people in need employment.

I have been pastor of Sheldon Baptist church (white) nearly 8 years, I think I know some of our needs here and elsewhere since I have been in the ministry nearly 18 years. We have here in Beaufort county, S.C., about 10 to 1, negro to white population. I think for a few whites and nearly all negros we need better living conditions, better homes, schools, farms, living wages, new administration to administer to the real needs of our people here.

Labor wages; here is from 50 to 75 cents per day, carpenters and other skill labor receive 20 cents per hour. In the name of God and human fairness how can these people live, with advancing food prices, common white meat 25 cents per pound, with no time of their own to help them selves? How can you or any one lead out to better times if living conditions remain like the above named? Yours for service in these crises.

[signed] A. D. Prentiss

> Typed Letter Signed. President's Personal Files, Franklin D. Roosevelt Library and Archives, Hyde Park, N.Y.: Clergy Letters, South Carolina–Tennessee.

---

[7] Arthur David Prentiss (1892–1954), born in Hampton County, South Carolina, served as pastor of Baptist churches in Alabama, Georgia, and Louisiana, as well as a number of churches in the Charleston area.

DuBose Heyward, "Porgy and Bess Return on Wings of Song"

October 1935
New York, N.Y.

On the suggestion of composer George Gershwin, writer DuBose Heyward agreed to collaborate with him on a musical version of Heyward's 1925 Porgy, *a novel that depicts the hardscrabble lives of poor African Americans on Charleston's waterfront.*[8] *On the eve of its Broadway debut, Heyward penned this article for* Stage *magazine detailing the musical evolution of* Porgy and Bess.[9] *Heyward recalled his first impression of Gershwin as "a young man of enormous physical and emotional vitality, who possessed the faculty of seeing himself quite impersonally and realistically, and who knew exactly what he wanted and where he was going." Especially memorable to Heyward were the weeks they spent living at his Folly Beach home and visiting African American enclaves on nearby James Island "with its large population of primitive Gullah Negroes," which "furnished us with a laboratory in which to test our theories, as well as an inexhaustible source of folk material."*

Porgy and Bess *was praised for its gritty treatment of working-class life, though some critics argued that it relied too heavily on racist stereotypes. Featuring a cast of classically trained African American singers, the musical fared poorly on Broadway, but Gershwin's composition "Summertime" is considered an American standard.*

Nothing could be more ill-advised than the writing of this article. It exhibits all too clearly the decay of a human will, and it is strewn with the debris of broken resolutions. Out of a limited but illuminating Broadway experience, I have grasped the simple fact that a play does not exist until the critics and the public have looked upon it and found it good. Could there then be a more perfect example of artless, parental

---

[8] Edwin DuBose Heyward (1885–1940) was a Charleston-born writer who, as a young man, worked a variety of clerical jobs, including a stint as a ship checker on the waterfront. That experience informed his writing of the novel *Porgy* (1925), which he adapted into a play two years later. Heyward also wrote poetry and screen adaptations. Composer George Gershwin (1898–1937) looms large in the annals of American song. Born to Jewish immigrant parents in Brooklyn, New York, Gershwin began working as a Tin Pan Alley composer and "plugger," or promoter, and pianist while still in his teens. His compositions were animated by his desire to blend classical European and American folk and popular styles. In addition to *Porgy and Bess,* Gershwin is best known for *Rhapsody in Blue* (1924) and *An American in Paris* (1928).

[9] The article was illustrated with scenes from *Porgy* by Alexander King.

exhibitionism than the spectacle of a playwright prattling about his expected brainchild a full month before the hazardous accouchement?

How did it happen? I will tell you. I can at least expose the system of which I am a victim.

You leave the first rehearsal, hypnotized by the music of your own words. You are beguiled into the sanctum of an editor. Your fingers close of their own volition about a cocktail glass. You are told things about your work which, in your state of initial intoxication, you are fatuous enough to believe. You conclude that the editor is also a discriminating critic and altogether an excellent fellow. And then, since, in any event it is against nature for an author to say "no" to an editor, you find yourself committed. It is not until later that you realize your deadline for a monthly periodical is a month in advance of publication, and that your story may burst from the presses, not as a bright paean for the living, but a sad and ironical epitaph for the dead.

But the story of *Porgy* has a definite past, as well as a projected reincarnation, and the production of the opera is the materialization of an idea suggested by George Gershwin in a letter written to me nine years ago. The drama had not yet been produced, but was being written by my wife, Dorothy Heyward, and myself for the Theatre Guild, when George read the novel and suggested a meeting.[10]

My first impression of my collaborator remains with me and is singularly vivid. A young man of enormous physical and emotional vitality, who possessed the faculty of seeing himself quite impersonally and realistically, and who knew exactly what he wanted and where he was going. This characteristic put him beyond both modesty and conceit. About himself he would merely mention certain facts, aspirations, failings. They were usually right.

We discussed *Porgy*. He said that it would not matter about the dramatic production, as it would be a number of years before he would be prepared technically to compose an opera. At the time he had numerous Broadway successes to his credit, and his *Rhapsody in Blue*, published three years before, had placed him in the front rank of American composers. It was extraordinary, I thought, that, in view of a success that might well have dazzled any man, he could appraise his talent with such complete detachment. And so we decided then that some day when we were both prepared we would do an operatic version of my simple Negro beggar of the Charleston streets.

In the meantime, the play went into rehearsal at the Guild Theatre. Rouben Mamoulian, in his first appearance on Broadway, was entrusted with its direction.[11] A

---

[10]Dorothy Kuhns Heyward (1890–1961) was born in Wooster, Ohio. In 1922 she met novelist DuBose Heyward at the MacDowell art colony in Peterborough, New Hampshire, and they married within the year. She collaborated with her husband on the 1927 theatrical version of his novel *Porgy*.

[11]Rouben Mamoulian (1897–1987) was a film and stage director. He directed the stage version of *Porgy* as well as the musical.

cast was assembled from Negro night clubs and Harlem theatres. Then for six weeks, what we all believed to be Broadway's most highly speculative venture dragged its personnel through the extremes of hope and despair toward the opening night.

I suppose it is sheer physical exhaustion, plus the emotional bludgeoning an author undergoes during rehearsals, that reduces him to pessimistic witlessness on the night of the premiere. Out of that night, I remember only vaguely a few moments of startling beauty: Mamoulian's fantastic shadows, the heartbreaking quality of the funeral spiritual, Porgy's pathetic leave taking. But never to be forgotten was that awful moment when Crown shouted to the silent heavens, "Gawd laugh and Crown laugh back." Then, after an aching interval, came the belated clap of thunder that was supposed to be the laugh of God. The scene shifts seemed interminable. And lastly, and most crushing as we cowered at the back of the house under the protective wing of Philip Moeller, came the exit of Woollcott before the last scene of the play.[12]

I have never seen him since, but I could point him out immediately in any crowd, so vivid is my impression of him. He stands about forty feet in his stockings, is about thirty feet broad; and when he rises to his full height from the second row in the orchestra, he can blot out an entire proscenium arch. His mouth is that of a medieval executioner, and when he strides down a theatre aisle and past a terror-stricken playwright, his footsteps shake the building with the tread of doom.

Somebody might have warned us that he had an early deadline, and had to get his copy in, but nobody did. To us it was a walk out. He gave us a fine review. He proved that dramatic critics really are omniscient by knowing how the show ended. But the mischief had been done. Thirty months later, when the play closed after a run in America and a successful journey across the Atlantic, the authors were still more or less nervous wrecks.

Time passes and Porgy and the goat lay comfortably dossed down in Cain's warehouse. But every year, between novels with me, and Broadway productions with George, I would journey North and we would meet and discuss our opera. I remember George saying once—it was, I think, when he was planning to stage *An American in Paris*—that he would stay abroad and put in some intensive study in counterpoint.[13] As always, he knew just where he was going. The success of his symphonic poem in Paris was flattering, but the main idea was to build toward the opera.

Later he worked with Joseph Schillinger, the musicologist, who carried him from Bach to Schoenberg, concentrating his attention on polytonality—modern harmony, and counterpoint.[14]

---

[12] Philip Moeller (1880–1958) founded the Theatre Guild, which staged *Porgy* on Broadway. Alexander Woollcott (1887–1943) was a drama critic.

[13] *An American in Paris* (1928) is a symphonic poem and among George Gershwin's best-known compositions.

[14] Joseph Moiseyevich Schillinger (1895–1943) was a Russian-born composer and musical theorist. He also created a system of musical composition and analysis known as the Schillinger System of Musical Analysis.

And then in October, exactly two years ago, our impatience got the better of what may prove to have been our better judgment, and the actual adventure of composing began.

It is the fashion in America to lament the prostitution of art by the big magazine, the radio, the moving pictures. With this I have little patience. Properly utilized, the radio and the pictures may be to the present-day writer what his prince was to Villon, the king of Bavaria was to Wagner.[15]

At no other time has it been possible for a writer to earn by hiring himself out as a skilled technician for, say, two months, sufficient income to sustain him for a year. And yet the moving pictures have made it possible. I decided that the silver screen should be my Maecenas, and George elected to serve the radio.[16]

During my first year I wrote the screen version of *The Emperor Jones*. For this I may have lost the friendship of Eugene O'Neill.[17] I haven't dared to look him up since. And to finance my second year I made a pilgrimage to Hollywood to tinker at Pearl Buck's *Good Earth*. My selection for this assignment presented a perfect example of motion picture logic. When I arrived on the lot and asked why I had been offered the job, it was made perfectly plain to me. Negroes were not a Caucasian people. Neither were Chinamen. I wrote understandingly of Negroes. It was obvious then that I would understand the Chinese. I suspect that before my engagement closed their faith in their reasoning power was shaken. But I gave them my best, and when I left for the East I was free to complete my work on the opera.

Statistics record the fact that there are 25,000,000 radios in America. Their contribution to the opera was indirect but important. Out of them for half an hour each week poured the glad tidings that Feenamint could be wheedled away from virtually any drug clerk in America for one dime—the tenth part of a dollar. And with the authentic medicine-man flair, the manufacturer distributed his information in an irresistible wrapper of Gershwin hits, with the composer at the piano.

There is, I imagine, a worse fate than that which derives from the use of a laxative gum. And, anyhow, we felt that the end justified the means, and that they also served who only sat and waited.

At the outset we were faced by a difficult problem. I was firm in my refusal to leave the South and live in New York. Gershwin was bound for the duration of his contract to the microphone at Radio City. The matter of effecting a happy union between words and music across a thousand miles of Atlantic seaboard baffled us for a moment. The solution came quite naturally when we associated Ira Gershwin with us.[18]

---

[15]Ludwig II of Bavaria was a patron of the German composer Richard Wagner.
[16]Maecenas was a patron to Roman poets.
[17]Playwright Eugene O'Neill wrote *The Emperor Jones* in 1920.
[18]George Gershwin's older brother, Ira Gershwin (1896–1983), cowrote the lyrics for *Porgy and Bess*.

Presently we evolved a system by which, between my visits North, or George's dash to Charleston, I could send scenes and lyrics. Then the brothers Gershwin, after their extraordinary fashion, would get at the piano, pound, wrangle, swear, burst into weird snatches of song, and eventually emerge with a polished lyric. Then too, Ira's gift for the more sophisticated lyric was exactly suited to the task of writing the songs for Sporting Life, the Harlem gambler who had drifted into Catfish Row.

I imagine that in after years when George looks back upon this time, he will feel that the summer of 1934 furnished him with one of the most satisfying as well as exciting experiences of his career. Under the baking suns of July and August we established ourselves on Folly Island, a small barrier island ten miles from Charleston. James Island with its large population of primitive Gullah Negroes lay adjacent, and furnished us with a laboratory in which to test our theories, as well as an inexhaustible source of folk material. But the most interesting discovery to me, as we sat listening to their spirituals, or watched a group shuffling before a cabin or country store, was that to George it was more like a homecoming than an exploration. The quality in him which had produced the *Rhapsody in Blue* in the most sophisticated city in America, found its counterpart in the impulse behind the music and bodily rhythms of the simple Negro peasant of the South.

The Gullah Negro prides himself on what he calls "shouting." This is a complicated rhythmic pattern beaten out by feet and hands as an accompaniment to the spirituals, and is indubitably an African survival. I shall never forget the night when, at a Negro meeting on a remote sea-island, George started "shouting" with them. And eventually to their huge delight stole the show from their champion "shouter." I think that he is probably the only white man in America who could have done it.

Another night as we were about to enter a dilapidated cabin that had been taken as a meeting house by a group of Negro Holy Rollers, George caught my arm and held me. The sound that had arrested him was one to which, through long familiarity, I attached no special importance. But now, listening to it with him, and noticing his excitement, I began to catch its extraordinary quality. It consisted of perhaps a dozen voices raised in loud rhythmic prayer. The odd thing about it was that while each had started at a different time, upon a different theme, they formed a clearly defined rhythmic pattern, and that this, with the actual words lost, and the inevitable pounding of the rhythm, produced an effect almost terrifying in its primitive intensity. Inspired by the extraordinary effect, George wrote six simultaneous prayers producing a terrifying primitive invocation to God in the face of the hurricane.

We had hoped, and it was logical, that the Theatre Guild would produce the opera. An excursion into that field of the theatre was a new idea to the directors. But then they had gambled once on *Porgy* and won. There was a sort of indulgent affection for the cripple and his goat on Fifty-second Street. Most certainly they did not want anybody else to do it, and so contracts were signed.

Having committed themselves, the Guild proceeded to deprive us of all alibis in the event of failure by giving us a free hand in the casting and a star producing staff.

Mamoulian returned from Hollywood to assume the direction. Alexander Smallens, who had conducted the Philharmonic Stadium Concerts, and the Philadelphia symphony, and who, in spite of having conducted the orchestra of *Four Saints in Three Acts*, still made his wants known in comprehensible English, was made conductor.[19]

Alexander Steinert, pianist and composer, with a Prix de Rome to his credit, was intrusted with the coaching of the principals.[20]

For a year George had been cast-hunting. It had been an exciting, if at times a strenuous sport. But last April, when I journeyed North to hear the aspirants and advise on the final decisions, I was amazed at the amount of promising talent exhibited. The cast was assembled. Steinert took them in hand, and at the first rehearsal he had them ready to read the difficult score from beginning to end.

We were in rather a dither about the name. The composer and author both felt that the opera should be called simply *Porgy*. But there was a feeling in the publicity department that this would lead to a confusion in that amorphous region known as the public mind, and that *Porgy* in lights might be construed as a revival of the original play, rather than as the Gershwin opus.

There had of course been Pelleas and Melisande, Samson and Delilah, Tristan and Isolde.[21]

"And so," said Heyward, with the humility characteristic of those who draw their sustenance from the theatre, "why not *Porgy and Bess*?"

To which Gershwin replied with the detachment to which I have referred and which could not possibly be mistaken for conceit, "Of course, it's right in the operatic tradition."

Two years! It doesn't seem that long. There has been so much to do. The published version of the piano and vocal score, fresh from the press, runs to five hundred and sixty pages. And when that was finished, George tackled the orchestration single handed. The resulting manuscript is impressive. It contains seven hundred pages of closely written music, and it is the fruit of nine months of unremitting labor.

For my own part, I had a play which needed to be cut forty per-cent for the libretto, yet nothing of dramatic value could be sacrificed. The dialogue had to follow that of drama, but it had to be arranged to form a new pattern, to escape monotony and adapt itself to the music. And then there were the spirituals, and the lyrics upon which Ira and I worked.

---

[19] Alexander Smallens (1889–1972) was born in St. Petersburg, Russia, and immigrated to the United States as a child. He served as conductor of *Porgy and Bess* in 1935 and for several of its revivals, including 1956 performances in Moscow and Leningrad.

[20] Alexander Steinert was a composer, conductor, and pianist. He was born in Boston, Massachusetts, and studied music at Harvard University.

[21] Heyward referred to several romantic operas.

In the theatre every production is a gamble. In some, naturally, the odds are greater than in others. *Porgy and Bess* has, I believe, a fair chance of scoring. But whether it does or not, we who have written and composed the opera cannot lose. We have spent two years doing exactly what we wanted to. It has been very especial sort of adventure. That, at any rate, is in the bag.

Published Document. *Stage 13* (October 1935): 25–28.

Elijah J. Curry to Franklin D. Roosevelt

5 October 1935
St. George, S.C.

Curry, an African American minister from St. George, responded to the president's 24 September request for guidance from the nation's ministers.[22] *He raised several criticisms of the president's social programs, including the Social Security Act's exclusion of domestic and agricultural workers, as well as the implementation of many New Deal programs that left control in the hands of employers who "show favoritism to certain people."*

The Hon. F. D. Roosevelt
President of the U.S.A.
Washington, D. C.

Dear president:

In reply to your letter of September 24th, I wish to say that I shall gladly furnish the desired information as best I can.

Concerning the Social Security Legislation, I can not give counsel as I desire because I have not read it in its finished form. I had the privilege of reading some of the clauses, through the newspapers while it was in the making. I particularly noted the exemption clauses at that time and must say that some of those exempted are the very ones that should receive pension in their old age. In this, "The land of the Free" it seems that we would still retain slavery when it comes to a certain group if those clauses were retained.

Now concerning the Works program I wish to say that the ones who really need the jobs at a living wage do not get it. It is rather unfortunate for the group as a whole that the matter of jobs and wages is handled, in the final stages, by local representatives who in most cases either by coercion or choice, will show favoritism to certain people. By way of parentheses, Have you thought seriously that one of the reasons why the war-veterans are contending for the immediate payment of the bonus is,

---

[22]Elijah Joseph Curry (1881–1945) was born in Denmark, South Carolina.

because the money or check, comes directly from Washington and is sure to get into the hands for which it was intended without local interferences.

On account of the high federal taxes and the enforcement of the provisions of the Bankhead cotton law, the farmers are unable to pay their debts.[23] That means that there is nothing for the minister of the gospel because he lives on what the people give and when they are unable to meet their demands, there is nothing to give.

Think of a poor farmer, with his wife and children who have worked all the year, who gins a 500 weight bale, receives a fraction over $45, pays the government $25. There he has approximately $20. to pay his debts and by his [strikethrough] family's winter clothing. perhaps you will ask what of the exemption certificates? My answer is: just as in other cases they or most of them get into the hands that least need them.

With the hope that these statements may be of assistance and with my prayers for your success, I remain

Respectfully yours,
(Rev) E. J. Curry

Autographed Letter Signed. President's Personal Files, Franklin D. Roosevelt Library and Archives, Hyde Park, N.Y.: Clergy Letters, South Carolina–Tennessee.

Franklin D. Roosevelt, Remarks at the Citadel: The Military College of South Carolina

23 October 1935
Charleston, S.C.

Following a three-week vacation at sea, President Roosevelt disembarked at Charleston en route to Washington. More than twenty thousand people gathered to hear the president speak on the parade ground of the Citadel.[24] In his remarks, reproduced here from a typescript, Roosevelt heralded his administration's economic recovery efforts: "We are on our way back—not just by pure chance, my friends, not just by a turn of the wheel, of the cycle. We are coming back more soundly than ever before because we are planning it that way. Don't let anybody tell you differently."[25]

---

[23]The Bankhead Cotton Control Act of 1934 sought to stabilize cotton prices by taxing farmers who ginned cotton in excess of their quotas.

[24]Charles W. Hurd, "President Renews Pledge of No War," *New York Times*, 24 October 1935.

[25]The week after his visit to Charleston, Roosevelt requested that Citadel president Charles P. Summerall cancel "all unserved punishments" in keeping with a military school tradition that allowed visiting dignitaries to grant amnesty to cadets facing disciplinary action. Summerall

During a press conference preceding his visit to the college, Roosevelt deflected a reporter's suggestion that his unemployment relief program was running behind schedule. "The President fixed an icy stare at the questioner" and insisted that hiring targets would be met by the deadline more than one month away, according to one press account.[26]

Informal Extemporaneous Remarks of the President, the Citadel, Charleston, South Carolina

October 23, 1935, 4.30 P.M.
(Mayor Maybank introduced Governor Johnston of South Carolina, who, in turn, introduced the President.)[27]

Governor Johnston, Mr. Mayor, my friends of Charleston and of South Carolina:

You have given me a very wonderful welcome home to the continental limits of the United States. It is a very happy ending to a very happy vacation.

I am glad to come back here after many years, for, as some of you will remember, in the old days when I was associated with the United States Navy under the Administration of that great American President, Woodrow Wilson, I had the opportunity of coming here on several occasions and of helping to build up, to some degree at least, this splendid Navy Yard in Charleston.[28]

When I heard that I was to speak at The Citadel, old memories came back to me, memories not only of my own visit to the old school but memories also of the great historic tradition of that school, an historical record, a war record, if you please, of

---

agreed to do so and thanked Roosevelt for his visit: "Your presence on our campus has consecrated the spot to nobler aspirations and greater endeavor, and your words of approval will live eternally in the hearts of Citadel men" (see Roosevelt to Summerall, 1 November 1935, and Summerall to Roosevelt, 4 November 1935, both documents in Charles P. Summerall Papers, Citadel Archives and Museum, Charleston, S.C.: Box 5).

[26]Walter Trohan, "Roosevelt Back in U.S.; Definite Revival Claimed," *Chicago Daily Tribune*, 24 October 1935. The press conference took place on board the USS *Houston*, the navy cruiser that transported the president during his vacation.

[27]In his introduction of Roosevelt, Governor Olin Johnston reportedly said, "I feel as if he was sent by God in order to lead the people of the United States back to normalcy." Turning to the president, he promised, "You will find the people of South Carolina in 1936 voting like they did in 1932, almost 100 percent for you" (Hurd, "President Renews Pledge of No War"). A strong New Deal supporter, Olin D. Johnston served as governor of South Carolina from 1935 to 1939 and 1943 to 1945 and as a U.S. senator from 1945 until his death in 1965.

[28]As assistant secretary of the navy, Roosevelt inspected the Charleston Navy Yard in 1913. He also attended the annual meeting of the American Historical Association, which was held at the Citadel. Roosevelt spoke briefly on the importance of preserving historic navy records ("Charleston Yard is Admirable One," *Charleston News and Courier*, 31 December 1913).

The Citadel boys that ought to be known to every boy in the United States. Then when I learned that The Citadel had moved, somehow I got a little choky over that, wondering what it would be like and yet here I come and I find the old Citadel reproduced. It is reproduced, I am confident, for generations to come for the continuance of this splendid institution and I am happy indeed that you have moved it here to these very fitting surroundings, and that The Citadel is under the command of my old friend General Summerall.[29]

I was glad to be welcomed not only by the Governor and the Mayor but by my old friend Senator Smith, but I was sorry indeed that another old friend of mine, the Junior Senator, Senator Byrnes, could not be here at the same time.[30] I have an idea that Jimmie Byrnes went away so that he would not have to hear fishing stories from me. (Laughter) We have fished together. I am a much better fisherman than he is, only he would never admit it. (Laughter) I could tell you a great many fishing stories, of fishing in Mexican waters and of fishing at the Treasure Island of Cocos in the Pacific Ocean, of fishing near Panama, of fishing down among the San Blas Indians in the Atlantic Ocean, in the Caribbean Sea. I don't know whether you would believe them all or not. I could tell you about fish that got away and about fish that were caught. (Laughter)

We have had a very happy three weeks and I am glad, in coming back here to the Southern Atlantic Coast, to find a very definite evidence of what I found in my trip across the Continent, starting from Washington and going out through the Middle West, out into the Great Plains country, through the Rocky Mountain States and finally to the Pacific Coast. There was not one dissenting word—there was general admission that this country was coming back. You could see it with your own eyes.

Today, on landing, I am told the same story about South Carolina.

---

[29]In 1922 the Citadel moved to its present location adjacent to Hampton Park and along the Ashley River. The move from its original campus on Marion Square in downtown Charleston allowed the school to increase the size of the student body. Charles Pelot Summerall (1867–1955) was born in Blunts Ferry, Florida. He graduated from the Porter Military Academy in Charleston (1885) and the U.S. Military Academy (1892). Summerall served in the U.S. Army from 1892 to 1931, retiring as a four-star general. Following a stint as the U.S. Army chief of staff (1926–30), Summerall became president of the Citadel, serving from 1931 until 1953.

[30]Senator Ellison D. "Cotton Ed" Smith served South Carolina in the U.S. Senate from 1909 to 1944. He supported some elements of the New Deal but became an outspoken conservative opponent of the president's policies. Charleston-born senator James Francis Byrnes (1882–1972) was a key New Deal supporter in the U.S. Senate, in which he served from 1931 to 1941, when he was nominated by Roosevelt for the U.S. Supreme Court. After Byrnes had served on the court for a little over a year, Roosevelt tapped him to lead the Office of Economic Stabilization and the Office of War Mobilization. He was U.S. secretary of state from 1945 to 1947 during the Truman presidency and served one term as governor of South Carolina (1951–55).

Yes, we are on our way back—not just by pure chance, my friends, not just by a turn of the wheel, of the cycle. We are coming back more soundly than ever before because we are planning it that way. Don't let anybody tell you differently.

There are many grave problems ahead. As you know, I spoke in San Diego, in California, three weeks ago today. I spoke in regard to the affairs of the world and I tried to make it clear then, as I continue to make it clear today, that it shall be my earnest effort to keep this country free and unentangled from any possible war that may occur across the seas.[31]

I have come back very much sun-burned, very much full of health and ready to tackle a great many things. I wish I could stay with you longer but I have to be back in Washington tomorrow. I shall always bear with me a very happy recollection of this coming back home, back into our country, and a very happy recollection of all the kind things you have said and that you have done, of your coming out to greet me, of my opportunity once more to see this historic city, to see those delightful and splendid old homes—homes that belong not just to you who are fortunate to live in Charleston, but homes and churches and public buildings that belong to all of us Americans, all of us who care for the great traditions of the United States.

I hope you will always keep those homes, keep them for yourselves and for your fellow countrymen as you would keep the splendid traditions of Charleston and the splendid traditions of South Carolina. I know that more and more people all over the United States are going to come to visit you just as your welcome today makes me want to come back every possible chance that I may get. Many thanks.

Typed Document. Charles P. Summerall Papers,
Citadel Archives and Museum, Charleston, S.C.: Box 5.

---

[31] Speaking to 45,000 people in San Diego, the president declared that despite rising conflict abroad, "the American people can have but one concern and speak but one sentiment: Despite what happens in continents overseas, the United States of America shall and must remain, as long ago the Father of Our Country prayed that it might remain, unentangled and free" (Charles W. Hurd, "President Warns Nation," *New York Times*, 3 October 1935).

1936

H. P. Lovecraft to Herman Charles Koenig

12 January 1936
[Providence, R.I.]
Upon visiting Charleston for the first time in the spring of 1930, writer H. P. Lovecraft was awestruck by the city's beauty.[1] *He wrote an extensive unpublished travelogue that included a mapped walking tour with sketches of various historic sites. Lovecraft revised that travelogue for this letter to his associate Herman C. Koenig, who was a collector of fantasy literature. In the letter, Lovecraft enthused that Charleston was "the only city except Providence in which I feel perfectly at home."*[2] *He used a phonetic representation of Koenig's initials for the salutation as well as for his own signature.*

---

[1] Howard Phillips Lovecraft (1890–1937) was a horror writer who was mostly unknown in his lifetime, publishing mostly in pulp magazines, including *Weird Tales*. He was born in Providence, Rhode Island, to parents who suffered from mental illness. Lovecraft also suffered from mental illness, physical ailments, and poverty. Following his death, a small group of associates kept his legacy alive, and through their efforts Lovecraft has been a continuing influence for horror writers.

[2] Herman Charles Koenig (1893–1959) was a laboratory manager in New York City and collector of fantasy literature. He typed and mimeographed the original handwritten copy of this letter for wider distribution. The Edison Company of New Jersey may have obtained a copy through Koenig. The company published Lovecraft's sketches in a travel brochure for company employees (see "Visit to Charleston of Edison Companies' Special Train Party," 25 January 1936, H. P. Lovecraft, Charleston County Public Library, Charleston, S.C.; and Lovecraft, "Account of a Visit to Charleston, S.C.," 28 April 1930, "An Account of Charleston, in His Majty's Province of South-Carolina," 1930, and "Charleston," in H. P. Lovecraft, *Collected Essays*, vol. 4, ed. S. T. Joshi (New York: Hippocampus Press 2005), 67–106, 261–83.

Dear Ech-Si-Kheh:

Before I do anything else, I must hasten to give you a few Charleston pointers. I'd envy you bitterly if you were going to spend any real time in the ancient city—or in Florida—though as it is, I extend as much sympathy as felicitation. I simply couldn't content myself with so tantalizing a glimpse. Yes—there are sightseeing facilities in the form of a rubberneck 'bus (Gray Line) which operates from the 'bus station in King Street, next to the corner of Calhoun (Marion square), but I doubt if such a service could do the old town justice. Nothing but a good pedestrian tour could do it—hence, I'm going to outline one for you in a few moments. I'd advise you to get a free city map at the Chamber of Commerce (Broad and Church Streets), but in case you can't, I'll make a rough sketch which may possibly suffice. I'll outline an abridged sightseeing route in red pencil. If you have any more than a day or two in Charleston, I advise you to get a full guide book which includes virtually everything of interest—"Street Strolls around Charleston, S.C." by Miriam Belhaugee Wilson.[3] This will set you back .75¢ at any good stationery store (such as Lightharts's on the east side of King Street just below George), but is worth every cent of it. It not only tells where to find all sights but gives the history and traditions centering around everything described. These itineraries could be covered in 3 or 4 days, though to receive justice, they ought to have at least a week.

Charleston, as you probably know, was first founded in 1670 on a site somewhat removed (across the Ashley River) from its present peninsular location. The colony of Carolina was chartered by Charles II in 1663, though then containing only some straggling settlements of Virginian and West Indian planters in its northern parts. In its government, the enterprise adopted a very formal and oligarchical plan called the "Grand Model," derived from the philosophical ideas of John Locke, and providing for fixed ranks (landgrave, cassique, baron) dependent upon land tenure. These distributions were never clear and finally fell into desuetude. The first new colonists—a group of 160 in two ships under Capt. Wm. Sales—were sent out in 1669 to build a "Towne of Trade" and in 1670 settled at their first location. The two great ben, Kiawah and Wando, were renamed respectively Ashley and Cooper in honor of the greatest of the Lords Proprietor (who never visited the colony)—Anthony Ashley Cooper, later first Earl of Shaftesbury. Within a year of the settlement many persons questioned the wisdom of the site and after 1672 a sprinkling of colonists began to drift across to "Oyster Point," the peninsula betwixt the Ashley and Cooper. By 1679 a change of site was agreed on and in 1680 the new Charles-Town (like the first named from Charles II, though Carolina was named from Charles IX of France because of abortive Huguenot settlements in 1562–5) was laid out according to a

---

[3] Lovecraft referred to Miriam Bellangee Wilson's self-published guide to the city. Wilson's collection of artifacts related to slavery formed the basis of the Slave Mart Museum at 6 Chalmers Street.

carefully preconceived plan. From this second planting the real history of Charleston dates. For protection against Spaniards and Indians the town was fortified with strong breastworks which soon developed into city walls, with bastions, salients and guard posts at the gates. Under these influences the town soon developed into a narrow parallelogram four squares long and three wide, fronting on the Cooper River and bounded on the south by Van der Hasel's [Vanderhorst] Creek—now filled in and forming the line of Water Street. The western boundary corresponded to the present Meeting Street, having here a wall, gate and drawbridge. Places were reserved for a church, a town hall and a parade-ground. The North and South streets were Church and Meeting; the East and West ones, from the South boundary up, were Tradd (named for the first white child born in the town), Elliott, Broad and Dock (later Queen).

The town soon outgrew its walls, and by 1700 had spread westward desultorily to the Ashley River. The decade 1679–1689 brought heavy immigration, especially of dissenters after the accession of James II. West Indian planters also flocked in, founding families still in existence. In 1693 the culture of rice was introduced and soon became the leading pursuit of the inhabitants. In 1741 the introduction of indigo provided another major industry—both lasting until the 19th century age of cotton.

Churches were early appeared—Anglican, Baptist, Presbyterian, Quaker and Huguenot. The Charleston Quakers are now extinct, but an Huguenot church still exists at Church and Queen Sts.—the only one surviving in the U.S. The Huguenots —so influential in Charleston history—came mostly between 1680 and 1688, uprooted by oppression in France. Some Dutch from Niew Nederland also appeared, followed by Germans and Swiss who established the wrought-iron industry. Buildings of a good type were erected, though no specimens earlier than 1722 survive.

Early Carolina history was turbulent. In 1686 the Spanish from St. Augustine destroyed a Scottish settlement farther down the coast—Port Royal—and went unpunished only because of religious discord in the colony. This discord eventually led to the abolition of the proprietary government and the establishment of Carolina as a royal province in 1719. In 1699 fever, hurricane and flood ravaged the colony. These scourges recur all down the centuries, though modern medical science has stamped out yellow fever, while 18th century engineering provided stouter sea-walls and better houses to resist the September tempests.

It was in the 18th century that the ripe culture of old Charles-Town fully flowered. Architecture flourished and all the attributes of a mellow civilization appeared. In 1702 Gov. [James] Moore led an expedition against the Florida Spaniards, holding all of St. Augustine except the fort for a time. Indians and pirates also harassed the colony. At one time Col. [William] Rhett hanged 57 of the latter at once on a spot near the tip of the peninsula, where Church and Meeting now intersect. In 1719 the colony became a royal province and a decade later its present division into North Carolina and South Carolina was made. By 1720 Charles-Town had largely overflowed its walls and these barriers now began to be demolished bit by bit. Today only a fragment of them remains—the ancient bastion in Cumberland Street, built in 1703 and now called the "Old Powder Magazine."

At this period the city began to assume much of its present aspect. Houses as early as the 1730's are still very numerous; and we still see the town, as far as general impressions go, as it was in the middle and later Georgian era. Block on block of the ancient edifices may still be descried in the region below Broad Street—to an extent not duplicated in any other American city. Roof-tiling a rare thing in early American houses—was introduced about 1735, and gave to the steep gables of the houses their characteristic aspect. Early experiments with porches were suggested by the warm climate, and before the end of the 18th century we see Charleston as a town of outdoor living . . . . with great verandahs on all three storeys of the south or west sides of the houses, opening on exquisite walled gardens which passers-by might glimpse through gates of magnificent wrought-iron grille-work. The brick-and-stucco houses generally followed Georgian models, but in an individual and localized way; so that no other colonial city looks just like Charleston. We find the city's gardens first mentioned about 1740. In 1748 the present proprietary library was founded, attesting to the good scholarship of a people more urban than the Virginians because of the heat and fever which drove them from their inland plantations to their town houses during a great part of the summer. Theatres appear about the middle of the 18th century (the first in 1736)—or before—the principal one being at the corner of Dock (Queen) and Church Streets. In 1752 a great storm damaged the town and produced much rebuilding—giving the streets a good deal of their present form.

Charles-Town weathered the revolution with considerable poise, though largely rebel in sympathies. It was defended by a strong fort on Sullivan's Island, commanded by Col. [William] Moultrie and later named for him. On June 28th, 1776, occurred that attack by His Majesty's fleet during which the rebel sergeant Jasper leapt outside the breastworks and saved his colours under fire. Charles-Town held out under the rebels till 1780, when the forces of Sir Henry Clinton and Lord Camden moved in and took up headquarters at the splendid Brewton Pringle mansion in lower King Street—a place still standing and open as a museum for the exorbitant fee of a full dollar.[4] There was some friction between troops and populace, for which blame seems evenly divided. Charles-Town was used as a base of supplies by the regulars during most of the Southern campaign—a campaign in which the chief obstacles were the Rhode Island General Nathanael Greene and the local South Carolina guerillas Francis Marion, Sumter, and Pickens. After the disaster to Lord Cornwallis's army in October 1781 the town was evacuated—the troops bearing away the chimes of St. Michael's church to London, whence they were afterward regained by purchase.

---

[4]Lovecraft likely referred to Lord Charles Cornwallis, who led British forces to victory in the Battle of Camden.

In 1783 the city's name was officially changed from Charles-Town to its exact present form of Charleston. Its general culture had been very little impaired by the upheavals of war, and the old social order continued to flourish. In 1792 the negro uprising in St. Domingo sent to Charleston a great number of French gentlefolk who were instantly made welcome, and who formed a highly civilizing influence. About this time Charleston was superseded by the inland town of Columbia as capital of South Carolina—the new place being laid out especially for that purpose.

This age—the late 18th and early 19th centuries—marks the heyday of Charleston's social glory and material prosperity. Culture was promoted by isolation from the hinterland and free communication with Europe—so that to this day the town avoids the characteristic negroid accent of the South. 18th century taste survived with remarkable tenacity, and classic revival architecture flourished with more than normal vigour. Victorian decadence was longer postponed than it was anywhere else. In 1800 Charleston was the leading centre of culture on this continent, with graceful institutions and a high level of taste such as no other American region is ever likely to parallel. The social season extended from May to November, when malaria drove the planters to town from their inland estates; and was supplemented by a shorter period around the end of January called the "Gay Season." The great social institution of the town whose meetings and functions determined the recreative life of the greatest families, and whose judgments determined the status of every person of consequence, was (and still is) an organization originally of musical purpose, called the St. Cecelia Society. The St. Cecelia's Day concerts and balls of this society and its Thursday functions that began at 9 P.M. soon became by-words of exclusiveness, till at length its musical character was merged in its social dictatorship. Various other dancing assemblies were frequented by the gay, and the Philharmonic Concerts were also well attended. Jockey balls attested the importance of racing, as did the Annual Race Week, which formed a sort of Charleston carnival. Much of this atmosphere is reflected in Du Bose Heyward's fairly recent novel "Peter Ashley." Business was transacted during the "Gay Season"—advantage being taken of the presence of many planters in town. Everyone was generally back in the country by the end of March, not to see Charleston again till May.

The gentry comprising the civilization were almost all planters of rice and cotton —the latter having replaced indigo as a major staple. Their cultivation greatly exceeded that of the Virginians, and they left mercantile pursuits to a bourgeois class largely from England and Scotland. Public education increased and individual taste developed. Favorite authors, apart from the omnipresent Graeco-Roman classics, were Shakespeare and Montaigne. Coaches now appear in frequent use, and on every hand we behold the ideal of gentlemanly carelessness uppermost. No man knew how much he was worth in cash—trade and calculation being left to hired "factors" from the north. Personal honour was very carefully guarded, and duelling was frequent.

In those days the factors offices and merchant's warehouses formed a distinct district along Bay Street, which faces the Cooper River or principal waterfront. Popular shopping streets were the east ends of Broad and Tradd and Elliott. General stores carrying all manner of goods were the rule, the jewelry shops forming the main exception. Country trade was conducted by long, white-topped wagons with four or six horses or mules, piled high with cotton-bales, high up in King Street near the present railway station. Most of the town was below, or only slightly above, Calhoun (then called Boundary) Street; just as before the Revolution it had been largely below Broad—or at West Queen or Cumberland. It should be noted that Charleston is a narrow penisula like the island of Manhattan, so that urban expansion (checked by marshes on the western or Ashley River side) is invariably northward. There was no one residence section, homes being scattered and surrounded by large gardens or tracts of land. The Battery, lower Meeting St., Legare St. and so on, were then as now favored by fine dwellings. Indeed, we may say that the social complexion of the town has changed but little in the 136 years since those gorgeous days of 1800. The Battery (or White Point gardens) was, as it still is a chosen place of promenade.

In 1822 a threatened negro insurrection alarmed the town, but the plot came to nothing.[5] Shortly afterward tension with the North was increased by the tariff troubles culminating in the nullification agitation of 1832 et seq. Slaves were in general very well treated, so that to this day the blacks of Charleston are orderly and well disposed. Much African superstition was picked up from them, so that to this day the region abounds in weird folklore. Arts and literary life continued to flourish, producing such figures as the graceful poet Henry Timerod.[6]

The Civil War naturally harassed Charleston greatly, though no actual land fighting occurred there. Secession began in South Carolina and the first shots of the war were fired at Fort Sumter in Charleston Harbour. Almost coincident with these events was the local fire of 1861, which created a vast burned district west of Meeting St. and above and below Broad, although it was of accidental origin and totally unconnected with the conflict. The fire destroyed St. Andrew's Hall in Broad St., formerly the leading place of public assemblage; and the site has never been built upon. The whole burned district remained a desert for years—dividing the town into two parts.

Wartime hardships—blockades and siege and all their consequences—pressed heavily upon Charleston, but the population carried on well. Because of Federal gunfire in the harbour, the lower end of the town was left almost deserted during the hostilities—the inhabitants congregating north of the burned district. With the war went Charleston's material prosperity, but despite external change the basic civilization proved too deep to eradicate. Perspectives and institutions persisted, and the nightmare of "reconstruction" was weathered without flinching. At length a limited prosperity began to dawn. Broad Street again bristled with banks, brokers and

---

[5]Denmark Vesey and dozens of alleged coconspirators were hanged in 1822 after they were accused of plotting an uprising of enslaved and free black Charlestonians.

[6]Henry Timrod (1829–1867) was a Charleston-born journalist and poet.

barristers, and King Street became a fashionable shopping promenade of the elegant '80's. Meeting Street drove a thriving jobbing trade in dry-goods, clothing, shoes and crockery, whilst the East Bay Street waterfront buzzed anew with the bulk of grocers and ship-chandlers. The rice and cotton industries, however, never reached their former state of opulence.

In 1886 Charleston experienced the severest earthquake ever known on the Atlantic coast—a thing which destroyed many buildings and public works, and severely impaired many more—including the splendid old edifice of St. Michael's Church. Recuperation, however, was very swift.

Today Charleston is probably the most civilized spot in the United States—the place where genuine values most amply survive, and where the false glitter and confusion of mechanized barbarism are least to be found. The original families still hold sway—Rhetts, Izards, Pringles, Bulls, Hugers, Ravenels, Manigaults, Draytons, Storeys [Stoneys], Pinckneys, Rutledges, Middletons and so on—and still uphold the basic truths and standards of a civilization which is genuine because it represents a settled adjustment betwixt people and landscape, old enough to have created the overtones useful to a sense of interest and significance. Gentlefolk in Charleston still pursue their ways for pleasure and not for show or profit, and are still decently anxious to keep their names and personal affairs out of the papers. The Charleston dailies are the only ones today without a vulgar "society column" to spy upon the comings and goings of important people.

Foreigners are not numerous, though Italian and Jewish colonies exist. Blacks, of course, abound but they are extremely civil and obliging. The street cries of Charleston, all uttered by negro vendors, were once very famous, but are now declining despite artificial efforts to revive them. The town contains many wealthy northerners who have bought old estates, but so far the newcomers have been very appreciative and assimilable. There is the nucleus of an "art colony" in and around lower Church Street, but fortunately no large-scale "Greenwich Village" has developed.

Architecturally, Charleston is the most remarkable town in the U.S.— possessing unique colonial features and having retained an astonishing proportion of early buildings. West Indian and French Huguenot features, plus native climatic adaptations, produce striking variants of English Georgian architecture—hence the tiers of verandahs, the gay titles, the painted stucco over brickwork, the peculiar gallic gables, the carved eaves, the deeply recessed windows and the occasional pixie-head roofs. No one, having seen a Charleston house, can ever mistake the type. The side verandahs with their classical doorway openings on the street are utterly characteristic of the place—as are the wrought-iron grilles and gates, and the great walled gardens. Railed double flights of steps curving above an arched passageway— a pleasant Renaissance affect—are nowhere else as numerous as here. In classic revival architecture Charleston excels. She bred the eminent architect Robert Mills and much of his work is to be found in his native place. There were, too, great numbers of amateur or gentleman architects like Gabriel Manigault. As the 19th century advanced, Charleston largely escaped the general collapse of architectural taste, though a certain heaviness and decadence are visible in later buildings. Some of the coarseness in details can be attributed to the replacement of expert white cabinet-makers by unskilled negro laborers. Today Charleston is refreshingly free from "modernistic" architecture and seems like Providence determined to remain true to its own heritage. During the past years there has been an encouraging reclamation of deserted and half-ruinous landmarks (like the splendid Georgian Vanderhorst Row (1802) in East Bay Street and the historic Planter's Hotel at Church and Queen) in connection with CWA, ERA, PWA and WPA projects—a work which one hopes may not be interrupted by any reactionary political move.[7]

Charleston occupies a flat—and originally marshy and creek-threaded—tongue of land betwixt the mouths of two great rivers which here flow into one of the most spacious harbours on the Atlantic coast,—a harbour seven miles across and separated from the open sea by several islands. The city is the natural part of a spacious inland region of subtropical climate and fertility, cut by many rivers and once the seat of extensive plantation. Here are gardens of figs, pomegranates, peaches, oranges, oleanders, myrtles, azaleas, camellias, acacias, jujubes and roses; and outside the towns one beholds the wild-rose, the wild yellow jessamine, the magnolia and the twisted and curious live-oak festoons of grey Spanish moss hanging from spectral branches. Observing Charleston horticulture, one does not wonder at its fame, or at the circumstance that two of our most celebrated flowers, the poinsettia and the gardenia, were named from gentlemen of Charleston, who cultivated them. The piquant and bristling palmetto-tree is very frequently met with, and more clearly than anything else proclaims our nearness to the tropics.

The city lies in N. latitude 32°45° and W. longitude 79°57° Approached from the sea, its flatness gives it a very curious and engaging aspect; the many spires and roofs seeming to rise directly out of the water, as if forming the topmost pinnacles of submerged Atlantis. St. Michael's and St. Philip's steeples are dominant and traditional pictures of the skyline. The general arrangement of the streets is like that of New York—with cross streets and long north and south streets ending at the Battery with a sea-wall. The social topography, however, is very different. Inasmuch as the Battery and vicinity form a sumptuous residential section (on account of the cool breeze) while business flourishes on the two great north and south streets (King and Meeting), about midway in their course. The principal cross-streets, from the Battery up, are Tradd, (a thoroughfare wholly colonial), Broad, (the street of bankers and brokers), and Calhoun (which marks the focus of the main business section, and crosses Meeting and King at an open park called Marion Square). The great North and South streets, from the Cooper River or principal waterfront westward, are East Bay, Church, Meeting, King, Legare (which runs north into Archdale and St. Philip),

---

[7]For more on the restoration of the Planter's Hotel, see Program, "The Recruiting Officer," Dock Street Theatre Dedication, 26 November 1937, pp. 131–133, this volume.

Rutledge Avenue and Ashley Avenue. The region below Broad Street is very largely colonial. Along the line of Meeting Street and around the Battery it is exceedingly fashionable and beautiful; whilst east of this, along the line of Church Street, it is quaint and homelike except for occasional book shops and artists studios. As one gets north of Stoll's Alley, a dismal slum district of abandoned warehouses and dirty tenements begins to develop along the Cooper waterfront; but this is well worth exploration because of the age and picturesqueness of the houses. But at Broad and Calhoun lies a region which may be called semi-colonial, and which ought to be thoroughly covered by the visitor, since it contains the leading public edifices. The focal point of this and the older southerly region is the historic intersection of Broad and Meeting Streets, once the principal gate of the original walled town, and for two centuries the real civic centre. On the four corners of this intersection will be found ancient St. Michael's Church (1761) (S.E.) the City Hall (1801) (N.E.), the Court House (1788) (N.W.) and the modern but sightly post office (S.W.). Adjacent to it and having gates on both Meeting and Broad Streets (as well as on Charles St. to the N.), is the old City Park or Washington Square, which lies behind the City Hall and forms the principal downtown resting-place besides the Battery. Here we find an excellent statue of William Pitt, Esq., set up in 1770 and moved to the present site from elsewhere; also a monument to the graceful Charleston poet Henry Timerod, and one to the great Confederate General Pierre-Gustave Toutant Beauregard. The park extends through to Chalmers Street on the north, and on the east is bounded by a very picturesque and ancient Georgian wall.

We now come to consider the actual observation of the city, for which a good map is eminently desirable. The slower one can go, the better, since colour and atmosphere can be best absorbed if one has leisure to savour and digest each sight to the fullest extent—correlating it with one's historical, literary and imaginative background. If a preliminary orientation tour is desired as a preface to real exploration, that offered by the Gray Line sightseeing coaches will be found excellent. Before beginning any actual trip, it would be wise to prepare in advance for what one is to see—either through this hasty sketch, or through the Wilson guide book previously mentioned. A minimum of time will then be lost. In this sketch only the most salient things will be touched upon. No attempt will be made to describe the multiplicity of rural sights around Charleston—sights which include many fine plantations, the ancient Goose Creek Church (1711), St. Andrews' Parish Church (1706) and the famous Magnolia, Middleton and Cypress Gardens, which are open to the public in the early spring. These latter, however, deserve a special expedition.

Arriving in Charleston, the visitor beholds a city which is alive in every sense despite the omnipresent aura of the past. Though suggesting Salem and Newport in its physical aspect, it has not the somnolence of those venerable towns, but is indeed the present metropolis of a large and opulent region, in which it stands alone and unchallenged. Accordingly, it will be found to contain a variety of urban refinements and facilities, and to harbour a metropolitan self-sufficiency, which would not be found in a northern town of equal size. The population, including the blacks, does as found, exceed 62,000; yet the general atmosphere is that of a large town of vast assurance and maturity. There are—allowing for the depression—signs of a commercial revival in the immediate future; and an increasing flow of appreciative tourists heightens the aspect of liveliness during the early spring season. The great Cooper River bridge serves, in connection with another bridge over the Ashley, to place Charleston on a direct coastal route betwixt Florida and the North; a circumstance very favourable to its economic outlook. Charleston's chief industries have latterly been the manufacture of phosphate fertilisers and asbestos products, and the export of varied agricultural commodities. The agricultural trade is very brisk, owing to the excellence and healthfulness of South Carolina vegetable produce—the fruit of a soil rich in the dietetically necessary element of iodine.

Regarding hotel accommodations, the traveler of modest needs will be very well served by the excellent YMCA on the north side of George Street between King and Meeting, and not far from the 'bus station in Marion Square. Those desiring a degree less of austerity may try the home-like Timerod Inn in Meeting Street near Broad—just across the street from ancient City Park. More modern hotel facilities are provide by the well-appointed Francis Marion Hotel in Marion Square, while still greater luxury can be had at the Fort Sumter—a definitely vacationist hostelry on the Battery at the foot of King Street. Most aristocratic of all, perhaps is the Villa Margharita, a made-over pirate mansion in South Battery St—the street running just north of the park and overlooking the harbour.

Issuing forth to observe his environment, the stranger cannot but note the civilized and distinctive atmosphere of the city around him. The pace of life is sensible and leisurely and there is no needless noise or bustle or excitement. The abundance of negroes is picturesque, and now and then the sweet chimes of Old St. Michael's can be heard striking the hours, halves, and quarters as they have done since 1779. Odd characters and quaint beggars abound to an extent unheard of in the efficient and dehumanized North. As for climate, most cannot but find it very much to their taste; it being mild in winter, and in summer cooled by the breezes of the neighboring ocean. The annual mean temperature is 67 F, and there are on the average only six freezing days in a year. The Battery is never warm enough to justify coatlessness. The sun in Charleston shines more continuously than in any other American city except Los Angeles. The one drawback is the prevalency toward gales and hurricanes in late August and September, a thing largely offset by stout building construction and massive sea-walls. The beaches of Charleston—Folly Beach, Sullivan's Island and the Isle of Palms—are among the finest in the South. Sullivan's Island, with Fort Moultrie, ought certainly to be visited because of its association with [Edgar Allan] Poe (who served in the army there) and its part in his celebrated tale "The Gold Bug"; and its possession of the grave of the unfortunate Seminole chieftain Osceola, who was confined in the dungeons of the fort. One of the Gray Line tours includes Sullivan's Island.

The best way to see Charleston is first to drift aimlessly about the ancient streets below Broad, picking up random impressions of certain charm and exotic tradition without the psychological hindrance of a preconceived or systematic plan, and then—having reached the palmetto-fringed and live-oak-dotted Battery with its numerous monuments—to begin the regular following of some stated sightseeing route. In the random Batteryward stroll a very good idea of old Charleston may be secured. One will stumble on the quaintest conceivable streets, alleys, squares, and hidden courtyards, and will encounter the most sumptuous mansions embedded in walled tropical gardens. Along the principal waterfront, that on the Cooper side he will discern the many abandoned and ruined brick warehouses which speak so eloquently of former shipping prosperity. As in Newport and Salem, relatively few of the ancient houses are ever demolished; though many are in a state of desertion or decrepitude. The exhibition of the old tiled and stuccoed buildings, with their occasionally bright hues, will engage the eye from the outset; suggesting something oddly French or Latin or foreign in some obscure way. The great blackness of most of the negroes will be remarked; it being evidently the custom for mulattos to keep to themselves in the newer far-northern part of the town. Foreign faces, except for a sprinkling of Greeks, Jews and Italians, are very seldom noticeable; the city being obviously still dominated by old Nordic stock. Now and then a classic, old-fashioned public building or church will attract notice; and at all times one is looking for glimpses of the two dominant landmarks—St. Michael's and St. Philip's spires. Wrought-iron work produces a deep impression because of its universal profusion—gates, balconies, window grilles, railings and the like; all of the finest craftsmanship. The gates are especially numerous because of the prevalence of high-walled gardens in this land of luxurious flowers, rambling vines and opulent trees that weave an omnipresent green twilight redolent of perfume and musical with bird-song when the sun goes down. Bronze street signs set in the sidewalk at intersections are a typical feature of modern Charleston. Most important buildings and historic sites are marked by tablets or placards.

We are now ready for our systematic itinerary. The route about to be outlined, beginning at the Battery, is designed to cover the whole city in a single walk with as few repetitions as possible; but it is of course merely fragmentary as compared with all the sites to be seen. I devised it with considerable care some five years ago, when preparing our friend Martonius for his first trip to Charleston.[8] It may be followed in one long tramp—a full day's pedestrian quota—or taken in sections; or in any order whatsoever. It is not meant to include everything in old Charleston, and it would be a pity if one were to follow it blindly without consulting the guide books, and ascertaining what else is to be seen. Likewise, it leaves to these fuller guide-books the task of supplying ampler descriptions of the few things which are touched upon.

[8]Lovecraft referred to anarchist writer and activist James Ferdinand Morton Jr., who belonged to the Kalem Club, a literary circle that included Lovecraft and Koenig.

For a detailed knowledge of Charleston, history and traditions, one should consult volumes at the excellent library in King Street, betwixt Clifford and Queen. Those by Mazyck and Mrs. St. Julien Ravenel (wife of the noted physician who eradicated yellow fever from the city) are especially good.[9] On the following crude map, the route is shown in red.

Especially important thoroughfares underlined.

Principal north and south Charleston streets or lines of streets, reading east to west from Cooper River front toward the Ashley:-East Bay W., Church St., Meeting St., King St., Legare, Ashdale [Archdale], St. Philip, Lockwood, Logan, Mazyck, Coming, Franklin-, Pott [Pitt], South St., Rutledge Ave., Ashley Ave., President St.

Principal cross streets or lines of streets of Charleston readings north from the battery. S. Battery, Lamboll-Atlantic, Ladson-Water, Tradd, Broad, Queen, Cumberland, Horlbeck, Clifford, Market, Beaufain-, Hasall [Hasell], Wentworth, George, Calhoun; Vanderhorst, Charlotte, Morris Mary, Cannon, Spring, Bogard, Columbus.

Principal Squares. Marion Square or Citadel Green, Calhoun, King and Meeting Streets, City Park, or Washington Square, Meeting, Broad and Chalmers Sts. Battery or White Point Gardens, foot of King, Meeting, Church and E. Bay Sts.

Beginning at the Battery, the visitor should observe the semi-tropical scenery of that pleasing area, and pay good attention to the mansions fronting on it. Looking down the harbour somewhat in the distance, and see to the left of it Fort Moultrie, occupying a point of land on Sullivan's Island. Turning inland, there is to be seen at #8 South Battery (on the left-hand corner of Church St.) the elegant private mansion built in 1768 by Thos. Savage, Esq., and in 1785 bought by Col. Wm. Washington of the celebrated Virginia family. If one choose to go up King St., to #27 and explore the ancient Brewton-Pringle house (headquarters of His Majesty's forces 1780–81), he may well do so; though this edifice will be encountered later in the circuitous route. If not, it is advisable to begin the tour by turning up Church St., though not without looking carefully up Meeting St., and observing the spacious mansions and estates lining both the sides. Advancing along Church St., which is very narrow, we pass by quaint ancient houses and stables, and notice the town dwellings of artists as we cross Atlantic St. After this we encounter a bend, on the left-hand side of which are some very ancient houses. No. 35 once inhabited by a local historian, was built in 1745. No. 37 was built before 1733. No. 39, the well-known George Eveleigh house, was built in the decade 1743–53, and had a secret stairway to the second floor! All three of these houses once had a secret passage to Vanderhorst Creek, which followed the line of the present Water St. We now come to Water St., which in

---

[9]Harriott Horry Ravenel, *Charleston: The Place and the People* (New York: Macmillan, 1906); Arthur Mazyck, *Charleston South Carolina in 1883* (Boston: Heliotype, 1883); *Guide to Charleston Illustrated: Being a Sketch of the History of Charleston, S.C.* (Charleston: Walker, Evans & Cogswell, 1875).

its—aqueous days was crossed by a bridge. That part of Church St., we have just been traversing was anciently called Fort St. The large round object in the sidewalk at this intersection is a <u>tidal drain</u>, ma necessary by the low and watery nature of the region. Somewhat west of this is the spot where Col. Rhett caused 57 pirates to be hanged in a single afternoon. Advancing around the bend, we now encounter on our right the entrance to Stoll's Alley, once a slum, but now tastefully restored as an habitation for artists. It is to be hoped that this colony will not sink to the status of a Greenwich Village. An exploration of Stoll's Alley is well worth one's while, nor is it a vain digression to go all the way through the narrow part to <u>East Bay St.</u> In the wider part the Georgian restorations are very clever and agreeable, though this artificiality is manifest. At East Bay St. we turn to the left and find the abandoned and ruined warehousing along the waterfront. We soon come to <u>Longitude Lane,</u> leading back to Church St., opposite which—on the water side of the street—is an exceedingly sightly edifice of brick, of Adam-period design and in a pathetic state of desertion and decrepitude until its recent P.W.A. restoration. This is <u>Vanderhorst Row,</u> put up in 1801 and said to be the oldest apartment-house in America. Now turning into Longitude Lane, we pass by the moss-grown brick walls of half-abandoned cotton warehouses; noting the cobble stones set for mules' feet, the flagstones for the dray-wheel, and the snubbing-posts at the warehouse doors. One of these posts is an old ship's cannon. Once back on Church St., we look to the left and digress backward to see the entrance of an old warehouse on the eastern side, and the classic facade of the <u>First Baptist Church</u> (1822—designed by Robert Mills) opposite it. Next the church and opposite the mouth of Longitude Lane, is #69 the <u>Jacob Motte House,</u> built in 1760 and having a pink colour which it has borne since the earliest times. Next door at #71—is the <u>Robert Brewton House</u> built in 1740 and forming a fine example of the smaller "single" house of early Charleston. Still farther along—at #73—is the <u>Miles Brewton</u> house (1733—a typical old Charleston "double" house). Across the street from it, at #78 is an old house with a fine wrought-iron balcony from which General Washington is reputed to have given an address. A study of this balcony tends to disprove the tradition since (although the house is ancient) the craftsmanship points to a later date than 1791, the period of the general's visit. One singular thing about the house is the symmetrical <u>central</u> portion of the doorway; a thing universally met within Georgian—New England, but very uncommon in the South. We come now to quaint and ancient Tradd St., which is so picturesque that it will pay us to stroll down it to the river and return. On both sides we may see very ancient houses, built flush with the street and with walls adjoining, as a protection (says local tradition) against the raids of pirates, Spaniards and Indians. <u>Bedon's Alley,</u> a very old and curious by-way containing a large three storey brick house which may possibly be the oldest in Charleston, extends northward from a point half-way to the river; on its western corner being the site once holding the <u>Carolina Coffee-House.</u> Here, in 1790, the St. Cecelia Society held one of its concerts; and in 1793 the Ugly Club (which must have had its inspiration in Wm. Steele's <u>Spectator</u> papers, and to which I would have enjoyed belonging) used it as a dining place.[10] At East Bay St. we again behold Vanderhorst Row and note on the northern corner of Tradd St. the site of the birthplace of the first white child in the town—Robert Tradd, from whom the street was named. Looking out over the river past Adger's Wharf, we behold the island called Castle-Pinckney, and the farther off, the opposite shore of Mt. Pleasant and part of Sullivan's Island. Returning now to Church St. and resuming a northerly course, we behold on the left at #87 the Heyward house, a fine brick Georgian mansion of generalised rather than Charlestonian architecture, some time ago restored as a public museum. This house was built in the 1770's or before, and was used by General Washington during his Charleston visit of May 1791. Adjoining this structure is an old house which in 1791–1810 was the French Theatre, afterward the City Theatre. The auditorium was in the rear, reached by crossing through an archway and traversing an inner court. In more recent times, the place had sunk to a slum and was used by negroes as a vending-place of vegetables, being commonly known as "Cabbage-Row" and presented in the novel "Porgy" by Du Bose Heyward, as "Catfish Row." The interior of this building is now familiar to northern audiences through the stage setting of the opera "Porgy and Bess." Some years ago it was restored to its original neatness, and it has at times housed various art and book shops. Proceeding onward, we should note the quaint alleys on either side of the street— St. Michael's Place to the left, and Elliott St. to the right. We now come to Broad St. the leading transverse thoroughfare of the town, and an abode of bankers and brokers. On the N.E. corner is the modern bank building which has most unfortunately replaced the old and historic Shepheard's Tavern, where the first Masonic Lodge in America was organized in 1736. On the N.W. corner, the Chamber of Commerce occupies the brick structure erected in 1784 for the Bank of South Carolina and used from 1835 to 1914 as a library. It will be worth our while to walk down Broad St. to the river and study the ancient and remarkable public building which squarely faces the end of the street. This is the Old Exchange, built in 1767 on the site of the old guard post called "Half-Moon Bastion," and used as executive headquarters by His Majesty's forces in 1780–81. It was later a post-office, and is now an headquarters of the D.A.R.—open as a museum and also housing certain federal clerical activities. During the Revolution prisoners were confined in the basement of this building; and on the northern end, close to the ground, can still be seen the small square hole, with heavy grating, which afforded scanty light and air to some of the dungeons. The architecture of the building in general is very fine. To the right of the Old Exchange, across a seaward lane and from the water side of East Bay St. at #114–116, will be found a group of very ancient buildings, two of which have cupolas or observation-towers. These towers were used by observers to watch the incoming shipping and transmit the news to the public. Ships were first sighted from a tower on Sullivan's

---

[10] The Ugly Club was a Charleston social group. Richard Steele copublished the *Spectator*, an early-eighteenth-century London periodical.

Island, whose watchman relayed the news to these urban towers by raising ball signals on a pole—a black ball for a square rigger, and a white ball for a schooner-rigged vessel. These signals were repeated by the urban watchers, the signal balls being left up until the ships they represented came to anchor. The small buildings on the corner, next the tall cupola'd building, is the old French Coffee-House, or Harriss Tavern. Beneath this structure may still be found the ancient wine-cellars, which form a tunnel extending far out under East Bay St., and then turning toward the Battery in an arm reaching half a block. We now, after a glance at the classic bank facade on the landward side of East Bay above Broad, turn back along Broad St. for one block; then turning northward into State St., originally called Union St. Following this to the first intersection, we there turn to the left into ancient and picturesque Chalmers St., a broad cobblestoned thoroughfare, at whose farther end can be seen in the distance the splendid classic pillars of Hibernian Hall (1841) in Meeting St. Almost all the houses along Chalmers St. are colonial. At #8, the small, low archway adjoining a pretentiously turreted building, is the Old Slave Market at which trained servants and skilled artisans were sold—the common field negroes being procurable at "Vendue Range," the foot of Queen St. where the Clyde Lines wharves now extend. Nearly opposite the "Slave Mart" is that curious pink-coloured building which possesses (perhaps) the only gambrel roof in Charleston. This is a very old house and was a tavern before the Revolution. It has 3 storeys, but only one room to a floor. We are now back at Church St. though it would do no harm to walk along Chalmers to Meeting and back in order to observe ancient houses. Turning up Church, we next come to Queen St. (formerly Dock St), at whose S.E. corner is the slightly Gothic church (1845) and churchyard of the Huguenots. This is today the only Huguenot church in the country, and deserves the support (which it sorely needs) of every surviving group of Huguenot descendants. Across the street from the church is the deserted and long dilapidated shell of the Planter's Hotel, built about 1805 and famous in the great cotton era as a rendezvous of neighboring planters and their families. It is now under restoration as a W.P.A. project. On the N.W. corner, and extending a considerable space along Church St. is a group of five small houses built of brick and Bermuda coral-stone, and known to have been standing prior to 1742. These are the so-called "Pirate Houses"; reputed to have been the haunt of freebooters in the old days, and said to have received visits at a later date from Poe. They are now all converted into fashionable shops, and the courtyard behind them has been developed as a highly fascinating by-way. Beyond these comes the bend in the street, with the five porticoes and steeple of St. Philip's Episcopal church looming up in the foreground, and sections of the churchyard stretching off on both sides of the way. St. Philip's present edifice does not antedate 1835, but it is a fine late-Georgian specimen whose steeple shares honors with St. Michael's as a landmark of the city and a welcoming symbol to the mariner approaching the port. The tower, with its triple portico, is very notable. When this fane was built, Church St. did not extend in front of it, the bend being made to accommodate it. The present street cuts the old churchyard in two, separating the larger part (which contains the grave of John C. Calhoun) from the edifice itself. We now push on to Cumberland St., choosing whether or not we shall stroll down toward the waterfront to see the old house (on the N. side) with the elaborate ironwork, and the wrought-iron emblem of the Iron Workers Guild—which was probably the residence and shop of a master craftsman. With this side-trip made or omitted, we follow Cumberland St. west of Church toward Meeting, noting on the left hand side the Old Powder Magazine in its limited but pleasing grounds. This squat, peaked-gabled bit of Cyclopean vaulted masonry is the oldest structure in Charleston, dating from 1703 and having formed a bastion of the city wall. It is the only surviving fragment of that wall. The Colonial Dames are in charge of it, and visitors are admitted to the heavily vaulted interior for a 25¢ fee. We now follow Cumberland to Meeting and turn northward to Market St. beholding in the middle of that thoroughfare the high classic facade of the old Market House, whose upper part is now a Confederate Museum. This edifice, built in 1841, is typical of old Charleston public architecture; having the characteristic double flight of steps with the mouth of an arched tunnel beneath. Behind the building the low-roofed shed of the Market (erected 1800) extends all the way to the river, along a line of what was once Fish Market Creek. In earlier times the refuse of this market attracted a famous array of buzzards, which became incredibly tame. Following the market shed to East Bay St. after a glance upward along Meeting St. at the classic facade of the old Charleston Hotel, we behold—somewhat to the right and set near the water—the massive and splendid Custom House with its classic architecture, begun in 1850 and finished after the Civil War. From the seaward side of this building an impressive view of the harbour may be obtained. We now proceed three squares up East Bay to Hasell St., here turning to the left and proceeding again toward Meeting St. on the north or right-hand site, at #54, is what is perhaps (the claim of the Bedon's Alley house not withstanding) the oldest dwelling in Charleston, built in 1722 or before by the old pirate-fighter Col. Wm Rhett, and later forming the birthplace of the eminent soldier and statesman General Wade Hampton. Reaching Meeting St., we may if we wish make a side-trip beyond to see the venerable classic facade of the Jew's Synagogue (1841) on the right and St. Mary's Catholic Church (1938) on the left. We then turn northward along Meeting toward George, passing on the left the stately columns of Trinity Ave. Episcopal Church (1875), called "the youngest church below Calhoun St." At George St. we note on the N.W. corner the fine but dilapidated King Mansions with its walled grounds, built in 1806 and later used as a high-school. Making a side trip eastward along George, we see on the north side the grounds and building of the local water works—which is the old Elliott-Pinckney-Middleton house, finished in 1797 and forming one of the finest possible specimens of Adam-period architecture. The interior, defaced though it is by industrial uses, still retains much fine woodwork and proportioning—especially the circular stairway and the oval room upstairs. Travelers should explore this mansion, since opportunities for seeing Charleston interiors are somewhat limited for strangers without local introductions. The section immediately around it was once known as "Auson [Anson] Borough" (still commemorated in Auson [Anson] St.)—most of the northerly and erstwhile suburban parts of Charleston having such individual local names. Returning now to Meeting St., we follow it northward again till we come to Calhoun St. (formerly Boundary St.) and the easterly end of the open park or parade-ground known successively as Inspection Square, Citadel Green and Marion Square. This was formerly the line of the city's northernmost defenses and in the midst of the part may be seen a single remaining bit of the old "Horn Wall"—made of a mixture of lime and sea shells—which formed the fortifications of 1780. On the north side of the green is the long, battlemented line of the old Citadel (1822) which formed the home of the Military College of S.C. from its foundation in 1842 to its removal (1924) to new quarters in the extreme northwestern part of the city. The building still houses military activities. The King St. side of the green is the focus of modern mercantile life and the seat of the principal hotel. The Meeting St. side marks the local district once known as Louisburgh. Continuing along Meeting St. beyond the square, we see above Charlotte St. the splendid avenue of approach to the Second Presbyterian Church, which was built in 1811. Just beyond this, at the corner of Ashmead St., and now defaced by an encroaching filling-station, is the fine old Peter Manigault mansion, with its striking circular gate-lodge (a typical old Charleston feature, though only two now survive), built in 1790.[11] We have now reached a logical northerly circuit of travel, though we may wish to proceed westward through Hudson and Vanderhorst Sts. to Coming St. up which, on the right-hand side, is St. Paul's Episcopal Church, a spacious fane built in 1810–12. This district was once known as Radcliffeborough. Proceeding south to Calhoun St. we may, if we desire, go westward several blocks to Rutledge Ave. in the old Cannonsborough section (south of which lay Hartestonborough [Harlestonborough]), where we will find the Charleston Museum with its many antiquarian and other exhibits. Typical old Charleston rooms and apothecary shops are shown in the gallery of this celebrated institution. The museum is the oldest in America, having been founded in 1778. Returning along Calhoun St. to St. Philip St., we see in the next block, on the north side of Calhoun and extending to the Francis Marion Hotel, the spacious grounds and venerable building (1792), of the Charleston Orphan Home. The early prevalence of cholera, fever and smallpox in the district left so many orphans that this institution was deemed a necessity. It still serves its original purpose—though the inroads of disease have long since been reduced to normal proportions through the progress of medical science. Descending St. Philip Street we come, at George St., upon the grounds, edifice and gate-lodge (the latter the only surviving specimen of the kind save that of the Manigault house aforementioned) of the stately and reposeful College of Charleston, erected in 1828. Proceeding eastward through George to King St., we turn to the right and descend that business thoroughfare for many

---

[11]Lovecraft referred to the Joseph Manigault house.

blocks. In the course of our walk we shall see two surviving instances of ancient shop signs; the drum clock over the jewelry shop at #285, betwixt Society and Wentworth Sts. on the western side, and the plough over McIntosh's Seed Store next the Masonic Temple on the eastern side betwixt Wentworth and Hasell. At Clifford St. we turn to the right, proceeding through to Archdale St. (a thoroughfare known for a time and so designated on many signs and maps, as Charles St. which causes considerable confusion). On the S.E. corner we behold the ancient edifice (1817) and picturesque churchyard of St. John's Lutheran Church; which is directly adjoined on the south—in Archdale St.—by the gothic precincts of the famous Unitarian Church (1772). This edifice is very remarkable as being one of the few serious Gothic specimens erected in the 18th century. Its churchyard, together with the neighboring churchyard of St. John's, which is virtually one with it, is the supreme epitome of exotic glamour; a perfumed green tropic twilight of twisted branches, overarching live-oak and hanging vines, with ancient slabs and altar-stones peeping through a vivid, verdurous undergrowth threaded by curious winding walks. It is truly something out of a dream—such things do not belong to the waking world! Recognizing this quality of fascination in the old Archdale St. churchyard, as well as in other churchyards and garden plots to the east, the president of the Charleston Garden Club some years ago formed the notion of mapping out an idyllic crosstown walk which might include as many as possible of them with a fair degree of continuity. The Unitarian churchyard had already established a walk through to King St., opposite the library, with a fine wrought-iron gate on the latter thoroughfare; and now a similar walk with gates was provided in the garden area just across the way—extending from the library grounds in King St. to the yard of the Gibbs [Gibbes] Art Gallery in Meeting St. Still further cooperating, the Circular Congregational Church in Meeting St. opposite the Gibbs Gallery (an ugly pseudo-Romanesque Victorian church but having a delightful old-Charleston chapel, (1867) with classic facade and double entrance flights, in its grounds) opened its spacious churchyard as a continuation of the garden stroll; being seconded by St. Philip's Church, whose westerly churchyard spreads form Church St. (as before mentioned) to meet the rear of the Congregational churchyard. Thus the walk is made continuous from Archdale St. across King and Meeting to Church St. and now there is some talk of continuing it though St. Philip's easterly churchyard—behind the church, and emerging in Cumberland St., through a future gate. Such is the Gateway Path or Gateway Walk, so-called; and every visitor to Charleston ought at some time or other to thread its entire length from St. John's to St. Philip's. For our present tour, we follow it from the Unitarian churchyard out to King St. and the library; there turning to the right and following King St. southward. On the easterly side of King below Queen, at #138, is the site of the old Quaker Meeting-House, enclosed by a tall iron fence. The first meeting-house was built in 1694, but there has been no edifice on the site since the fire of 1861; the Quakers being extinct in Charleston. The churchyard, however, is owned and kept in good condition by the central organization of Friends in

Philadelphia, and two of the ancient graves may yet be seen. Having inspected the place, we advance down to Broad St., making a short side-trip down that thoroughfare to the right to see the Robert Izard House, at #110 (1750) the later Izard house (1827) at #114 (now occupied by the Catholic Bischop), the Rutledge House (1760), and the still vacant site (#118) of St. Andrew's Hall, built in 1814 and burned in the fire of 1861. It is melancholy to observe the decaying garden walls and the mossy bricks of the long-disused walks. This was, in its day, the principal auditorium of the town; a distinction now falling to Hibernian Hall in Meeting St. The St. Andrew's Society which built it, was organized by Caledonians in 1729, and is still in a flourishing state—having ceremoniously observed its 200th anniversary seven years ago. General Lafayette was entertained in this vanished building in 1825. Beyond this site may be seen the modern Catholic Cathedral of St. John the Divine, but we must now return eastward, retracing out steps to King St. (on the N.W. cor. of which is the oldest pharmacy in America) and proceeding beyond to the important Meeting St. intersection. On the left-hand side of Broad, just back of the Court-House, is a small street known as Court-House Square. The large Georgian double house visible at the end, with a peculiarly Charlestonian arrangement of steps, and twin colonial doorways with transoms having double rows of lights, is the house exploited in the novel "Lady Baltimore" by Owen Wister. Approaching this house and proceeding through the green gateway on the left, we encounter a quasi-rustic lane which leads to a hidden group of idyllically embowered houses—a sylvan oasis not a stone's throw from the busy civic center of the city. Emerging thence to the intersection of Broad and Meeting, we are indeed at the very heart of Charleston. On the N.W. corner is the Court House, built in 1788 on the site of the burned-down state-house in the days of Charleston's state capitalship. Across on the N.E. corner is the City Hall, built in 1801 as the United States Bank, and used as a city hall since 1818. On the S. E. corner is ancient St. Michael's Episcopal Church (1761), with its glorious steeple, exquisite chimes, and quaint old churchyard with wrought-iron gates by Iasti.[12] And on the S.W. corner is the modern but not unsightly Post-Office. Back of the City Hall is City Park or Washington-Square, with its walks, benches, Pitt, Timerod and Beauregard monuments, and ancient rear wall with arched embrasures. In the N.W. corner of the park, on the S.E. corner of Meeting and Chalmers Sts. stands the classic hall of records; put up in 1826 and called the Fire-proof Building because it was the first of that type erected in America. The work of Robert Mills, it proved its worth in the earthquake of 1886, when—alone of all, the structures in this region it remained uninjured. Opposite the park in Meeting St. is the homelike old Timerod Inn with its archaic portico extending over the sidewalk. On the same western side of the street opposite the end of Chalmers is the stately classic facade of Hibernian Hall (1841) the city's principal auditorium and the home of a society of gentlemen of Irish

---

[12] J. A. W. Iusti was a German-born blacksmith.

descent who alternately elect a Protestant and a Catholic as president in their annual balloting. Hence, proceeding south down Meeting St. we behold on our left, below St. Michael's Place, the splendid edifice of the South Carolina Society, built in 1804 and designed by Gabriel Manigault. This is a masterpiece in the true Charleston tradition, with double steps flanked by wrought-iron lamps. The colossal portico over the sidewalk is very justly esteemed, and is of a somewhat later date than the building proper. The society which this building houses, was formed for charitable purposes in 1736, and is still vigorously flourishing. Descending to Tradd St., we behold on the N.W. corner an ancient mansion with a two-storeyed porch (probably of much later date) overshadowing the street. This is the Governor Branford or Horry House, built in 1751–7.[13] On the S.W. corner is the old South or First Presbyterian Church and churchyard, the present sightly edifice dating from 1819. Just below this, on the same side of the street at #51, is the splendid Nathaniel Russell mansion of un-stuccoed brick. Over the doorway the initials "N.R." are woven into the wrought-iron balcony. The interior (not open to the public alas!) is very celebrated and includes a magnificent circular stairway lighted by two vast and unusual windows (externally visible on the N. side). Descending Meeting St. still farther, we must not neglect to glance into any quaint alleys we may pass. At Water St. we are again near the spot where Rhett hanged his 57 pirates. Here were anciently the sources of Vanderhorst Creek. All along the street, on both sides, are now seen residences of the greatest beauty and antiquity. No. 39, on the right-hand side, was built in 1767. No. 35 was the residence of Wm. Bull, a Charleston gentlemen who was Lt.-Gov. of the Province at the time of the Revolution. Just across the street, at #34, resided the last Royal Gov. of the Province, Lt. Wm. Campbell, who at length was so threatened by seditions mobs that he withdrew secretely, through a hidden passage, to a small boat in Vanderhorst Creek, by which he was conveyed to His Majesty's vessel Tamar, then lying in the harbour. We now turn to the right through Ladson St., though not without a glance down Meeting (to meet the upward glance we made when starting from the Battery) at the many fine mansions and gardens. Proceeding through Ladson to its end in King St., we find ourselves at the sumptuous Miles Brewton (his second home, built after he left the house in Church St. previously mentioned) or Pringle house (#27), a spacious brick mansion with walled garden, coach-house, and slave quarters, built in 1765 and displaying the best British architecture modified for Charleston needs with a two-storeyed portico. It was used as a headquarters for His Majesty's officers in 1780–81, and is open to the public for the somewhat excessive fee of one dollar. The interior, from a vaulted basement to raftered attic, is well worth inspection. All the great rooms are finely decorated and panelled, and show early phases of the Adam influence—rare in the colonies as early as 1765. There are some notably fine mantels and much good furniture is present. The gardens and outbuildings are all highly interesting—especially the coach-house

---

[13]The home was built for William Branford, a wealthy plantation owner.

fronting on the street just above the mansion, which displays very fully that curious whimsical use of Gothic architecture for ignominious purposes (doghouses, coach-houses, and etc) which prevailed in 18th century Charleston. We now proceed southward along King St., noting as we cross it, the extreme narrowness (on the left-hand side) of Lamboll St. which despite its alley-like dimensions betwixt Meeting and King, is a residential thoroughfare of the first order. As we approach the Battery, we may well pause to observe <u>#3 King St.</u> on our right; this ancient house being called by guide-books the <u>narrowest</u> residence in Charleston, and perhaps in the whole South. Arrived at the Battery, we turn to the right, or westward; pausing as we do so to reflect that on this spot in 1718 were hanged the celebrated pirate captain Stede Bonnet, and some 40 of his men, It is said that the invincible Col. Rhett compelled these malefactors to dig their own graves, so that upon being cut down their bodies fell into them, where they still lie. Another account has it that they were hanged above the water, and cut down so that the ebb of the tide might carry them away. At all events, it is certain that Col. Rhett's efforts made Charleston remarkably free from pirates. There is much of doubt, confusion and hearsay in all these tales; and this hanging on the Battery is often mixed up with that other hanging of the 57 near Vanderhorst Creek at about the same time. Several guide-books declare that it was Capt. Bonnet's hanging which took place on the creek; appearing to join the facts of the two events in one. It is not well to place too much reliance on any statement made concerning these traditional matters. We now proceed westward, or toward the Ashley River, for a single square; there turning to the right up <u>Legare St.</u> This is equal to lower Meeting St. in the taste and elegance of its dwellings, and is altogether inhabited by families of consequence. Like all places long tenanted by a vivid gentry, it is full of all legends which guide-books still relate; amongst them being that of a duel fought with pistols from opposite upper windows across the street. On every hand are exquisite specimens of wrought-iron work, old granite hitching posts (very typical of Charleston), fine polished knockers, graceful gates and doorways, pleasing house-facades, and walled gardens of unutterable charm. At the head of <u>Gibbes St.</u> we observe in a wall one the most famous pairs of <u>wrought-iron gates</u> in Charleston. At #19, on the eastern or right-hand side of the street, we come to the <u>George Edward's house</u> in its walled grounds, noticing the famous gates with their pineapple-topped posts, which were erected in 1820. Into the ironwork around the doorway are woven the script initials "G" & "E." The ironwork of the gate is pieced out with cypress-wood, but so cunningly that the difference cannot be told. Cypress was at one time a great medium of construction in Charleston, many entire houses being built of it. Such an one is now seen, on the left at #15 Legare St., this being one of the houses figuring in the duel just mentioned. On the right, the <u>knockers</u> of the Edward's house and of its neighbour at #16 are deserving of special notice. We ought also to observe the ancient iron lanterns over the entrance gates, the finest of which will be found at #18. Approaching <u>Tradd St.</u>, we see in the high brick wall on our right, at #32, the famous <u>Simonton Sword gates</u>, which are perhaps the most beautiful specimens of their kind in Charleston, or in the country. They derive their name from the central horizontal bars of their design, which are in the form of Roman short swords, on which are vertical supports in the form of Roman javelins. The scroll work supplementing these is of the most graceful description, and the whole is topped by a fine lantern. Behind the gates—which date from about 1820—are spacious and well-ordered grounds, and an old-fashioned avenue of magnolias leading to a mansion built before 1776. In the late 18th century this estate became a fashionable girls' school conducted by a French gentlewoman, Mme. Talmande, who fled hither from the San Domingo massacre. Later the place was owned by a young Englishman whose revelry and gaming made it a scene of nightly resort for Charleston's gayest young blood. We now reach the corner of Tradd St., and may if we wish digress westward toward the Ashley River to observe some of the old houses and gateways. At No. 129, on the left, is a fine recessed gate with a curving wall on either side. Next it, at #131, is another excellent specimen. Across the street is #128 is a fine old house built in 1760 and reached by curved steps climbing to a high porch. Around the corner, to the right, in Legare St. is the ancient churchyard of a vanished church—old St. Peter's. This is in the burned district of 1861, hence beyond it most of the houses are new. At #141 Tradd St., however, is a fine old recessed home with a splendid gate of cluster-and-arrow ironwork at the inner bend of the curve. Behind it is a deep garden with trees, at the end of which the mansions may be seen at a distance. Now retracing our steps toward Meeting, we re-cross Legare and note some more objects of interest. On our left Orange St. runs up to Broad and we may behold at its end the previously-mentioned younger Izard house now tenanted by the Catholic Bishop. On the N.W. corner, at #104 Tradd, is the Stuart House, built in 1772 and owned by a Royalist. At King St. we note the fine tiling of the three-storey edifice on the N.W. corner. Beyond this, on our left, we see at #72 Tradd Street, a fine old English double house with steps, built in 1734, and now inhabited by Miss Esly P. Willis, artist and historian of the Charleston stage.[14] Next door, at #70, is the Robert Pringle house, built in 1774 and since defaced by the addition of a bay-window. The next corner is Meeting Street with the Branford-Horry house on our left and the First Presbyterian Church on our right. These we beheld before upon descending Meeting Street and we are at last aware that the end of our sightseeing route has been reached.

Such, in briefest and most inadequate outline, is Old Charleston. It remains to add a partial list of some old local pronunciations of proper names constantly met with: Fraser, fra-zier; Hasell, ha-zel; Huger, yu-jēe; Legare, lĕ-gree; Manigault, man-i-go; Moultrie, mōō-tri; Vanderhorst, van-derost or van-drōst; Mispronunciation of these names marks one very definitely as a stranger in Charleston. So far as general language is concerned, the speech of Charleston does not differ greatly from that of

---

[14] Eola Willis is the author of *The Charleston Stage in the 18th Century* (Columbia, S.C.: State Company, 1925).

New England—contact with England and isolation from the rest of the south having prevented the growth of a typical "southern accent." Local idiosyncracies are very slight and subtle, involving minutiae of cadence and quantity. Among the humbler classes, largely derived from Georgia and the Carolina interior, a "Southern accent" does exist.

Well—I hope all of this will be of assistance in giving you a quick and understanding grasp of old Charleston. Hope it won't arrive too late to be of benefit . . . I wonder if I ought to send it to Boca Raton? Writing all of this up has made me quite "homesick" for the place—which never wanes in fascination no matter how often I visit it. Will you also see St. Augustine? If forced to choose betwixt the two, I'd advise <u>Charleston</u> by all means. There's no place quite like Charleston—and it's the only city except <u>Providence</u> in which I feel <u>perfectly</u> at home. It divides honours with <u>Quebec</u> as the most distinctive and fascinating city in North America (north of Mexico, at least) and of the two I tend to prefer it in the long run.

Meanwhile, let me once more express my regret that I could not see you last week—and my congratulations anent your forthcoming trip. Hope the notes on Charleston will prove of assistance. Fearing that I've been too verbose, I'm adding a skeleton itinerary in simpler form, you really need the background of the fuller text.

Well, Bon Voyage!

Yours by the Elder Sign,
Ech-Pi-El

Typed Letter. Charleston County Public Library, Charleston, S.C.: H. P. Lovecraft.

Walker Evans, *19th Century Shop-Front, Charleston, S.C.*

March 1936
Charleston, S.C.

Established in 1937 as a subagency of the U.S. Department of Agriculture, the Farm Security Administration was a New Deal agency that sought to alleviate rural poverty and assist struggling farmers. The FSA hired some of the nation's most talented photographers to document its programs and to draw public attention to the plight of the American farmer.[15] *The photographers, including Walker Evans, Marion Post Wolcott, Arthur*

---

[15]The FSA photography project built on earlier efforts of the Resettlement Agency and continued under the auspices of the Office of War Information.

Rothstein, and Dorothea Lange, shot more than 175,000 photographs, only a fraction of which were ever printed.[16]

There are thirty extant FSA photographs of Charleston. Evans visited in March 1936 and captured this image of a store front.[17]

Allen Jones Jr., Diary

6 March 1936
Charleston, S.C.

During the 1935–36 school year, Citadel sophomore Allen Jones Jr. maintained a diary detailing his experiences over the course of several months.[18] In this entry, Jones described

[16]The photographs and unpublished negatives are now available online through the Library of Congress. For two of Wolcott's photographs, see pp. 138–139, this volume.

[17]Walker Evans (1903–1975), born in St. Louis, Missouri, was a writer and documentary photographer best known for his photographs chronicling American life during the Great Depression. In 1936 Evans teamed with writer James Agee to produce the book *Let Us Now Praise Famous Men*, a deeply moving account of rural poverty in Hale County, Alabama. As an FSA-affiliated photographer, Evans had a particular interest in taking photographs of rural churches, vernacular architecture, barbershops, and cemeteries.

[18]Allen Jones Jr. (1916–2005) was born in Columbia, South Carolina, and graduated from the Citadel (1938) before earning a graduate degree in engineering from the University of Tennessee the following year. Jones served in the U.S. Army and was deployed to the Pacific Theater during World War II. He later worked as a consulting structural engineer until his retirement.

a "great argument" with his roommate, Thomas "Dick" Daniel, in which they debated the New Deal, the Civil War, and college football.[19] "We spoke heatedly at times," he wrote, "and were bitter towards each other, sarcasm and irony playing no small part."[20]

Friday, March 6—Got up feeling very, very sleepy. Only five hours sleep, I should be a bit under the weather! It all started just after "taps" last night when I happened to mention Roosevelt to Oakey: "I don't know what you think about him," I said, "but I'm agin' him."

So we started. And for three solid hours we argued! Finally at 1:30 we called it quits, both of us being tired, sleepy, and exhausted. But it was a great argument—we spoke very heatedly at times and were bitter towards each other, sarcasm and irony playing no small part. We're both stubborn—too stubborn for our own good—and it's with difficulty often that we are able to hold our tempers. We don't always hold them either!

We began by wrangling over Roosevelt's policies—Dick defended his spending of money while I attacked it. It wasn't long before the bonus came up—something else that I was against. The words "Professional Patriotism" got him! I held that the bonus should have been paid within five years after the war; that if a man couldn't "settle down" after twenty years, he doesn't deserve money from the government any more than any one else; that any decent man would be ashamed to attack the government demanding money in the midst of such a depression.[21]

Finally we began to fight the Civil War all over again. Our sarcasm and cutting remarks towards each other prompted by sectional pride became very insulting I'm ashamed of them now. Well, Dick looked at slavery from the moral stand point while I tried to defend it from a practical stand point—not that slavery is right and lawful of course, but that it would have been highly impractical to free them. In answering

---

[19] English major Thomas Richard Daniel of Augusta, Georgia, graduated from the Citadel (1938) and served in World War II.

[20] First-year student Hugh Henderson maintained a diary during the same school year. In an excerpt from his second semester on campus, he described the escalating tension between the cadets and administrators that culminated in some late-night hijinks involving glass, trash, and projectiles: "I knew something was going to happen last night and sure enough about 3 o'clock it sounded as if the whole barracks were going to fall in." Henderson reported that "somebody had thrown some trash cans off. It was sure planned well—you couldn't hear anybody running or any doors slam." Among other complaints, the cadets were upset after having been restricted to campus because of an influenza outbreak (Hugh H. Henderson, Diary, 1935–36, Citadel Archives and Museum, Charleston, S.C.).

[21] In the summer of 1932 up to twenty thousand World War I veterans marched on Washington, D.C., demanding early payment of bonuses that were due to them in 1945. Their demands were rebuffed by the U.S. Senate, and the violent routing of the Bonus Marchers from the capital was a political embarrassment for the Hoover administration.

his charge that the Southerners were "pig-headed," I said: "Suppose you owned a thousand acre plantation, had slaves working your cotton, and someone came along to take them (the slaves) away from you. What would you do?"

Our discussion of slavery led to the negro question and to the equality of races. We argued back and forth—where did the expression "yes, Ma'am" originate? Is it a barbarism?—until the subject of football came up. I got some good points in about Pitt's defeat in the Rose Bowl, about Georgia's victory jinx over Yale.[22] Meanwhile he tried to convince me that a team fights twice as hard if they have traditions—if they have won in the Rose Bowl before—behind them. Finally we decided to quit Alabama's victories in the Rose Bowl . . . .[23] "Nothing to it," I said . . . . "Sure," he answered, "just a swap . . . . . ."

And so I was pretty sleepy this morning. A couple of cups of coffee, however, made me feel better, and I went down to English class to find that I had made an A for the first month of this semester. If I don't make an A in Military, that will be the only one on my report card. And to think that last year for this month I had six A's—all A's!

During the vacant period following, I shaved then dropped over to the library to return Larry and to read a little about the life of Thomas Wolfe. Into physics—my grade really surprised me: an 83 on the quizz, a lower one on the make-up test, giving me a C for the month! To further provoke me, [Charles T.] Razor gave us a "pop test"—his first this year—on the day's assignment. All I could do was to write the numbers of the questions on the paper and hand it in! My attitude towards my studies has been anything but that becoming a former "gold-star" man! I've got to snap out of it.

There was no mail when I came by the post office. After getting my laundry, I spent the rest of the hour preparing for inspection. Boy, I thought I was really a "spoony-file" when I reached the quadrangle! I did get commended for appearance (my new shoes gave me that), but I was pulled for dusty bore! I forget that very often—my rifle may be perfect, but I leave the bore to look out for itself.

After lunch I walked up to [William J.] Dewitt's room with him and stayed a while. He has a very attractive picture of Charlotte—I think I'll write her and see what the chances are of getting one for myself. Not so good, I guess. Seeing the picture made me feel sort of funny—just as if I were seeing her personally, talking to her. I sure hope she'll send me one. Incidentally, Dewitt says she's thinking about going to Agnes Scott next year, I mean this fall.

My shoulder took some hard knocks at practice this afternoon. Coach [A. W. "Rock"] Norman had us do a little tackling: we paired off, each taking several tackles from the front and sides. [Clough Farrar "Mutt"] Gee was my partner; I was sure

---

[22] The University of Southern California defeated Pittsburgh in the 1930 and 1933 Rose Bowls. The University of Georgia defeated Yale University six straight times between 1929 and 1934.

[23] The University of Alabama won the 1926, 1931, and 1935 Rose Bowls.

glad he's light; I managed to hit him with my good shoulder and drag him down with my good arm. I hurt myself several times though—that aching pain returning making me feel sick and tired of it all. After dummy scrimmaging a while, we donned helmets—[Herman "Red"] Smith had me in there at defensive end—and roughed it up for about fifteen minutes. Again I went the route without making a tackle; I have enough trouble playing football with <u>two</u> arms much less one! Well, only two weeks more . . . .

Tonight I went down to the motion-picture room directly below us and listened to [Oliver K.] Marshall play the piano. It's one of my biggest regrets that I never learned to play while I was young. While we were there, Nat Sims came in and also played a little. He's from Charlotte and belongs to St. Peter's Church where I was confirmed.

Yes, sir, the more I think about it the more I want to learn piano. Think of what pleasure it would be, what relaxation it would give you, to sit down to the piano when you're tired and discouraged and just play. When football is over, I can practice down there I guess—I can get in some over the week ends—even perhaps during the morning and afternoon study periods. I hope I can establish and keep up an interest in it. That's been my trouble all my life—I lose interest in a new toy before very long.

The eleven o'clock confinement formation is meeting, I'm awfully sleepy, so I think I'll go on to bed. AJ

Autographed Document. Citadel Archives
and Museum, Charleston, S.C.

The State v. Benjamin J. Rivers

25 September 1936
Charleston, S.C.

Shortly before 1 A.M. on Tuesday, 14 July 1936, Charleston police detective Purse A. Wansley was shot and killed following an altercation with two African American men.[24] Wansley had been told they were on their way to commit a crime. Isaac Brown turned himself in within forty-eight hours and implicated his friend Benjamin Rivers as the gunman. Rivers was arrested following a week-long manhunt.[25] After an angry crowd of several hundred

---

[24]Purse Ashley Wansley (1892–1936) was born in Elberton, Georgia, and had been a detective for the Charleston Police Department for nearly twelve years prior to his death. The chairman of the city police commission called Wansley "the most reliable officer we had, attentive to his duties, and courteous at all times" ("Police Search for Suspects," *Charleston Evening Post*, 14 July 1936).

[25]According to the *Charleston Evening Post*, "many colored people expressed satisfaction upon the capture of Rivers. During the long search the homes of many negroes were visited

white Charlestonians gathered outside the county jail on Magazine Street, Rivers and Brown were removed to Columbia.[26]

Rivers returned to Charleston two months later for his 24–25 September trial, which was presided over by circuit court judge Marvin M. Mann and prosecuted by solicitor Robert M. Figg.[27] In his testimony, reproduced below, Rivers claimed that he fired in self-defense after having been shot by Wansley. Earlier in the trial, the court-appointed defense attorney, B. Allston Moore, established that Wansley was not in uniform and had no arrest warrant for Brown or Rivers.[28] Contrary to earlier press reports, Wansley was driving an unmarked vehicle rather than a patrol car. Witnesses for the state offered contradictory testimony, at times asserting that Rivers shot first and at other times that he had only returned Wansley's fire. After fifty-five minutes of deliberation, the all-white jury convicted Rivers of murder, and he was put to death by electrocution at the State Penitentiary on 29 April 1938.[29]

---

by the police officers and they were constantly uneasy because of these raids." The Charleston police also arrested and held for questioning dozens of African American men with the same surnames as the suspects (see "Healy Plans Second Quiz," *Charleston Evening Post*, 22 July 1936; and "Police Search for Suspects"). Benjamin J. Rivers (1891–1938) was born on Wadmalaw Island, South Carolina. After arriving in Charleston shortly before World War I, he worked a variety of maritime-related jobs.

[26]Rivers was initially questioned at police headquarters at Vanderhorst and St. Philips Streets until a crowd there prompted police to remove him to the county jail, which was thought to be more secure. As the second crowd grew in size and intensity, the county sheriff requested a detachment of U.S. Marines to secure the jail. After being informed that only the governor could make such a request, he sent the prisoners to Columbia ("Two Lodged in Columbia Jail," *Charleston Evening Post*, 21 July 1936).

[27]Marvin McAlister Mann (1877–1965) retired in December 1949, after serving twenty-five years as a circuit court judge. Before being elected to the bench, he had been the clerk of the state senate for more than twenty years. In addition to leading the prosecution, Robert McCormick Figg Jr. (1901–1991) interrogated Rivers on the night of his arrest. Figg later represented the Clarendon County School District in the historic *Briggs v. Elliot* (1952) case that would later be incorporated into the U.S. Supreme Court's historic Brown decision, overturning public school segregation. From 1959 to 1970, he served as dean of the University of South Carolina Law School.

[28]Benjamin Allston Moore (1900–1988) was a Charleston attorney specializing in maritime law. Frank Herndon Bailey (1902–1986) served as his cocounsel.

[29]Rivers spent his last moments singing hymns. "Tell mother and father I will meet them in heaven," he said on his way to the execution chamber ("Rivers Pays with His Life," *Charleston Evening Post*, 29 April 1938). Rivers had exhausted his appeals and a request for clemency was denied (for the full trial transcript, including the failed appeal and clemency request, see *State of South Carolina v. Benjamin Rivers*, 24–26 September 1936, Governor Olin D. Johnston Papers (1935–1939), South Carolina Department of Archives and History, Columbia: Pardons,

BENJAMIN RIVERS (black) was called as a witness on behalf of the Defendant, and having been duly sworn, testified as follows:

DIRECT EXAMINATION
By Mr. Moore:
Q. Now, Ben, talk out so these gentlemen can hear you clearly.
A. All right, sir.
Q. How old are you?
A. Forty-five.
Q. Where were you born?
A. Wadmalaw Island.
Q. Wadmalaw Island?
A. Yes, sir.
Q. How long did you live at Wadmalaw Island?
A. I lived there until 1915; I moved to Charleston in 1915.
Q. What does your family consist of?
A. They is farmers.
Q. You didn't understand my question. What family have you?
A. Mother, father and daughter.[30]
Q. Where do they live?
A. Wadmalaw Island.
Q. Is your father in court?
A. He should be here, sir.
Q. When you came to Charleston, Ben, where did you start to work?
A. On the Clyde Line.
Q. How long did you work there?
A. I worked around there several days on the Clyde line.
Q. What was your next job?
A. The next job, I worked for the telephone Company; Southern Bell.
Q. The Southern Bell Telephone Company?
A. Yes, sir.
Q. After that, where did you work?
A. After that, I worked for F. W. Wagener & Company.
Q. What sort of work?

Paroles, and Commutations Files, Box 6. In a separate trial several weeks after Rivers's conviction, Isaac Brown was found guilty of murder and sentenced to life in prison ("Brown Gets Life Term for Killing," *Charleston News and Courier*, 12 December 1936).

[30]Rivers referred to his mother, Darkus Rivers (1879–1945); his father, Allen Rivers (1883–1942); and his daughter, Albertha Rivers Mack (1919–2006). His parents served as character witnesses for their son and testified that he provided them with groceries. Several white co-workers also testified to Rivers's positive temperament and reliability.

A. Help around the shop.
Q. What did you do for the Southern Bell Telephone Company?
A. Put up posts; run wire.
Q. What did you do for the Clyde Line?
A. Stevedore work.
Q. Where did you work after you left the Wagener Company?
A. Went to the Cypress.
Q. What is that?
A. Government work.
Q. What did you do?
A. Buoy tender.
Q. Does the Cypress or not go out from Charleston and bring back to bring in and repair buoys?
A. Yes, sir.
Q. What sort of work did you do on the Cypress?
A. I used to be fireman. I went back as mess boy.
Q. How long did you work on the Cypress then?
A. Five or six months. I went back on the longshoreman work a couple of years, and went back to the Cypress as mess boy.
Q. How long did you work on the Cypress?
A. Around thirteen years.
Q. Were you or not working on the Cypress on the night of the 13th of July?
A. Yes, sir.
Q. You had been working on the Cypress thirettn years prior to that time?
A. Yes, sir.
Q. What time did you leave the Cypress in the afternoon on that day?
A. I leave there about five o'clock, and got home about five-thirty.
Q. Where did you join Brown?
A. He come home when I knock off.
Q. How long have you known Brown?
A. Several years; ten or fifteen years; never been in no company with him up to now.
Q. Where were you living the 13th of July?
A. Three Clifford Alley.
Q. Bottle Alley?
A. Yes, sir.
Q. Where did Brown live?
A. One and a half Bottle Alley.
Q. What divides three and one and a half?
A. Stairs go upstairs, and a partition between both.
Q. If you come out of one and a half Bottle Alley like that (indicating), on the step like that (indicating), you are right at the door of three?
A. Yes, sir.

Q. What time did you and Brown leave Bottle Alley?
A. About six o'clock.
Q. Where did you go?
A. Went down to his mother's house.
Q. Where did you go from there?
A. Came back and stopped at home.
Q. Bottle Alley?
A. Yes, sir.
Q. Then where did you go?
A. Then went around on Locan [Logan] Street. Went to Beaufain Street. We stopped there; just stopped there.
Q. Where did you go from there?
A. Cumberland Alley.
Q. Where did you go from there?
A. Come around, went through Short Street, come back to Logan and Magazine Street.
Q. Were you armed at the time?
A. No, sir, I wasn't armed.
Q. Do you know whether or not Brown had any arms on him?
A. No, sir.
Q. Were you visiting around then?
A. I stopped in there to see my first cousin, Ethel Simmons; she live at the corner.
Q. She lived at the corner of Magazine and Logan?
A. Yes, sir.
Q. What relation is she to you?
A. First cousin.
Q. You go there frequently to see her?
A. Yes, sir.
Q. Does she live on the first or second floor?
A. Second floor.
Q. You and Brown went to the second floor?
A. Yes, sir.
Q. Who did you find up there?
A. Simmons, String, Henry Middleton; all the boys up there; Ted Robinson and two girls.[31]
Q. What were they doing?
A. Playing cards.
Q. Did you and Brown play?
A. No, sir.
Q. Was there any whiskey there?

---

[31] Francis "String" Middleton and Lymus "Spark" Simmons.

A. Yes, sir, they had some whiskey there.

Q. How much did you see?

A. About a pint.

Q. How much did you drink?

A. Took one drink.

Q. Ben, in your own words, after I ask you one more question, tell me what took place in that room. Did you in that room get mixed up in any fuss or altercation with anybody in that room?

A. No, sir; Henry made joke about this fellow knocking him, slapping him in the restaurant.

Q. You all laughed about it?

A. Yes, sir.

Q. Then what occurred?

A. Then Simmons get mad and get in an argument with me; said I can't beat him; "Come on down stairs." I said, "I don't want to fight you; I never fight anybody in my life." We come on down stairs; I was going home—

Q. Who went out first?

A. Simmons. I come down behind Simmons, me and Brown; Simmons beat me to the steps.

Q. You were between Simmons and Brown?

A. Yes, sir.

Q. Did you have a knife?

A. No, sir.

Q. Then what occurred?

A. I come on down the steps. Simmons kept wanting to fight; come out on the street. I said, "I don't want to fight you." I went down on the corner; he went to the south side of Magazine Street, and String come up behind me and hit me. I looked around to see who hit me—

Q. Did you know who hit you?

A. I didn't know until I was hit.

Q. When you looked who did you see?

A. String. When I look around String run up on Magazine Street and said, "You son of a bitch, I will kill you." I started at him, and he run.

Q. At that time Simmons and String disappeared?

A. Yes, sir.

Q. Then what did you do?

A. Then Brown said, "Come on let's go home and get my gun." When I get to the door, Mary come to the door, and she see blood on my shirt.[32] She handed me another shirt, and Brown was standing in the doorway. I throwed the shirt over in the next room. Shen she catch me, I bump her and come on out. Brown got

---

[32] Rivers lived with Mary Wiggins at 3 Clifford Alley.

the gun. We come on out. He put the bullets on the dresser. You can put anything on the dresser without coming inside. He fired the gun on Magazine Street, and I took the gun—
Q. Who did?
A. Brown.
Q. Who did he fire at?
A. Nobody; just fired so.
Q. Did you see String at that time?
A. No, sir, nobody.
Q. How many times did he fire?
A. Twice.
Q. Were those shots fired in sight of the jail?
A. Yes, sir, this side of the jail, on Magazine Street.
Q. You could see the jail from where the gun was fired?
A. Yes, sir.
Q. Then you took the gun from Brown?
A. Yes, sir. Brown reloaded the gun; he took out the empty cartridges—
Q. What caliber gun was it?
A. A thirty-eight.
Q. How many chambers did it have?
A. Six.
Q. Anything like this gun (indicating)?
A. Yes, sir, like that.
Q. This has six chamgers?
A. Yes, sir.
Q. Was it a revolver?
A. Yes, sir.
Q. So Brown reloaded the gun?
A. Yes, sir.
Q. Had six chambers full?
A. Yes, sir.
Q. What did you do with the gun?
A. I took it and stuck it in my bosom, in my shirt, and started to the—
Q. Where did you put it?
A. Inside my bosom.
Q. You didn't stick it in your pants?
A. Inside here (indicating).
Q. You let the handle, all go in?
A. Yes, sir.
Q. Didn't just stick it down like that (indicating)?
A. No, sir.
Q. Were you or not looking for String?

A. We went on—
Q. Were you looking for String?
A. Looking for String.
Q. Where did you go?
A. To his sister [Annie Simmons] house.
Q. What were you going to do to him?
A. If I found him, I was going to 'put him on the peg', shoot him in the leg.
Q. You and Brown were looking for String?
A. Yes, sir.
Q. When you put somebody on the peg, what do you do?
A. Shoot him in the foot.
Q. Then where did you go?
A. We leave there, went to Magazine, Magazine into Wilson, Wilson into Beaufain, Beaufain into Pitt, to 10½ Pitt.
Q. That is where String and Spark Live?
A. Supposed to live there. I ask Annie where was String, and she said they was out; I said, "If I find him I am going to put him on the peg,"
Q. Did you tell her that?
A. Yes, sir; I said, "If I find him I am going to put him on the peg."
Q. Then where did you go?
A. Went to Montague Street, Montague into Coming, Coming to 51.
Q. Who lives there?
A. Viola Simmons.[33]
Q. What did you do there?
A. I told her concerning this boy knocking me, and tell her if I find him I was going to put him on the peg.
Q. Did you show her the pistol there?
A. Yes, sir.
Q. How long did you stay there?
A. Not very long.
Q. When you left there, where did you go?
A. Headed for Montague Street, coming on home.
Q. Had you given up finding String and Simmons?
A. Yes, sir. I said I couldn't find them and I would get them next day.
Q. When you left 51 Coming to go home, what street did you take?
A. Montague Street.
Q. You went down Montague Street?
A. Yes, sir.
Q. On which side?
A. The South side.

---

[33] Viola Simmons was the wife of Lymus Simmons.

Q. On which side were you walking?
A. I was on the inside of the pavement; Brown on the outside.
Q. Were you walking fast or slow?
A. Moderate.
Q. Do you remember talking to Brown as you walked?
A. No, sir.
Q. You were walking toward Pitt, on the South side of Montague Street?
A. Yes, sir.
Q. You were inside and Brown on the outside?
A. Yes, sir.
Q. Then what happened?
A. I saw this car coming toward me.
Q. On which side?
A. On this side (indicating).
Q. South Side?
A. Yes, sir.
Q. At that time, when you first saw this car, where were you towards Pitt Street?
A. Over the middle of the block. I didn't pay any attention to the car—
Q. Kept on walking?
A. Yes, sir, kept on walking.
Q. Were the lights on you?
A. They cut off the lights when they stopped.
Q. The lights were cut off?
A. Yes, sir.
Q. How about the motor?
A. I don't remember about the motor.
Q. Then what happened?
A. I saw a man step out and walk around to the front of the car and rush to the sidewalk.
Q. Was it dark?
A. Yes, sir.
Q. Could you see him clearly?
A. No, sir, not clearly.
Q. Could you see whether he was a fat or thin man?
A. No, sir.
Q. Could you see whether he was tall or short man?
A. No, sir.
Q. Could you see whether he was a white or a colored man?
A. No, sir.
Q. He walked out to the front of the car and rushed up on the sidewalk?
A. Yes, sir.
Q. Then what happened?

A. When he walked up, I thought he was going in the yard there; Brown stepped aside to let him go between us, and I didn't pay attention until I seen him reach at Brown, and He started to reach at me, then I throwed my hand up, and he said, "Don't you run," and I said, "No, I ain't going to run," and he said, "You run, I will shoot you," and then he shot me.
Q. Did you know who the man was?
A. No, sir, I did not.
Q. Did you see what kind of clothes he had on?
A. No, sir.
Q. You just saw it was a man?
A. Yes, sir.
Q. You thought he was going into the yard until he put his hand on Brown?
A. Yes, sir.
Q. Did he address his remarks to you?
A. He said, "Don't run, if you do I will shoot you;" about that time he shot me.
Q. What happened then?
A. I leaned over like that (indicating), and reached in and brought my gun out—
Q. Are you accustomed to carrying a gun?
A. No, sir.
Q. Ever walk around with a gun in your possession?
A. No, sir.
Q. Do they let you have a gun on the government boat?
A. No, sir.
Q. When you leaned over like that, what did you do?
A. I shot where that other shot come from; I didn't know whether I hit him or not.
Q. How many times did you shoot?
A. I just shoot fast; I don't know how many.
Q. Did you see anybody fall?
A. No, sir.
Q. Did you know you had hit anybody?
A. I didn't know whether I hit anybody or not.
Q. What did you do?
A. I went from Montague to Coming to Wentworth—
Q. Have you the gun with you?
A. No, sir.
Q. What did you do with it?
A. Throwed it away on Wentworth Street.
Q. You threw it down and ran?
A. Yes, sir.
Q. Why did you run?
A. I didn't know whether I hit him or not, and I just got scared.
Q. Then where did you go?

A. To Ashley Avenue, and from Ashley to Anderson and turned back.[34]
Q. Were you headed for the boat?
A. Yes, sir.
Q. Then where did you go?
A. Come back to Pitt Street to Duncan Street, and went to that house where I was.
Q. You stayed where?
A. Inside an empty house on Duncan Street, on the corner.
Q. With a yard closed in?
A. Yes, sir.
Q. Did you know that house was empty?
A. I had seen it empty.
Q. That is why you went in there?
A. Yes, sir.
Q. Was it still dark?
A. Yes, sir.
Q. How long did you stay there?
A. I stayed in that house the whole balance of that week.
Q. This was on Monday night, and you stayed in that house the balance of that week?
A. Yes, sir.
Q. When did you get any water?
A. I got water Monday morning; I come out to get some water; I been thirsty.
Q. Couldn't stand it any longer?
A. No, sir.
Q. Did you have any food?
A. No, sir, not in the house.
Q. Did you get hungry?
A. Yes, sir.
Q. Which was worse, the thirst or the hunger?
A. Both bad.
Q. Do you remember when you went in that house?
A. Early part of the morning when I came back up the street.
Q. Do you remember what day it was you left that house?
A. It was on the 20th.
Q. You went in there Monday night, and you stayed the rest of the week; do you know what day it was you came out? Had you seen a newspaper?
A. No, sir.
Q. Did you know anybody was looking for you?
A. No, sir.
Q. Did you know you had hit anybody?

---

[34] Anderson Lumber Company was at the west end of Broad Street.

A. No, sir.
Q. Why did you stay in there?
A. I was scared.
Q. You stayed in there the rest of the week?
A. I come out, one time and got some water, and went back and got under a house until they come.
Q. Were you inside that last house, or under it?
A. Under that last house.
Q. Did somebody look under the house?
A. I heard a little boy say, "Look, a man under the house," but I didn't move.
Q. That was what time?
A. In the afternoon.
Q. You didn't move?
A. No, sir.
Q. It was that same night you were caught?
A. Yes, sir.
Q. What were you doing when they caught you?
A. Doing nothing; laying down under the house on my side.
Q. State what happened?
A. I was laying there, and some men come and said, "This must be the house," and a man looked under the house with a flash light, and said, "Is that you Rivers?" and I said, "Yes," and they said, "Come on out," and I come on out.
Q. Did that wound in your side hurt you much?
A. Yes, sir, hurt very much.
Q. Bleed much?
A. Yes, sir.
Q. Did you do anything for that?
A. No, sir, didn't done anything at all.
Q. What food did you have from the time you went in the house until the officers got you?
A. No food, except some crackers and bread.
Q. Where did you get it?
A. Some little boys playing out there, come to the edge of the fence, and I asked them to get it for me, and I give them the money and they got it.
Q. That is all you had until they got you and took you to the police station?
A. Where did they take you?
A. Upstairs to the second floor, I think.
Q. They treated you all right?
A. Yes, sir.
Q. You have no complaints against the police?
A. No, sir.
Q. Did you see this gentlemen up there (indicating)?

A. Yes, sir.
Q. Did he ask you to make a statement?
A. I told him I wanted to make a statement.
Q. And you told him about it?
A. Yes, sir.[35]
Q. Did he ask you some questions when you got there?
A. I don't know; I been so scared and nervous, I don't remember.
Q. Did you know there was a crowd of people outside?
A. I heard them.
Q. Did you think they were going to get hold of you?
A. Yes, sir.
Q. Did they bring the paper back to you?
A. I don't remember; I been so nervous and scared.
Q. How long did you stay in the police station?
A. I reckon—
Q. Did you sign your name at the police station?
A. No, sir. I signed it at the jail.
Q. Did they show you any paper and start reading it to you at the police station?
A. I was so scared, I don't remember.
Q. When they took you to the jail, they took you what way?
A. Took me around on Vanderhorst Street.
Q. Did you hear a lot of people out there?
A. Yes, sir.
Q. They put you in jail?
A. Yes, sir; put me in the office and ring up for the Sheriff, and the Sheriff come, then called for the doctor.[36]
Q. You heard Dr. Scharlock testify?[37]
A. Yes, sir.
Q. He is the one who examined you?
A. Yes, sir.

---

[35] Rivers's trial testimony was consistent with the statement he made to the police as well as the testimony he offered during the trial of Isaac Brown in December. Brown, unlike Rivers, complained of being beaten by the police. He also alleged that the police commissioner, Henry W. Lockwood, ordered him to "say something or he would burn" ("Brown on Stand in Murder Trial," *Charleston News and Courier*, 11 December 1936).

[36] Joseph M. Poulnot served as Charleston County sheriff from 1921 to 1948.

[37] Theodore M. Scharloock, who examined Rivers shortly after his arrest and administered a tetanus shot, countered a Columbia physician's testimony suggesting that Rivers's wound was either nonexistent or perhaps self-inflicted. "I don't think the fellow had the nerve to inflict it on himself like that," said Scharloock, the city jail physician for more than thirty years. "When I gave him the antitoxin, no sooner than I touched him with the needle, he sprang out of his chair, showing that he was hypersensitive to pain."

Q. What happened after the doctor looked after you? Had you had any food then?
A. No, sir.
Q. Any water?
A. No, sir.
Q. The doctor gave you something?
A. Yes, sir.
Q. Food or something to drink?
A. He said it would act in the place of food.
Q. How much was it?
A. I think it was a glass full.
Q. That is all you had?
A. Yes, sir.
Q. Then they took you upstairs?
A. Yes, sir.
Q. Then what happened?
A. They come back and read that paper to me.
Q. When they read that paper was there a table there?
A. Yes, sir.
Q. Had the paper on the table?
A. Had it in his hand when he read it to me.
Q. Could you read?
A. I could read, but they read it.
Q. Did they ask you to read it?
A. No, sir.
Q. They read it line by line?
A. Yes, sir.
Q. Did you sign it?
A. Yes, sir
Q. Would you or would you not have done what they told you to do that night?
A. Yes, sir, because I was really scared.
Q. Ben, have you sent money to your family?
A. Yes, sir, I support my mother and father and daughter every month.
Q. You ever been arrested by the police before this?
A. No, sir.
Q. Ever been charged with anything before this?
A. No, sir.
Q. Ever been charged with anything?
A. No, sir.
Q. Did you ever have a difficulty with your wife?
A. Yes, sir, one. I told her about it, and she said it didn't happen.
Q. What did you tell her she was doing?
A. Running a two-handed game.

Q. What was that?
A. Being in company with another man.
Q. Did you or not come in and find you wife in bed with another man?
A. Yes, sir.
Q. What did you do?
A. He run out the door, and I run after him, and he got away.
Q. When you came back to your house, what did you do?
A. I cut my wife with a straight razor.
Q. What for?
A. Because I had give her warning and she paid not mind to it. I been a man always looked after my home.
Q. You did that to teach her a lesson?
A. Yes, sir.
Q. Were you arrested?
A. No, sir.
Q. Any charge made against you for that?
A. No, sir.
Q. Did you ever live with your wife after that?
A. No, sir.
Q. Was she taken to the hospital?
A. So I learned.
Q. Did you hear how long she stayed there?
A. No, sir, I don't know; about two or three weeks, I think.
Q. Do you know how many stitches were taken in her?
A. I read in the papers ninety-five stitches.[38]
Q. That is the only trouble you ever had in your life?
A. Only trouble I ever had in my life.
Q. Do you like to fight, Ben?
A. No, sir.
Q. Ben, how many times have you ever shot a pistol?
A. I never did shot a pistol; never did own one, except one, and it was broke and I never did get it fixed.
Q. You never fired a pistol?
A. No, sir.
Q. Do you know how to handle a rifle?
A. I can handle a shotgun, going rabbit hunting.
Q. But you are not experienced with a pistol?
A. No, sir.

---

[38] Martha Rivers was treated at Roper Hospital for wounds to her head, neck, right arm, and back ("Use 95 Stitches to Close Wounds," *Charleston News and Courier*, 18 December 1931).

Q. Now, Ben, you ever lived with—are you married now? Did you ever marry again after you left your wife?
A. No, sir.
Q. Have you lived with other women?
A. Yes, sir.
Q. How many?
A. One.
Q. Were you living with a woman on Bottle Alley at the time this shooting took place?
A. Yes, sir.
Q. You ever fooled with Spark's wife?
A. I got in company with her after they parted.
Q. They have been separated sometime?
A. Yes, sir.
Q. How long?
A. About a year before I got in company with her.
Q. You never had any trouble with Spark about it?
A. No, sir.
Q. He never got mad with you, did he?
A. Not to my knowing.

CROSS EXAMINATION
By the Solicitor:
Q. Rivers, you say you only lived with one woman after you left your wife; how many did you keep company with?
A. One.
Q. Viola Simmons?
A. Yes, sir.
Q. That is all?
A. Yes, sir.
Q. Why did you go to Viola Simmons's house looking for String?
A. I just went up there to talk with her and tell her concerning String knocking me.
Q. Did you think you might find Simmons and String at Simmons' wife's house?
A. No, sir.
Q. You were just paying a social call?
A. Yes, sir.
Q. Just going there showing her the gun and telling her what you were going to do with it, and went to String's house. Did you have to go from Montague to Pit to get to Bottle Alley?
A. I was going back home then, sir.
Q. Going to your house, do you have to go Coming to Wentworth, or Coming to Beaufain, then to Bottle Alley?

A. I knew there be the officer up on the corner of Logan and Beaufain, so I went the other way.
Q. You were not anxious to meet a policeman then?
A. No, sir, I just wanted to go back home.
Q. About this wife; you say they took ninety-five stitches?
A. That is what I read in the paper.
Q. You think she stayed in the hospital about two or three weeks?
A. I reckon so; I don't know.
Q. You figured that from what happened to her?
A. I know how I cut her.
Q. How many times did you slice her with that razor?
A. I don't know.
Q. Plenty of times? You ran the man off and went back and got the razor and proceeded to slice your wife up?
A. I had the razor.
Q. Do you know who took your wife to the hospital?
A. No, sir, I don't; I took the little child with me.
Q. You don't know it was Mr. Wansley who took your wife to the hospital?
A. No, sir.
Q. He never did speak to you about that?
A. No, sir; nobody ever spoke to me at all about that.
Q. Just forgot about you in the shuffle? You didn't know he was the one who took your wife to the hospital and handled that case?
A. No, sir, I don't know that.
Q. Now, you say—let's go back a little further; what kind of place is this your first-cousin, Ethel Simmons, maintains up at Logan and Magazine Street?
A. That is her residence.
Q. The boys play cards there very often?
A. No, sir, not often; sometimes.
Q. How often?
A. Just sometimes with me up there.
Q. How often you go up there and have drinks?
A. Not very often; sometime they come to my house.
Q. They had quite a crowd there, didn't they?
A. Yes, sir.
Q. They had a card game going on?
A. Yes, sir.
Q. You and Brown came in; you were not interested in the card game?
A. No, sir.
Q. Why did you go there?
A. I just stopped to see Ethel on my way home.
Q. Were you there when Limus and String came?

A. No, sir.
Q. They were there when you got there?
A. Yes, sir.
Q. You all took drinks?
A. I took one.
Q. How many did Brown take?
A. He didn't take but one.
Q. How many did Limus and String take?
A. I don't know; I meet them there.
Q. Simmons went first down the stairs?
A. Yes, sir.
Q. You next?
A. Yes, sir.
Q. Brown next?
A. Yes, sir.
Q. String next?
A. No, sir, he went out when Simmons was arguing with me about let's fight and I told him I didn't want to fight.
Q. Simmons went ahead of you?
A. Yes, sir.
Q. You followed him?
A. I went out to go home.
Q. Didn't Brown slip you a knife?
A. No, sir.
Q. Did you feel in your pocket and find a knife?
A. No, sir.
Q. You did feel in your pocket?
A. Yes, sir.
Q. You didn't find a knife?
A. No, sir.
Q. When Simmons got out, where did he go?
A. Run south on Logan Street.
Q. He was the man who invited you out to fight?
A. Yes, sir.
Q. He ran to the corner?
A. Yes, sir.
Q. What did you do?
A. I walked towards the corner; I went the south side.
Q. Simmons run into the telephone post?
A. I don't know about that. String hit me, and Simmons went west on Magazine, and String went south on Logan.
Q. String and Simmons took out?

A. Yes, sir.
Q. That is when Brown said "Let's go get my gun and hunt them up?"
A. Yes, sir.
Q. You got the gun?
A. Yes, sir.
Q. You went in your house?
A. Yes, sir.
Q. Isiah went into his place?[39]
A. Yes, sir.
Q. Isiah got the gun and loaded the gun?
A. Yes, sir.
Q. Loaded it right out of this box of bullets?
A. Yes, sir.
Q. And put it in your house after he loaded it?
A. Yes, sir.
Q. In the meantime, you were changing your shirt?
A. Yes, sir.
Q. Didn't you live with Mary?
A. Yes, sir.
Q. Mary asked you what the trouble was and you said nothing?
A. Yes, sir.
Q. When you started out, Mary said, "Where you going?"
A. Yes, sir.
Q. She said "Mind trouble," and tried to hold you, and you pushed her back and went on out?
A. Yes, sir.
Q. That is the frame of mind you were in when you went out that night?
A. After them boys?
Q. Now, you all got on Magazine Street, and Isiah Brown shot twice?
A. Yes, sir.
Q. Where did he shoot?
A. Up in the air.
Q. As a matter of fact, didn't he shoot at that lot String had run through when you chased him?
A. No, sir.
Q. What was he shooting up in the air for?
A. Just shooting up by that lot.
Q. What, lot, the one String had run in?
A. Yes, sir.
Q. Did he see anybody up there?

---

[39]Isaac Brown was known to some associates as Isiah or Isaiah.

A. No, sir.
Q. How do you know?
A. I don't think he seen anybody.
Q. He shot the gun twice?
A. Yes, sir, up in the air.
Q. Did you see where the gun was pointing?
A. Yes, sir.
Q. What did he shoot up in the air for?
A. Just so.
Q. Just making a noise?
A. Yes, sir.
Q. You boys were feeling pretty good?
A. No, sir.
Q. You took the gun then?
A. Yes, sir.
Q. You went on around to 10½ Pitt Street?
A. Yes, sir.
Q. And asked Annie Simmons where String and Simmons were?
A. I said them two boys.
Q. You told her if you found String, you were going to put him on the peg?
A. Yes, sir.
Q. What did you say about Simmons?
A. I didn't say anything about Simmons.
Q. But you asked for 'them two boys'?
A. Yes, sir.
Q. What did Brown say about reading in the newspaper?
A. I didn't hear him say anything.
Q. Didn't he say to Annie Simmons they were going t read about that in the newspaper next morning?
A. No, sir.
Q. Did you say that?
A. No, sir.
Q. You don't know what Brown said?
A. No, sir.
Q. Then you went to Montague Street?
A. Yes, sir.
Q. Through Montague Street to Coming?
A. Yes, sir.
Q. On Coming a half block to 51 Coming?
A. Yes, sir.
Q. Went in Viola Simmons'?
A. Yes, sir.

Q. Pulled the gun out and showed it to her?
A. Yes, sir.
Q. What did you tell her?
A. I told her if I saw String I would put him on the peg.
Q. Still looking for String?
A. I give him up after we leave there.
Q. Did you expect to find them there?
A. No, sir.
Q. Why did you go there if you didn't expect to find them there?
A. Just to show her the gun.
Q. You showed her the gun and said you were looking for 'them two boys', and then you gave up?
A. Yes, sir, and started home.
Q. Walked to Montague Street toward Pitt Street?
A. Yes, sir.
Q. Where were you going?
A. Going home.
Q. Right down Pitt Street?
A. Yes, sir.
Q. You were not even going to ten and a half Pitt? As a matter of fact, weren't you headed right for those boys' house, and when you got there, you were going to shoot them?
A. I wasn't looking for them; I done give them up.
Q. Then the automobile came around the corner and the lights fell on you and Brown?
A. Lights cut out.
Q. Cut out before they fell on you or after?
A. Cut out before.
Q. The lights never did hit you?
A. No, sir.
Q. It was awfully dark?
A. Yes, sir.
Q. The light never fell on you?
A. No, sir.
Q. The man got out and came up to you?
A. Yes, sir.
Q. How did he know you in the dark?
A. He had seen us coming up the street.
Q. The man came up to you?
A. Walked around the car and rushed up on the sidewalk.
Q. In spite of the dark, you could see him?
A. Yes, sir.

Q. He reached for you with one hand and Brown with the other?
A. No, sir, he didn't reach for me. He started to put his hand on me and I threw up my hand.
Q. Didn't he say, "Consider yourselves under arrest?"
A. I don't know.
Q. Didn't he say that?
A. He probably did; I don't know.
Q. Didn't he say you were under arrest?
A. Yes, sir.
Q. Said that when he walked up to you.
A. Yes, sir.
Q. You say he said—he rushed up and said, "You are under arrest, I will shoot you," and he shot you; all happened at one time?
A. Yes, sir.
Q. When he reached for Brown, did Brown get away or stand still?
A. I don't know.
Q. Don't you know you were standing up there sometime arguing about it?
A. No, sir.
Q. Tussling?
A. No, sir, he never did have hold of me.
Q. You pushed his hand to one side. What did you do when you pushed his hand to one side? That is when you shot him?
A. No, sir. I just held up my hand and then he shot me.
Q. When he walked up to you, did he have a gun in his hand?
A. I don't know, sir.
Q. How could he reach for you with one hand and Brown with the other if he had a gun in his hand; wouldn't you have seen it?
A. He didn't reach for me.
Q. You said he reached for you.
A. He reached for Brown.
Q. When he reached for Brown, did he have a gun in his hand?
A. I don't know.
Q. When he started to reach for you with the other hand, did he have a gun in that hand?
A. No, sir.
Q. Then he didn't have a gun in either hand?
A. I just saw him reach his hand at Brown.
Q. Take this pistol and show me the way you had it when you got it from Brown on Magazine Street?
A. About like that (indicating).
Q. The handle wasn't even showing?
A. No, sir.

Q. How did you have it when you took it out at Viola Simmons', and how did you put it back?
A. The same way.
Q. Didn't you have it between your shirt and pants like this (indicating)?
A. No, sir; all on the inside.
Q. In the shirt like this (indicating)?
A. Yes, sir.
Q. Buttoned up?
A. One button open.
Q. Had it all the way in your shirt like this (indicating)?
A. Yes, sir.
Q. You had to fish around to get it?
A. Yes, sir.
Q. You say you didn't see anybody fall after you shot?
A. I don't know; I was so scared.
Q. You never did see anybody fall?
A. I don't know.
Q. You didn't fall?
A. No, sir, I just bowed from the bullet.
Q. How many times did you shoot the man after he fell by the fence?
A. I don't know.
Q. Didn't you shoot at him after he had fallen by the fence?
A. Yes, sir.
Q. Then you must have seen him fall. Don't you know you shot at him twice after he fell on his knees by the fence?
A. I don't know; I was so scared.
Q. I will ask you if you shot at him at all when he fell down by the fence?
A. I don't know whether I did or not.
Q. After Brown shot twice on Magazine Street, he reloaded the gun?
A. Yes, sir.
Q. How many bullets did the gun have in it?
A. It carries six.
Q. How many times did you shoot?
A. I don't know; I just shot fast.
Q. You just shot fast.
A. I was so scared.
Q. Did you stop shooting until the gun stopped shooting? Didn't you pull the trigger as long as there was anything in it?
A. I don't know.
Q. Didn't you shoot every ball out before you stopped?
A. I don't know.
Q. Now, where was the street light?

A. Arc light on Coming Street.
Q. As a matter of fact, isn't it on Pitt Street, at the corner?
A. I don't know; I never—
Q. Isn't that the light on the corner (indicating)?
A. I don't know.
Q. Look at the picture; isn't that the shop where this thing happened?
A. It been below the shop, I think.
Q. Isn't that the corner of Pit and Montague Street?
A. It seems that is.
Q. That light shines down to that street there (indicating)?
A. I don't know; it was dark.
Q. Was the motor running on that car?
A. I don't know.
Q. The lights were cut off?
A. Yes, sir.
Q. It was awfully dark?
A. Yes, sir.
Q. So dark that you couldn't tell whether he was a white or colored man?
A. I didn't know who he was.
Q. You didn't know whether he was a white or colored man, it was so dark, with that arc light at the corner?
A. I didn't know who he was.
Q. What did you think when he said you were under arrest?
A. I didn't know whether he was an officer or not; he didn't have on a uniform or anything.
Q. He didn't have on brassbuttons, but he said you were under arrest?
A. And shot me at the same time.
Q. You were looking for these two boys with a pistol, and you were so scared when he came up to you that you just shot and shot and shot?
A. He shot first.
Q. You don't know who many times you shot after he fell by the fence?
A. I was so scared.
Q. You said they treated you all right at the police station?
A. Yes, sir.
Q. Nobody mistreated you there?
A. No, sir.
Q. You were washing your hands when I got up there?
A. I don't know whether I was or not.
Q. You told how this thing happened; now you say this morning you were scared, that there was a crowd gathered outside?
A. Yes, sir.
Q. How did you know a crowd was outside?

A. I heard the noise, automobiles coming up and stopping.
Q. Why didn't you go on the boat where you worked, instead of going back up town?
A. I was just scared; I didn't know what to do.
Q. You were not scared at the time you put that razor on your wife?
A. No, sir, not then.
Q. You were not scared when you chased String after he hit you in the head with the pipe?
A. No, sir, I wasn't scared.
Q. You were not scared when you were looking for those two boys?
A. No, sir.
Q. You were not sneaking up behind them?
A. No, sir.
Q. You were not scared when you went to Mary's, and she told you to mind trouble?
A. No, sir.
Q. The only time you were scared was when you were doing that shooting and when you were telling about it up at the police station?
A. I was scared all along.
Q. You were scared all along. You say Simmons got mad up in that room?
A. Yes, sir.
Q. And he challenged you to to come out and fight it out?
A. Yes, sir; if Simmons has stayed in there—
Q. He went down before your did; he invited you down?
A. Yes, sir.
Q. The minute he got to the street he turned and ran?
A. He run after I got outside the gate; I wasn't after him.
Q. Then String ran up behind you and 'Bop'; yet you didn't have anything to do with that argument down there, and all of these people ran away from you?
A. No, sir, Simmons didn't run from me.
Q. String Ran?
A. String didn't run; he run out in the street after he hit me with the pipe.
Q. He had the pipe, you didn't have any weapon, and you chased him down the street?
A. He dropped the pipe; Brown picked it up.
Q. Now, as you boys came down the street from Coming to Pitt, on your way back to Pitt Street, you passed a light down at Montague Court, didn't you?
A. There is a light at Coming Street.
Q. There is an arc light at Coming; isn't there one in the middle of the block?
A. I don't know.
Q. You do know there is a light on the corner of PItt and Montague?
A. I didn't notice the light. There is an arc light on Comings, but—
Q. You know that, but you don't know whether there is an arc light on the corner of Pitt and Montague?

A. No, sir.

Q. That is how dark it was, eh?

A. Dark, yes, sir.

Q. When this man grabbed Brown, what did Brown do?

A. I don't know, sir—

Q. How long did he hold Brown?

A. He threw his hand out at Brown and Brown stepped aside to let him go between us.

Q. How long after he threw his hand out at Borwn, did he throw it at you?

A. He threw his hand out like that (indicatin) at Brown, and Brown stepped aside to let him pass between us; I was on this side and Brown was on that side, headed west.

Q. He walked right up in front of you?

A. Yes, sir.

Q. Did he grab Brown with the hand nearest Brown?

A. He grabbed him so.

Q. With his left hand?

A. Yes, sir.

Q. Which hand did he grab you with?

A. I don't know.

Q. His left hand?

A. Brown turned off like that (indicating); when Brown stopped I was already stopped.

Q. You are hazy on that?

A. He must have reached for Brown with his left hand and reached for me with his left hand, because Brown stopped; I was already stopped.

Q. Which hand did he shoot you with?

A. With his right hand.

Q. Did you see the pistol?

A. I saw the flash.

Q. Did you see the pistol in his hand?

A. I could see the fire out of his hand ahen he shot.

Q. Did you see the flame and the pistol, or just the flame?

A. I saw the flame from the pistol.

Q. You didn't see the pistol in his hand?

A. No, sir.

Q. Was Brown in front or behind him when you shot?

A. Brown behind him.

Q. Did he ever change the pistol from his right to his left hand?

A. I don't know what he done.

Q. You knew he fell?

A. I didn't know he fell.

A. You know that you shot him after he fell against the fence?
A. I don't know whether I did or not.
Q. How many shots did you hear?
A. I don't know, because I was scared.
Q. How many times did you shoot?
A. I don't know, I was so scared.
Q. Did you shoot one shot right after the other?
A. Bam-bam-bam-like that.
Q. How many times did you shoot?
A. I don't know how many times I shoot.
Q. You say you all were not scuffling there for some little time?
A. No, sir, we didn't had no scuffle.
Q. You were not arguing with him there for some little time?
A. No, sir.

RE-DIRECT EXAMINATION
By Mr. Moore:
Q. Your wife that you had the cutting scrape with is alive, isn't she?
A. Yes, sir.
Q. Did you or not cut her in the face?
A. No, sir.
Q. Did you try to avoid cutting her in the face?
A. Yes, sir.
Q. Where does she live?
A. On Coming Street; I don't know what number.
Q. Ben, you knew the officers, the police, had a beat that was traveled down Coming Street, did you not?
A. Police always be on the corner of Beaufain and Logan, so I didn't went that side.
Q. You had a gun on you?
A. Yes, sir.
Q. You knew you had no business with a gun on you?
A. Yes, sir.
Q. That is why you didn't want to go that way?
A. Yes, sir.
Q. You say you told Annie Simmons, when they were not there, you were going to get them tomorrow and peg them?
A. Yes, sir.
Q. After you left ehre, had you or not abandoned the idea of hunting them? As a matter of fact, were you hunting two or one people that night?
A. String.
Q. If you had met Simmons, would you have shot him?
A. No, sir, I had no animosity against Simmons; I had it for String.

Q. Did String, or not, come up behind you and hit you?
A. Yes, sir.
Q. You didn't see String until after he hit you?
A. No, sir.
Q. That was why you wanted to shoot String?
A. Yes, sir.
Q. Now, Ben, did you know Detective Wansley?
A. No, sir, I didn't know him.
Q. Had you ever seen him in your life?
A. No, sir.
Q. So far as you know, did he ever speak to you in his life?
A. No, sir, had no cause.
Q. When you got through cutting your wife, what did she do?
A. She run out; I took my daughter and went to No. 5, Duncan Street, to my first cousin's.
Q. You left there that night?
A. Yes, sir.
Q. You don't know what happened to her that night?
A. No, sir.
Q. Did any officer ever come to you about that night?
A. No, sir.
Q. Ben, when you started shooting, how did you shoot?
A. I just bam-bam-bam.
Q. Did you ever shoot any other time than that?
A. No, sir.
Q. Those are the only ones you shot?
A. Yes, sir.
Q. You don't know how many times you shot?
A. No, sir.
Q. Regardless of how many times you shot, you shot all at one time?
A. Yes, sir.
Q. Ben, you don't know whether there is an arc light on Pitt and Montague Street, or not, dod you?
A. No, sir.
Q. You won't swear there is not one?
A. No, sir.

RE-CROSS EXAMINATION
By the Solicitor:
Q. How did your wife get to the hospital?
A. I don't know; I just leave the house.

Q. Nobody came around to investigate it?
A. I don't know; I took my daughter, and taken her over to John Henry Mack house, and sent to the ship.

> Typed Document. Governor Olin D. Johnston Papers (1935–1939), South Carolina Department of Archives and History, Columbia: Pardons, Paroles, and Commutations Files, Box 6.

1937

John L. M. Irby to William Watts Ball

26 May 1937
Columbia, S.C.

A strong critic of the New Deal, Charleston News and Courier *editor W. W. Ball argued in a 25 May editorial that South Carolina had paid a disproportionate amount of the costs for state Public Works Administration projects: "Probably they have gotten something for the money. Probably most of it has been wisely spent, much of it on roads and schoolhouses, but did they really mean to borrow $50,000,000? Do they think it was good business?"[1] That day, Mayor Maybank forwarded the editorial to Irby, the state director of the PWA. Irby replied to Maybank the following day, explaining, "it was so much worse than I had expected that I have written Dr. Ball giving him a correct statement."[2]*

In his letter to Ball, Irby disputed the editor's math and defended PWA projects as beneficial to South Carolina: "As I glance at a state map showing the wide distribution of projects constructed it is with pride that I realize I have had a small part in the enactment of this program." Irby further explained that because of the collapse of the financial system "in a good many instances without the aid furnished by this office school districts would not have been able to build and equip adequately on account of their bonded

---

[1] "50,000,000 Deeper in Debt," *Charleston News and Courier,* 25 May 1937. William Watts Ball (1868–1952) was born in Laurens County, South Carolina, and graduated from South Carolina College in 1887. During his long journalism career, Ball edited four daily newspapers in South Carolina and served as dean of the School of Journalism at the University of South Carolina (1923–27). He became editor of the *Charleston News and Courier* in 1927 and frequently used the editorial page to express his opposition to democracy and African American equality.

[2] Maybank to Irby, 25 May 1937, and Irby to Maybank, 26 May 1937, Maybank Senatorial Papers.

indebtedness." While there is no extant reply from Ball, he published this letter on the News and Courier *editorial page*.[3]

Dr. W. W. Ball
Editor of the News and Courier
Charleston, S.C.

Dear Dr. Ball:

I have before me a copy of your editorial from your issue of May 25, entitled "$50,000,000 Deeper in Debt." In response to a statement in your first paragraph in which you call for an explanation, I wish to give you an analysis of the P.W.A. expenditures in South Carolina, knowing that although you are a bitter foe of the New Deal you have no desire to take advantage of incorrect figures to gain your point and thus do an injustice to a very worthy organization.

Since the organization of the Public Works Administration in June, 1933, we have had approved, exclusive of the Santee Cooper Project, 155 projects costing $19,598,561.00. Of this amount the Government gave as a grant $6,766,541.00, the applicant furnishing the $12,832,020.00 in cash or by sale of bonds; which is a ratio of 34.5% grant and 65.5% funds furnished by applicant.

The statement on which you based your editorial charged the entire cost of Santee Cooper, $37,500,000, with the exception of $225,000,00 against funds furnished by the applicant, an obvious error.[4] This project, if constructed, will cost the applicant 55% of the cost of the project provided the total cost does not exceed $37,500,000.00, in which case the proper figures for South Carolina expenditures would be:

156 projects approved, costing $57,098,561.00, of which the Government grant would be $23,641,541.00 and funds furnished by the applicant, $33,457,020.00. This gives a ratio of 41.4% grant and 58.6% funds furnished by applicant, giving South Carolina a grant about 7% higher than the general average of the United States.

The Public Works Administration has never solicited an application but has acted on those planned and submitted by the different sub-divisions of State Government. As I glance at a state map showing the wide distribution of projects constructed it is with pride that I realize I have had a small part in the enactment of this program. Take a mental trip with me over South Carolina and view the living monuments to this organization: New Dormitories and Agricultural Building at Clemson College, new High School at Greenville, County Hospital at Laurens, Roads in Newberry

---

[3] Irby, "PWA Analyzed," *Charleston News and Courier*, 28 May 1937.

[4] After several years of legal challenges from private energy companies, work on the Santee Cooper Power and Navigation Project began in 1939. Dams and power plants constructed on the Santee and Cooper Rivers generated electricity for tens of thousands of businesses, farms, and homes.

County, new and up to date T. B. Hospital at State Park, $700,000.00 spent in needed facilities at the South Carolina State Hospital, Dormitories at the University, Tri-County Hospital at Orangeburg, improvements to schools at Charleston, in addition to Chapel, Mess Hall and Officers' Quarters at The Citadel; or on any route over the State you have evidence of new waterworks and sewer systems, schools and hospitals.

I would also like to call your attention to some other interesting facts. When this organization came into being not a bond of any sub-division of the State would sell at par at 5% under our 1933 N.I.R.A. program, in addition to the grants provided, we had to buy the bonds of all but two out of the 57 projects although some of them were General Obligation Bonds of the richest districts of this State; under our 1935 E.R.A. program partly through our help in the improvement of economic conditions about 90% of the applicants were able to dispose of their bonds at better advantage than our terms, i.e., at par, 4%. In the handling of the bonds bought by the P.W.A. we have raised the applicants' credit for we have disposed of their bonds at a profit of $10,000,000.00 to the people of the United States and, further, to date not a single complaint has come in from an applicant claiming that his project is not useful or fails to fulfil the need for which it was constructed. On the contrary, we know that in a good many instances without the aid furnished by this office school districts would not have been able to build and equip adequately on account of their bonded indebtedness.

With kindest regards,

Yours very truly,
J. L. M. Irby
State Director, P.W.A.

> Typed Letter Copy. Burnet R. Maybank Senatorial Papers, Special Collections, Addlestone Library, College of Charleston, Charleston, S.C.: Box 142.

Susan Calder Hamilton, Interview by Augustus Ladson

[May–June 1937]
Charleston, S.C.

As part of the Federal Writers Project, unemployed journalists and writers were put to work compiling a series of state guides that spotlighted historical, geographic, and cultural features of each of the forty-eight states. As an offshoot of that effort, project writers interviewed African Americans who had lived under slavery. The resulting collection of slave narratives has served as an important first-hand source of information regarding the experience of enslavement.

Writers Project folklore advisor John Lomax instructed the interviewers to employ dialect that would represent their interviewees' speech patterns as closely as possible. He also recommended that they record their stories faithfully, insisting that "these old people have a right to speak their minds."[5] Project officials and contracted interviewers nevertheless employed a variety of interviewing practices. Historians note that the context for the interviews, most of which were conducted by white interviewers, shaped their tone and content. They continue to debate the meaning and usefulness of the Slave Narratives.

In this interview, Susan Hamilton shared her memories of enslavement with Augustus Ladson, an African American interviewer.[6] She provided graphic details of the torture of enslaved women and men and the breakup of enslaved families: "All time, night an' day, you could hear men an' women screamin' to de tip of dere voices as either ma, pa, sister, or brother wus take without any warnin' an' sell."

Ex-Slave 101 Years of Age Has Never Shaken Hands Since 1863
Was On Knees Scrubbing When Freedom Gun Fired

I'm a hund'ed an' one years old now, son. De only one livin' in my crowd frum de days I wus a slave. Mr. Fuller, my master, who was president of the Firs' National Bank, owned the fambly of us except my father.[7] There were eight men an' women with five girls an' six boys workin' for him.[8] Most o' them wus hired out. De house in which we stayed is still dere with de sisterns an' slave quarters. I always go to see de old home which is on St. Phillip Street.[9]

---

[5] See John Lomax to Mabel Montgomery, 26 May 1937, Federal Writers Project, Records of the Works Progress Administration, Record Group 69, National Archives and Records Administration, College Park, Md. (abbreviated below as FWP Records).

[6] According to press reports at the time of her death, Susan Calder Hamilton (1826–1942) witnessed John C. Calhoun's 1850 funeral procession and was among the founding members of Mother Emanuel AME Church. She was predeceased by her husband, Joseph, who died in 1885. Extant records provide conflicting evidence regarding her age, though the coroner accepted 1826 as the year of her birth ("Former Slave, 115 Years Old, Dies at Home of Friend Here," *Charleston Evening Post*, 11 January 1942). Augustus Ladson was among the ten African American writers hired by the Negro Writers Project to generate research material for a proposed *Negro Guide to South Carolina*, which was never completed. Ladson focused much of his work on the lowcountry.

[7] Edward N. Fuller (1820–1896) was born in Beaufort, South Carolina, and was an officer of the Southwestern Railroad Bank and an Edisto Island plantation owner. Following the Civil War, he worked as a clerk with various Charleston-based businesses.

[8] According to federal census records, Fuller owned seventeen human beings in 1860, six of whom were listed as fugitives from the state.

[9] The Fuller house was on St. Philip, north of Morris Street, according to the 1859 city directory.

My ma had t'ree boys an' t'ree girls who did well at their work. Hope Mikell, my eldest bredder, an' James wus de shoemaker. William Fuller, son of our master, wus de bricklayer.[10] Margurite an' Catharine wus de maids an' I look' at de children.

My pa b'long to a man on Edisto Island. Frum what he said, his master was very mean. Pa real name wus Adam Collins but he took his master' name; he was de coachman. Pa did supin one day en his master whipped him. De next day which wus Monday, pa carry him 'bout four miles frum home in de woods an' give him de same 'mount of lickin' he wus given on Sunday. He tied him to a tree an' unhitched de horse so it couldn't git tie-up an' kill e self. Pa den gone to de landin' an' catch a board dat wus comin' to Charleston wood fa'am products. He was permitted by his master to go to town on errands, which helped him to go on de boat without bein' question'. W'en he got here he gone on de water-front an' ax for a job on a ship so he could git to de North. He got de job an' sail' wood de ship. Dey search de island up an' down for him wood hounddogs en w'en it wus t'ought he wus drowned, 'cause dey track him to de river, did dey give up. One of his master' friend gone to New York en went in a store w'ere pa wus employed as a clerk. he reconize' pa is easy is pa reconize' him. He gone back home an' tell pa master who know den dat pa wusn't comin' back an' before he died he sign' papers dat pa wus free. Pa ma wus dead an' he come down to bury her by de permission of his master' son who had promised no ha'am would come to him, but dey wus fixin' plans to keep him, so he went to de Work House an' ax to be sold 'cause any slave could sell e self if e could git to de Work House. But it wus on record down dere so dey couldn't sell 'im an' told him his master' people couldn't hold him a slave.

People den use to do de same t'ings dey do now. Some marry an' some live together jus' like now. One t'ing, no minister nebber say in readin' de matrimony "let no man put asounder" 'cause a couple would be married tonight an' tomorrow one would be taken away en be sold. All slaves wus married in dere master house, in de livin' room where slaves an' dere missus an' mossa was to witness de ceremony. Brides use to wear some of de finest dress an' if dey could afford it, have de best kind of furniture. Your master nor your missus objected to good t'ings.

I'll always 'member Clory, de washer. She wus very high-tempered. She wus a mulatta with beautiful hair she could sit on; Clory didn't take foolishness frum anybody. One day our missus gone in de laundry an' find fault with de clothes.[11] Clory didn't do a t'ing but pick her up bodily an' throw 'er out de door. Dey had te sen' fur a doctor 'cause she pregnant an' less than two hours de baby wus bo'n. Afta dat she begged to be sold fur she didn't want to kill missus, but our master ain't nebber want to sell his slaves. But dat didn't keep Clory frum gittin' a brutal whippin'. Dey whip' 'er until

---

[10] According to the 1870 federal census, Susan Calder Hamilton lived with her brother William Fuller in Charleston. Both were identified as mulattoes; she was listed as a twenty-three-year-old dressmaker and Fuller, twenty-five years old, as a brick mason.

[11] Hamilton likely referred to Mary Ann Mikell Fuller (1822–1899).

dere wusn't a white spot on her body. Dat wus de worst I ebber see a human bein' got such a beatin'. I t'ought she wus goin' to die, but she got well an' didn't get any better but meaner until our master decide it wus bes' to rent her out. She willingly agree' since she wusn't 'round missus. She hated an' detest' both of them an' all de fambly.

W'en any slave wus whipped all de other slaves wus made to watch. I see women hung frum de ceilin' of buildin's an' whipped with only supin tied 'round her lower part of de body, until w'en day wus taken down, dere wusn't breath in de body. I had some terribly bad experiences.

Yankees use to come t'rough de streets, especially de Big Market, huntin' those who want to go to de "free country" as dey call' it. Men an' women wus always missin' an' nobody could give 'count of dere disappearance. De men wus train' up North fur sojus.

De white race is so brazen. Dey come here an' run de Indians frum dere own lan', but dey couldn't make dem slaves 'cause dey wouldn't stan' for it. Indians use to git up in trees an' shoot dem with poison arrow. W'en dey couldn't make dem slaves den dey gone to Africa an' bring dere black brother an' sister. Dey say 'mong themselves, "We gwine mix dem up en make ourselves king. Dats d only way we'll git even with de Indians."

All time, night an' day, you could hear men an' women screamin' to de tip of dere voices as either ma, pa, sister, or brother wus take without any warnin' an' sell. Some time mother who had only one chile wus separated fur life. People wus always dyin' frum a broken heart.

One night a couple married an' de next mornin' de boss sell de wife. De gal ma got in in de street an' cursed de white woman fur all she could find. She said: "dat damn white, pale-face bastard sell my daughter who jus' married las' night," an' other t'ings. The white man treaten' her to call de police if she didn't stop, but de collud woman said: "hit me or call de police. I redder die dan to stan' dis any longer." De police took her to de work House by de white woman orders an' what became of 'er, I never hear.

W'en de war began we wus taken to Aiken, South Ca'lina w'ere we stay' until de Yankees come t'rough. We could see balls sailin' t'rough de air w'en Sherman wus comin'. Bumbs hit trees in our yard. W'en de freedom gun wus fired, I wus on my 'nees scrubbin'. Dey tell me I wus free but I didn't b'lieve it.

In de days of slavery woman wus jus' given time 'nough to deliver dere babies. Dey deliver de baby 'bout eight in de mornin' an' twelve had too be back to work.

I wus a member of Emmanuel African Methodist Episcopal Church for 67 years. Big Zion, across de street wus my church before den an' before Old Bethel w'en I lived on de other end of town.[12]

---

[12] Emanuel AME Church was reestablished in 1865; it had been destroyed after one of its cofounders, Denmark Vesey, was implicated for plotting a slave rebellion in 1822. The church was then rebuilt and shut down by the city in 1834. Old Bethel United Methodist Church was

Sence Lincoln shook hands with his assassin who at de same time shoot him, frum dat day I stop shakin' hands, even in de church, an' you know how long dat wus. I don't b'lieve in kissin' neider fur all carry dere meannesses. De Master wus betrayed by one of his bosom frien' with a kiss.

SOURCE: Interview with (Mrs.) Susan Hamilton, 17 Henrietta Street, who claims to be 101 years of age. She has never been sick for twenty years and walks as though just 40. She was hired out by her master for seven dollars a month which had to be given her master.

> Published Document. Federal Writers Project, *Slave Narratives: A Folk History of Slavery in the United States from Interviews with Former Slaves, vol. 14, South Carolina Narratives, Part 2* (Washington, D.C.: Library of Congress, 1941).

Susan Calder Hamilton, Interview by Jessie A. Butler

6 July 1937
Charleston, S.C.

White Federal Writers Project officials in South Carolina were unhappy with Susan Hamilton's interview with African American interviewer Augustus Ladson. "It is my opinion that she made up a great part of the tale out of the whole cloth, apparently being glad of the opportunity to give vent to her bitterness," wrote Chalmers S. Murray, a Charleston project official to Mabel Montgomery, the state director.[13] *They arranged for Hamilton to be interrogated by a white woman, Jessie A. Butler, to whom she offered a much more favorable view of slavery and slave owner Fuller: "You know he good when even the little chillen cry and holler when he dead."*[14]

The results of this second interview were more satisfying to Murray and Montgomery. "It flatly contradicts almost all of the statements in the article filed by the negro worker Ladson," Murray later wrote. "It is just a thought; Ladson asked the woman a number of

---

founded in the late eighteenth century by black and white members but became an African American congregation during a church schism. Big Zion Presbyterian Church was founded in the 1840s as a mission church. From 1859 to 1959, it was located near the corner of Calhoun and Meeting Streets.

[13]Murray to Montgomery, 1 July 1937, FWP Records.

[14]Jessie Allison Butler (1882–1978) worked for the Charleston Food Administration during World War I and later served as a registered mesne conveyance officer for Charleston County. In her later years she was an outspoken supporter of conservative causes and defender of racial segregation.

leading questions and literally put the words in her mouth. . . . I only wish that all interviewers were as careful as Miss Butler about these ex-slave stories."[15]

Interview with Ex-Slave

On July 6th, I interviewed Susan Hamlin, ex-slave, at 17 Henrietta street, Charleston, S.C. She was sitting just inside of the front door, on a step leading up to the porch, and upon hearing me inquire for her she assumed that I was from the Welfare office, from which she had received aid prior to its closing. I did not correct this impression, and at no time did she suspect that the object of my visit was to get the story of her experience as a slave. During our conversation she mentioned her age. "Why that's very interesting, Susan," I told her, "If you are that old you probably remember. the Civil War and slavery days." "Yes Ma'am, I been a slave myself," she said and told me the following story:

"I kin remember some things like it was yesterday, but I is 104 years old now, and age is starting to get me, I can't remember everything like I use to. I getting old, old. You know I is old when I been a grown woman when the Civil War broke out. I was hired out then, to a Mr. McDonald, who lived on Atlantic Street, and I remembers when de first shot was fired, and the shells went right over de city.[16] I got seven dollars a month for looking after children, not taking them out, you understand, just minding them. I did not get the money, Mausa got it." "Don't you think that was fair?" I asked. "If you were fed and clothed by him, shouldn't he be paid for your work?" "Course it been fair," she answered, "I belong to him and he got to get something to take care of me."

"My name before I was married was Susan Calder, but I married a man name Hamlin. I belonged to Mr. Edward Fuller, he was president of the First National Bank. He was a good man to his people till de Lord took him. Mr. Fuller got his slaves by marriage. He married Miss Mikell, a lady what lived on Edisto Island, who was a slave owner, and we lived on Edisto on a plantation. I don't remember de name cause when Mr. Fuller got to be presdent of de bank we come to Charleston to live. He sell out the plantation and say them (the slaves) that want to come to Charleston with him could come and them what wants to stay can stay on the island with his wife's people. We had our choice. Some is come and some is stay, but my ma and us children come with Mr. Fuller.

We lived on St. Philip street. The house still there, good as ever, I go 'round there to see it all de time; the cistern still there too, where we used to sit 'round and drink the cold water, and eat, and talk and laugh. Mr. Fuller have lots of servants and the

---

[15] Murray to Montgomery, 8 July 1937, FWP Records
[16] Hamilton may have worked for William McDonald, a ship's pilot.

ones he didn't need hisself he hired out. The slaves had rooms in the back, the ones with children had two rooms and them that didn't have any children had one room, not to cook in but to sleep in. They all cooked and ate downstairs in the hall that they had for the colored people. I don't know about slavery but I know all the slavery I know about, the people was good to me. Mr. Fuller was a good man and his wife's people been grand people, all good to their slaves. Seem like Mr. Fuller just git his slaves so he could be good to dem. He made all the little colored chillen love him. If you don't believe they loved him what they all cry, and scream, and holler for when dey hear he dead? 'Oh, Mausa dead my Mausa dead, what I going to do, my Mausa dead.' Dey tell dem t'aint no use to cry, dat can't bring him back, but de chillen keep on crying. We used to call him Mausa Eddie but he named Mr. Edward Fuller, and he sure was a good man.

"A man come here about a month ago, say he from de Government, and dey send him to find out 'bout slavery. I give him most a book, and what he give me? A dime. He ask me all kind of questions. He hask me dis and he ask me dat, didn't de white people do dis and did dey do dat but Mr. Fuller was a good man, he was sure good to me and all his people, dey all like him, God bless him, he in de ground now but I ain't going to let nobody lie on him. You know he good when even the little chillen cry and holler when he dead. I tell you dey couldn't just fix us up any kind of way when we going to Sunday School. We had to be dressed nice, if you pass him and you ain't dress to suit him he send you right back and say tell your ma to see dat you dress right. Dey couldn't send you out in de cold barefoot neither. I 'member one day my ma want to send me wid some milk for her sister-in-law what live 'round de corner. I fuss cause it cold and say 'how you going to send me out wid no shoe, and it cold?' Mausa hear how I talking and turn he back and laugh, den he call to my ma to gone in de house and find shoe to put on my feet and don't let him see me barefoot again in cold weather.

When de war start going good and de shell fly over Charleston he take all us up to Aiken for protection. Talk 'bout marching through Georgia, dey sure march through Aiken, soldiers was everywhere.

"My ma had six children, three boys and three girls, but I de only one left, all my white people and all de colored people gone, not a soul left but me. I ain't been sick in 25 years. I is near my church and I don't miss service any Sunday, night or morning. I kin walk wherever I please, I kin walk to de Battery if I want to. The Welfare used to help me but dey shut down now, I can't find out if dey going to open again or not. Miss (Mrs.) Buist and Miss Pringle, dey help me when I can go there but all my own dead."

"Were most of the masters kind?" I asked. "Well you know," she answered, "times den was just like dey is now, some was kind and some was mean; heaps of wickedness went on just de same as now. All my people was good people. I see some wickedness and I hear 'bout all kinds of t'ings but you don't know whether it was lie or not. Mr. Fuller been a Christian man."

"Do you think it would have been better if the Negroes had never left Africa?" was the next question I asked. "No Ma'am," (emphatically) dem heathen didn't have no religion. I tell you how I t'ink it is. The Lord made t'ree nations, the white, the red and the black, and put dem in different places on de earth where dey was to stay. Dose black ignoramuses in Africa forgot God, and didn't have no religion and God blessed and prospered the white people dat did remember Him and sent dem to teach de black people even if dey have to grab dem and bring dem into bondage till dey learned some sense. The Indians forgot God and dey had to be taught better so dey land was taken away from dem. God sure bless and prosper de white people and He put de red and de black people under dem so dey could teach dem and bring dem into sense wid God. Dey had to get dere brains right, and honor God, and learn uprightness wid God cause ain't He make you, and ain't His Son redeem you and save you wid His precious blood. You kin plan all de wickedness you want and pull hard as you choose but when the Lord mek up His mind you is to change, He can change you dat quick (snapping her fingers) and easy. You got to believe on Him if it tek bondage to bring you to your knees.

You know I is got converted. I been in Big Bethel (church) on my knees praying under one of de preachers. I see a great, big, dark pack on my back, and it had me all bent over and my shoulders drawn down, all hunch up. I look up and I see de glory, I see a big beautiful light, a great light, and in de middle is de Sabior, hanging so (extending her arms) just like He died. Den I gone to praying good, and I can feel de sheckles (shackles) loose up and moving and de pack fall off. I don't know where it went to, I see de angels in de Heaven, and hear dem say 'Your sins are forgiven." I scream and fell off so. (Swoon.) When I come to dey has laid me out straight and I know I is converted cause you can't see no such sight and go on like you is before. I know I is still a sinner but I believe in de power of God and I trust his Holy name. Den dey put me wid de seekers but I know I is already saved."

"Did they take good care of the slaves when their babies were born?" she was asked. "If you want chickens for fat (to fatten) you got to feed dem," she said with a smile, "and if you want people to work dey got to be strong, you got to feed dem and take care of dem too. If dey can't work it come out of your pocket. Lots of wickedness gone on in dem days, just as it do now, some good, some mean, black and white, it just dere nature, if dey good dey going to be kind to everybody, if dey mean dey going to be mean to everybody. Sometimes chillen was sold away from dey parents. De Mausa would come and say "Where Jennie," tell um to put clothes on dat baby, I want um. He sell de baby and de ma scream and holler, you know how dey carry on. Geneally (generally) dey sold it when de ma wasn't dere. Mr. Fuller didn't sell none of us, we stay wid our ma's till we grown. I stay wid my ma till she dead.

"You know I is mix blood, my grandfather bin a white man and my grandmother a mulatto. She been marry to a black so dat how I get fix like I is. I got both blood, so how I going to quarrel wid either side?"

SOURCE: Interview with Susan Hamlin, 17 Henrietta Street.

NOTE: Susan lives with a mulatto family of the better type.[17] The name is Hamlin not Hamilton, and her name prior to her marriage was Calder not Collins. I paid particular attention to this and had them spell the names for me.[18] I would judge Susan to be in the late nineties but she is wonderfully well preserved. She now claims to be 104 years old.

> Published Document. Federal Writers Project, *Slave Narratives: A Folk History of Slavery in the United States from Interviews with Former Slaves*, vol. 14, South Carolina Narratives, Part 2 (Washington, D.C.: Library of Congress, 1941).

Susan Calder Hamilton, Interview by Jessie A. Butler

[November 1937]
Charleston, S.C.
Some months after their July interview, Butler met Hamilton on King Street and shared this exchange.

OLD SUSAN HAMLIN—EX SLAVE
(Verbatim Conversation)
Old Susan Hamlin, one hundred and four years old, was strolling down lower King St., about a mile from where she lives, when she was met by a white "friend," and the following conversation took place:

"How are you, Susan, do you remember me?"

"Yes, Ma'am, I 'member yo face, Missus, but I can't 'member yo name. I gettin' ole. Dis eye (touching the right one) leabin' me. Ole age you know. Somet'ing got tuh gie way."

"Don't you remember I came to see you one morning, and you told me all about old times?"

"Yes, Ma'am, (with enthusiasm) come tuh see me 'gain, I tell you some mo.' I like tuh talk 'bout dem days; 'taint many people left now kin tell 'bout dat time. Eberybody dead. I goes 'round tuh de ole house, an' I t'ink 'bout all dem little chillen I is nuss, (calling them by name) dey all sleep, all sleep in de groun.' Nobody lef' but ole Susan. All my fambly, de massa, de missus, all de little chillen, all sleep. Only me

---

[17]In her final years Hamilton was cared for by the Poinsette family, which included Septima Poinsette Clark, an educator and human rights activist. Clark's mother, Victoria Poinsette, considered Hamilton to be her "adopted mother" ("Hamilton," *Charleston Evening Post*, 12 January 1943).

[18]The source of this discrepancy is unclear. Her friends and her obituary, as well as public records, most often refer to her as Susan Hamilton.

one lef', only ole Susan. Sometime I wonder how it is. I ober a hund'ed, I stahtin' (starting) tuh forgit de years."

"Tell me one thing, Susan, you have lived a long time, do you think the young people of today are better or worse than in the old days?"

"Well, Missus, some is wuss but not all. Some stray jus' like dey always done but dey'll come back. I stray 'way myself but dey'll come back jus' like I did. Gib um time dey come back. I git converted you know."

"Yes, you told me about that."

"Yes, Ma'am, I see de Sabior. He show me hoe He die. I nebber forget dat day. Dere He hang,—so—(with arms outstretched) an' He show me de great brightness, an' He show me de big sin on my back, black as dat cyar (car). Den I pray an' I pray, an' it fall off. Den I praise Him. Nebber since dat day is I forget what I see. When I see dat reconcile Sabior countenance,—oh!—I nebber forget. No, Ma'am, I nebber forget dat reconcile countenance. As I tell yuh, I stray 'way, but not after I see dat reconcile countenance. I pray and praise Him. Sometimes all by myself I get so happy, jes t'inkin' on Him. I cyant forget all dat He done fuh me."

"People tell me I ought not walk 'round by myself so. I tell um I don't care where I drop. I 'member when my ma was dyin' I beg um not to leabe me, she say: "Wha' I got yuh, wha' I want tuh stay yuh fuh? I want tuh go, I want tuh see muh Jesus.' I know what she mean now. I don't care if I drop in de street, I don't care if I drop in my room, I don't care where I drop, I ready tuh go."

"All you got tuh do is libe right, yuh got tuh libe (live) de life. What is de life?—Purity.—What is Purity?—Righteousness.—What is Righteousness?—Tuh do de right t'ing.—Libe right,—pray an' praise. Beliebe on de delibrin (delivering) Sabior. Trus' Him. He lead yuh. He show yuh de way. Dat all yuh got tuh do. Beliebe—pray—praise. Ebery night befo' I lay on my bed I git on my knees an' look up tuh Him. Soon I wake in de mornin' I gibe Him t'anks. Eben sometime in de day I git on my knees an' pray. He been good to me all dese years. He aint forget me. I aint been sick for ober twenty-five years. Good t'ing too, nobody left tuh tek care of me. Dey all gone. But I don't care now, jus' so I kin see my Jesus when I gone."

"I goin' down now tuh see my people I use to cook fuh. I too ole now tuh cook, I use tuh cook fine. Come tuh see me again, missus, come tuh see de ole monkey, I tell yuh mo' 'bout dose times. You know I kin 'member dem when I been a big girl, most grown, when de bombardment come ober de city."

SOURCE: Writer's conversation with Susan Hamlin, 17 Henrietta Street, Charleston, S.C.

Published Document. Federal Writers Project, *Slave Narratives: A Folk History of Slavery in the United States from Interviews with Former Slaves*, vol. 14, South Carolina Narratives, Part 2 (Washington, D.C.: Library of Congress, 1941).

Program, *The Recruiting Officer*, Dock Street Theatre Dedication

26 November 1937
Charleston, S.C.

Culminating three years of work funded by the Works Progress Administration, the Dock Street Theatre on Church and Queen Streets was opened and dedicated before an audience of five hundred white residents. The Recruiting Officer was a fitting choice for the opening night performance as it was the first play staged at the theater when it opened in 1736.[19] *Purportedly the first building in North America constructed exclusively for theatrical performances, the Dock Street Theatre and a hotel on the same site had long since fallen into disrepair. WPA funding provided the opportunity to return the site to its original purpose, while serving as a symbol of economic and civic renewal for Charleston.*[20]

Before the play, WPA administrator Harry Hopkins told the audience that after reviewing the building he could "scarcely believe" the fine results. "There is no city in America where this could have been done other than Charleston," Hopkins said. "The city has escaped the ruthless march of the industrial system. Here a heritage of culture and arts is honored and respected. In dedicating this theater I would dedicate it to the people of Charleston—proud, fearless, courageous, intelligent." Hopkins then presented the key to the theater to Mayor Maybank "on behalf of the United States government."[21]

THE DOCK STREET THEATRE
CHARLESTON, SOUTH CAROLINA
BY APPOINTMENT OF HON. BURNET R. MAYBANK, MAYOR
AND FOLLOWING THE DEDICATION BY MR. HARRY L. HOPKINS
THE FOOTLIGHT PLAYERS
ON FRIDAY NOVEMBER THE TWENTY-SIXTH THROUGH WEDNESDAY THE FIRST OF DECEMBER, 1937
WILL PERFORM
A COMEDY

---

[19]*The Recruiting Officer*, written by Irish playwright George Farquhar (1667–1707), draws from his experience recruiting for the British army.

[20]The project cost $350,000 and employed more than eighty people for three years.

[21]E. M. Collison, "Performances at Dock Street Theater to be Repeated," *Charleston Evening Post*, 27 November 1937. The verso of this program included additional production credits.

CALLED THE
RECRUITING OFFICER
BY GEORGE FARQUHAR
ADAPTED BY EMMETT ROBINSON[22]

CAST		ACTORS
Justice Balance		Mr. Stewart
Justice Scale	*three justices of the Peace*	Mr. Day
Justice Scruple		Mr. Atkins
Mr. Worthy	*a Gentlemen of Shropshire*	Mr. Richter
Captain Plume	*two Recruiting Officers*	Mr. Worthington
Captain Braze		Mr. Halsall
Serjeant Kite	*Serjeant to Captain Plume*	Mr. Bunker
Bullock	*a Country Clown, Brother to Rose*	Mr. Spillars
Costar Pearmain	*two Recruits*	Mr. Jarvis
Thomas Appletree		Mr. Birlant
Constable		Mr. Reynolds
Tycho		Mr. Horres
Silvia	*Daughter to Justice Balance, in love with Captain Plume*	Miss Lyon
Melinda	*a Lady of Fortune, beloved by Mr. Worthy*	Miss Rhett
Lucy	*Maid to Melinda*	Miss Hagood
Rose	*a Country Girl, Sister to Bullock*	Miss Moisson
Mrs. Appletree		Mrs. Kinloch
Maria	*Servant to Justice Balance*	Miss Gowd
Lydia	*Servant to Melinda*	Mrs. McAlister

[22]Emmett E. Robinson (1914–1988) was the managing director (1935–77) of the Footlight Players, Charleston's longest continuously producing theater company.

The PROLOGUE was written especially for the OCCASION by DUBOSE HEYWARD and will be spoken by MR. Worthington
On Friday and Saturday evenings will be added at the end of the Play[23]

SONGS
By The SOCIETY for the PRESERVATION of SPIRTUALS
Music by the CHARLESTON STRING SYMPHONY[24]

"Ladies and Gentlemen are requested to desire their Servants to take up and set down with their Horses Heads towards the *Dock* to avoid confusion; also as soon as they are seated, to order their Servants out of the *Boxes*.
-:No Person to be admitted behind the Scenes on any Account whatever"
Vivat Respublica

Printed Document. Charleston County Public Library,
Charleston, S.C.: Charleston Vertical Files.

---

[23] Heyward's brief prologue concluded: "So let your laughter ring—these walls are strong Remembering that, though the years are long, A Charleston ancestor could not be wrong" (*Yearbook, City of Charleston, South Carolina, 1937*), 194.

[24] The Society for the Preservation of Spirituals, an exclusively white organization of prominent Charlestonians, was founded in 1923 to preserve and perform traditional African American religious songs. The Charleston String Symphony had formed the previous year.

1938–1940

Photographs from the Charleston Tornadoes

[September 1938]
Charleston, S.C.

On Thursday morning, 29 September 1938, one of the worst natural disasters in the city's history struck Charleston, killing thirty-two people and wreaking havoc on hundreds of homes, businesses, churches, and historic sites. Five tornadoes touched down in the area that day, causing more than two million dollars' worth of damage. The federal response to the catastrophe was both swift and significant. The Works Progress Administration provided a half-million dollars to assist with disaster relief and rebuilding. The photographs below were taken by J. Ernest Losse and published in the city yearbook for 1938.[1]

Weather station observers working at the Customs House were among the first to view the approaching tornadoes.[2] Robert C. Aldredge, the assistant observer, spotted the first tornado as it hit the ground at 8:06 A.M. and a second one two minutes later. "Here comes another one!" Aldredge announced to a United States meteorologist on the other end of the telephone line.[3] Watching from the ninth floor of the Francis Marion Hotel, out-of-town visitors described what appeared to them as a "big black thunderhead narrowing down to a funnel shape" as it crossed the Ashley River from James Island.[4]

Over the next several days, area residents surveyed the damage to their property, while local hospital staff treated injuries and city officials busied themselves with relief efforts.

---

[1]The city published a detailed account of the tornadoes in its annual report (see A. J. Tamsberg, "The Tornadoes," *Yearbook, City of Charleston, South Carolina*, 1938), 188–201.
[2]David Robinson, "Big Black Thunderhead," *Charleston Evening Post*, 30 September 1938.
[3]"Gets Report at Firsthand," *Charleston Evening Post*, 5 October 1938.
[4]Robinson, "Big Black Thunderhead."

Photograph of 38–42 South Battery.

Car turned over at 57 Broad Street.

Looking east on Market Street.   "Fiddlers Green" on Hagood Avenue.

President Roosevelt wired Mayor Maybank on Friday indicating that he had "been distressed to learn of the great loss of life and great damage in historic Charleston."[5] Roosevelt pledged to dispatch WPA director Harry Hopkins to the city to assess the damage and provide funds for repair and reconstruction.[6]

Upon arriving in Charleston, Hopkins outlined the WPA's strategy for recovery and assured residents that the rebuilding would respect the city's historic integrity. WPA-funded work teams cleared the streets of debris and the Disaster Loan Corporation provided property owners with loan money to rebuild. Many of those residents who did not qualify for WPA support were assisted by the American Red Cross.[7]

---

[5] Senator James Byrnes and several South Carolina mayors were among dozens of public officials who wired messages of support to Charleston (see "Roosevelt Sends Wire," *Charleston Evening Post*, 30 September 1938).

[6] "WPA to Restore Public Property," *Charleston News and Courier*, 1 October 1938.

[7] "Hopkins Offers Immediate Help to Rebuild Here," *Charleston News and Courier*, 1 October 1938.

Marion Post Wolcott, *Negro Home near Charleston, South Carolina*

December 1938
[Charleston, S.C.]

Over the winter holiday in 1938–39, photographer Marion Post Wolcott documented Charleston's waterfront and area housing conditions on behalf of the Farm Security Administration. She was the first woman to be hired by the FSA as a full-time photographer.[8]

[8] Marion Post Wolcott (1910–1990) was born in Montclair, New Jersey, and raised by a mother who was a social activist. While studying dance at the University of Vienna in the early 1930s, she was encouraged to take up photography but returned to the United States in 1934, dismayed by the rise of fascism. She worked for several years as a documentary photographer before joining the FSA in 1938. She produced thousands of images during her tenure with the FSA.

Marion Post Wolcott, *The Cook on a Fishing Boat in Charleston, South Carolina, Peeling Potatoes for Christmas Dinner*

[25 December 1938]
Charleston, S.C.

Ruby and John Lomax, Field Notes

6–8 June 1939
Murrells Inlet, S.C.

Folklorists John and Ruby Lomax traveled across the South in the spring and summer of 1939 collecting stories and songs for the Library of Congress.[9] *The couple covered over sixty-five hundred miles in their 1939 Plymouth, recording singers and storytellers in Alabama, Arkansas, Florida, Louisiana, Mississippi, South Carolina, and Texas.*[10] *Towards the end of their ten-week trip, the Lomaxes spent three days in Murrells Inlet, a coastal community between Georgetown and Myrtle Beach. There they were the guests of writer and preservationist Genevieve Chandler.*[11]

This excerpt from the Lomax's field notes describes some of the challenges they faced in collecting folk material. A polio outbreak prevented them from "gathering little Negro children together... for playparty songs." Efforts to transport their heavy recording equipment to a nearby island were made impossible "as only rowboats were available." Further, some of the singers with whom Chandler had prearranged performances declined to sing for the Lomaxes. A handwritten note at the top of the page indicates that this text was drawn from a letter that Ruby Lomax wrote to family.[12] *Additional field notes from the trip included a list of songs and transcribed lyrics.*[13]

From Raiford we went up the coast highway through Brunswick, Savannah, Charles[ton] where we spent the night, though I think we should not have stopped,

---

[9] John Avery Lomax (1867–1948) was born in Goodman, Mississippi, and raised in central Texas, where he developed an interest in cowboy songs. In 1903 he began teaching English at Texas A&M, leaving in 1910 to accept a post at the University of Texas. In the early 1930s he began recording songs for the Archive of American Folksong of the Library of Congress. During the New Deal he served as folklore advisor to the Works Progress Administration's Historical Records Survey and Federal Writers' Project. Ruby Terrill Lomax (1881–1961) was born in Denton, Texas. After receiving an M.A. from Columbia University (1925), she was named associate professor of classical languages and dean of women at the University of Texas. She accompanied her husband on field recording trips to the South in 1937 and 1939.

[10] John Lomax, Report, John and Ruby Lomax 1939 Southern States Recording Trip (AFC 1939/001), American Folklife Center, Library of Congress, Washington, D.C.

[11] Genevieve Willcox Chandler (1890–1980) served as custodian at Brookgreen Gardens for twenty-five years and collected oral histories and other folk material as a Works Progress Administration worker.

[12] The note reads: "Excerpt from letter of RTL to family."

[13] Many of the audio recordings are available online through the Library of Congress.

had we known about the polio epidemic, the worst in S.C. for many years.[14] For that reason we had to forego gathering little Negro children together at Murrells Inlet, as we had planned, for playparty songs,—twenty-five dollar fine for such. Tourist camps and houses were not allowed to take in children under twelve years without some kind of statement from a doctor. But we did get some good individual singers, among them our old friend Mrs. Floyd who learned to read when she received her first love-letter.[15]

If you or any of your family travel along Route 17 between Georgetown and Myrtle Beach (through Murrells Inlet), dont fail to drive into Brookgreen Garden, which is developed by Huntington, one of nine gardens which he has given to various regions of the United States.[16] His wife is the sculptor of the Diana which re-poses in the Univ. of Texas library, a copy of which is in Brookgreen Garden, among nearly a thousand fine pieces of American sculpture. Our friend, Mrs. Chandler, is curator of the museum on the grounds. The best part of the whole garden is the natural beauty grand old live-oaks with silvery moss, restful and quiet and dignified. For the flower gardens Mr. Huntington has specialized in native South Carolina flowers. Our trip all the way from Texas was made, most of the way, through canyons of green woods, with various sorts of wild flowers, and magnolia trees; the last day through the Blue Ridge our road was lined with azaleas in higher spots, and mountain laurel and rhododendron in addition to the gayer-colored smaller flowers. Wild honey-suckle and roses were profuse too.

Further notes on Murrells Inlet:
We had not seen the Chandlers since 1937. On our way to their home three miles north of the post office, we stopped at Brookgreen Gardens, eight miles south, to see Mrs. Chandler and make arrangements for recording. She did everything possible to help us in the short hours of leisure; besides her work at the Gardens, she has a family of five children to support and look after. She had already arranged for Mrs. Minnie Floyd to come sing. She tried to arrange for a trip over to the Island, where the people live in very primitive style and sing tunes that go back to slavery and earlier times. But transportation for our machine was and the heavy batteries needed for supplying the power was a problem that we did not [go?], as only rowboats were available. Another snag: Mrs. Chandler's maid, Lillie Knox, was not well

---

[14]The Lomaxes recorded prisoners at the state prison in Raiford, Florida.
[15]Minnie Lou Ingram Floyd (1883–1955), born in Davidson County, North Carolina, sang Anglo-American ballads she had learned as a child. She lived at Burgess, near Murrells Inlet, from 1926 until her death. The Lomaxes had also recorded Floyd for the Library of Congress in 1937.
[16]In 1932 sculptor Anna Hyatt Huntington and her husband, Archer Milton Huntington, the stepson of a railroad magnate, founded Brookgreen Gardens as a wildlife preserve and sculpture garden.

and was having family troubles; she was in a "not appreciated" mood and would not sing her spirituals for us in, as she had done previously for us in her own delightful and im pressive way. And her cousin Zackie, also, refused.[17] We set up our machine in the center of lovely moss hung liveoak grove, in the home of Mrs. Chandler's father, where we could get electric current. Mrs. Floyd came and sang, as did a Negro schoolteacher Annie Holmes, who brought two or three small children with her to sing game songs.[18]

We had been introduced to Mrs. Genevieve W. Chandler through Miss [Mabel] Montgomery of the WPA Writers Project. Mrs. Chandler had sent in interesting stories and texts of songs that she had gathered in her community, which is the setting of Julia Peterkin's novels about Negroes of S.C. Mrs. Chandler herself has stories rpinted in Scribner's and Ma'amoiselle[19]

Typed Document. American Folklife Center, Library of Congress, Washington, D.C.: John and Ruby Lomax, 1939 Southern States Recording Trip (AFC 1939/001).

Box Score, Columbus Red Birds vs. Charleston Rebels

24 July 1940
Charleston, S.C.

After an absence from the city of seventeen years, professional baseball returned to Charleston on 24 July 1940. More than four thousand fans endured one-hundred-degree heat and extra innings as they watched the Charleston Rebels fall to the Columbus Red Birds 5–2 at College Park Stadium in Hampton Park.[20] The remainder of the 1940 season proved to be a tough one as well, but the return of baseball to the city underscored a growing sense of revival at the end of a decade of uncertainty and hardship.

As reports of the Spartanburg Spartans' financial struggles became public in mid-June, the directors of the South Atlantic League opened up negotiations with Charleston officials regarding the possibility of relocating the team to College Park. After reaching

---

[17]Lillie Cogsdell Knox (b. 1902) and her cousin Zackie Knox (1910–1961) had worked for Genevieve Chandler's family. They provided Chandler and the Lomaxes with much material concerning African American folklife and song.

[18]Supplemental notes indicate that the Lomaxes recorded Annie Holmes singing "You Got's to Move," which is among the earliest recorded versions of a song later popularized by the Rolling Stones and Fred McDowell.

[19]Peterkin's 1928 Pulitzer Prize–winning novel, *Scarlet Sister Mary*, was set in the lowcountry.

[20]R. M. Hitt Jr., "Tenth-inning Uprising Gives Columbus Victory over Charleston, *Charleston News and Courier*, 25 July 1940.

an agreement to use College Park for the remainder of the season, the league awarded the team to Savannah businessman Bobby LaMotte, who retained player-manager Cecil "Dusty" Rhodes and many of his Spartanburg teammates.[21] Working under a tight deadline, local contractors erected a fence, constructed makeshift dugouts, and smoothed the playing surface.[22] Local retailers launched promotions to boost ticket sales and the Charleston Evening Post sponsored a contest to name the new team, which was still unnamed until the morning of the first game. Thirteen contestants, among hundreds who had offered suggestions, received free tickets for proposing "The Charleston Rebels."[23]

Though tickets went on sale just four days before the game, the stadium was packed well before the opening pitch. A section reserved for LaMotte's Savannah associates was quickly overrun by local fans. African American spectators were restricted to the Negro section of the stadium, a privilege for which they paid thirty cents; white bleacher seats cost forty-eight cents and grandstand seats sixty-five cents. Mayor Henry W. Lockwood offered a short welcome over a spotty public address system, and he threw out the ceremonial first pitch to the chairman of the Board of Parks and Playgrounds, Alfred H. von Kolnitz, who had a brief career in Major League Baseball.[24]

---

[21] See R. M. Hitt Jr., "Hitt's Runs and Errors," *Charleston News and Courier*, 12 July 1940; and R. M. Hitt Jr., "Charleston Gets Sally League Franchise," *Charleston News and Courier*, 15 July 1940. Robert Eugene "Bobby" LaMotte (1898–1970) was born in Savannah, Georgia, and played five seasons as an infielder for the Washington Senators and the St. Louis Browns. He was the owner of the Savannah Indians (1936–39) and was recognized by the *Sporting News* as an outstanding leader in baseball for breaking the minor league baseball attendance record in 1937. Cecil Conway "Dusty" Rhodes (1909–1986) was an infielder, manager, and briefly the president of the Spartanburg Spartans. After leaving the Rebels, Rhodes coached one season at the Citadel.

[22] LaMotte agreed to pay for the improvements for which Charleston officials had earlier declined to pay. "It's not hard to understand why the city doesn't want to spend the money," said the league president Roy Williams, noting that the team would likely lose money until lights could be installed (see "Hitt's Runs and Errors," *Charleston News and Courier*, 12 July 1940, and "Capacity Crowd Expected in Park," *Charleston News and Courier*, 24 July 1940). LaMotte also sought to acquire new talent to inject some life into the struggling lineup, predicting "we'll be in there fighting next year" (see "Charleston Gets Sally League Franchise," *Charleston News and Courier*, 15 July 1940).

[23] Nolly J. Sams, "Rebels is New Designation of Charleston Sally Leaguers," *Charleston Evening Post*, 24 July 1940. King Street retailer Taylor's Men's Wear, for instance, promised a suit to the first Rebel to hit a homerun (advertisement, Taylor's Men's Wear, *Charleston News and Courier*, 24 July 1940).

[24] R. M. Hitt Jr., "Tenth-inning Uprising Gives Columbus Victory over Charleston," *Charleston News and Courier*, 25 July 1940.

The Rebels squandered a gem by pitcher Mack Stewart, who scattered nine hits before being touched up for three unearned runs in the tenth inning. Other Rebels highlights included a long homerun by Doc Richmond and the first-base defense of Lyle Thompson. The Rebels dropped three of four to the Red Birds in that first home series and finished the season last in the "Sally League" with a record 106 losses. They rebounded by 1942, winning the league championship that year and again in 1948 but were forced to close down in 1953 after fans lost interest and stopped attending games.[25]

Exciting Game

COLUMBUS	a	b	r	h	o	a
Fresh,	lf	4	1	1	2	0
Stanton,	2b	5	1	1	0	2
Knoblauch,	cf	5	1	1	0	0
Triplett,	rf	5	0	1	1	0
Sanders,	1b	5	0	0	19	1
Richards,	ss	4	0	0	2	4
Beale,	c	5	0	1	5	1
Serafine,	3b	4	2	2	0	2
Martin,	p	3	0	2	1	8
Totals		40	5	9	30	18

CHARLESTON	a	b	r	h	o	a
Gardella,	lf	5	0	0	6	0
Hall,	ss	5	0	0	0	3
Richmond,	rf	4	1	1	3	0
McBryde,	cf	3	1	2	3	0
Hargrove,	3b	4	0	1	1	2
Thompson,	1b	4	0	1	12	0

[25] Professional baseball returned briefly to College Park when the Chicago White Sox made Charleston their Class A affiliate from 1959 to 1962. The Charleston team has also been affiliated with the Pittsburgh Pirates, Kansas City Royals, San Diego Padres, and Tampa Bay Devil Rays. The club moved to Joseph P. Riley Jr. Park in 1997 and has been affiliated with the New York Yankees since 2004. Among the former Rebels who enjoyed major league success were Boston Braves second baseman Roy Hartsfield and Frank Thomas, who was a three-time all-star for the Pittsburgh Pirates and was fourth in voting for the National League "Most Valuable Player" in 1958.

Table continued

CHARLESTON	a	b	r	h	o	a
Willoughby,	c	4	0	2	4	1
Rhodes,	2b	4	0	1	1	6
Stewart,	p	3	0	0	0	1
Moon,	p	1	0	1	0	0
Totals		36	2	9	30	13

Columbus   001 010 000 3–5
Charleston 000 200 000 0–2

Errors, Willoughby 2, Hall. Runs batted in, Willoughby, Richmond, Fresh, Martin, Stanton, Knoblauch, Triplett. Two-base hits, Fresh, Stanton, Moon. Three-base hit, Serafine. Home run, Richmond. Stolen base, Richards. Sacrifices, Martin, Stewart. Double play, Martin to Richards to Sanders. Left on bases, Columbus 8, Charleston 6. Bases on balls, off Stewart 2, off Martin 1. Strikeouts, Martin 5, Stewart 3. Hits off Stewart, 9 in 9 innings; off Moon 0 in 1 inning. Winning pitcher, Martin. Losing pitcher, Stewart. Umpires Hammond and Throgmorton. Time 2:12.

Published Document.
Charleston Evening Post, 25 July 1940.

1941

Leon Banov to Burnet R. Maybank

15 November 1941
Charleston, S.C.

As the United States moved closer to war, thousands of laborers and their families flocked to the area to work in the rapidly expanding Charleston Navy Yard. The influx of war workers led to housing shortages, overcrowded schools, transportation woes, and new public health threats. The spread of typhoid and venereal diseases were particular concerns during the fall of 1941. To combat the spread of these and other communicable diseases, the Charleston County health officer, Leon Banov, enlisted the help of Burnet Maybank, who had recently won a special election to fill the U.S. Senate seat of his friend James Byrnes.¹ That vacancy was created by Roosevelt's appointment of Byrnes to the U.S. Supreme Court.

In this letter to Maybank, Banov outlined Charleston's most pressing public health needs. He asked the senator to relay this information to Surgeon General Thomas Parran and Maybank did so in a 21 November letter.² Parran replied to Maybank on 1 December,

---

¹Leon Banov (1888–1971) was born in Poland and immigrated to Charleston as a child. He received degrees in pharmacy (1906) and medicine (1917) from the Medical College of South Carolina. For nearly fifty years Banov served the City and County of Charleston in a variety of public health roles until his retirement in 1961. His advocacy led to the passage of a 1919 ordinance requiring that all milk sold at market be pasteurized, and he was named the first county health officer in 1920.

²Maybank forwarded Banov's letter, explaining to Parran that it concerned "public health problems" in Charleston "which have been created by the sudden influx of population there incident to the Navy Yard activities and other defense work" (Maybank to Parran, 21 November 1941, Maybank Senatorial Papers). Thomas Parran Jr. (1892–1968) served as surgeon general of the United States from 1936 until 1948.

indicating that he had been in touch with Banov and had encouraged him to apply for funding for new public health facilities. Parran also recommended that Banov contact the state health officer to arrange for additional personnel. In a 10 December letter Banov reported to Maybank that he believed "that we are going to get some aid in our emergency" and that he had contacted the state health officer.[3]

Honorable Burnett R. Maybank
United States Senator
Washington, D.C.

Dear Senator Maybank:

I would like to enlist your interest and aid in the solving of some of our local public health problems created by the sudden increase of population incident to our National Defense.

Charleston, as you know, has a number of health hazards peculiar to an old seaport city; and for a great many years we have been attempting to cope with them under numerous handicaps—inadequate appropriations; a comparatively small staff of actual health workers with a number of superannuated persons who were middle aged or elderly even when Dr. Green was our Health Officer,—improvised quarters that are becoming more inadequate every day, any many other handicaps too numerous to mention.[4]

Now, that our population has suddenly expanded by thousands upon thousands of newcomers—some of them forced by a lack of housing to live most primitively —I am very much afraid that our health situation is going to get entirely our of bounds.

We have already experienced one typhoid outbreak in the newly crowded area in the vicinity of the Navy Yard; and scattered cases of typhoid fever have been reported throughout the summer. Just yesterday, another navy yard worker died of this disease.[5]

Typhus fever has, as you know, been endemic in Charleston for a number of years. With our present crowded condition, we may look forward to a marked increase of this disease.

---

[3] See Parran to Maybank, 1 December 1941, and Banov to Maybank, 10 December 1941, both documents in Maybank Senatorial Papers.

[4] John Mercier Green (1869–1931) served as city health officer for twenty-five years before being appointed city epidemiologist in 1926.

[5] Leroy Hendrix, a forty-nine-year-old pipefitter died of typhoid fever on 14 November 1941 (see "Leroy Hendrix," *Charleston News and Courier*, 15 November 1941; and Leroy Hendrix, State of South Carolina Standard Certificate of Death, 15 November 1941).

Our syphilis and gonorrhea rates have always been high. With this as a nucleus, a marked increase would be expected with soldiers and sailors in our midst and an influx of young male workers in our Navy Yard.

Our Federal Government has given us some aid in combating the venereal diseases; but this aid is inadequate to our needs.

We may sum up our needs as follows:-

(1) <u>More Adequate Quarters.</u> We need a properly constructed and adequately equipped Health Center in the City of Charleston, with a small branch health center at North Charleston and one small branch health center at Mt. Pleasant.
(2) Suitable detention facilities to house about fifteen infected prostitutes should be provided—preferably in conjunction with one of our local hospitals.
(3) A full time sanitary engineer and at least six (and preferably eight) additional sanitary inspectors for food supervision and sanitation.
(4) A full time epidemiologist.
(5) One additional full time clinician for Venereal Disease Control work.
(6) At least six additional public health nurses—two to be detailed for venereal disease control and four for our general public health program.
(7) One competent trained epidemiologist nurse and one medical social worker for the follow-up of venereal disease cases.
(8) At least three (and preferably four) additional clerks, one (or two) of whom to be detailed for venereal disease control.

Our State Board of Health is cognizant of and sympathetic to our needs, but while they helped us most generously for our peacetime program, they seem unable to assist us very much with the emergency situation which has arisen as the result of National Defense.

The State Board of Health sent us a sanitary engineer who stayed here about a month and left to enter the navy. An epidemiologist nurse for venereal disease was also detailed here and did splendid work for about eight months, until she resigned to take a more remunerative position. Nearly two months have elapsed, and her successor has not been assigned to Charleston, although we have an acute prostitution and venereal disease problem.[6]

I am writing you of our local situation, because I understand that the Community Facilities Bill (Public Law 137–77th Congress) was designed to meet just such problems.[7]

---

[6]Treatment for venereal diseases improved after penicillin became widely available in the mid-1940s.

[7]The Defense Housing and Community Facilities and Services Act, also known as the Lanham Act of 1940, provided for the construction of housing, schools, and public health and childcare facilities in areas affected by the rapid expansion of the defense industry.

I would therefore appreciate very much if you could advise me, as to how I may go about securing Federal aid to meet our present emergency.

If you think that it would help, I would be willing to run up to Washington and interview the proper officials with regard to our needs.

Any aid that you can give us in this matter will be greatly appreciated.

Yours sincerely,
[Signed]
Health Officer.
Leon Banov, M.D.
LB/ep.

Typed Letter Signed.
Burnet R. Maybank Senatorial Papers,
Special Collections, Addlestone Library,
College of Charleston, Charleston, S.C.

Elizabeth Maybank to Joseph Maybank

14 December 1941
[Washington, D.C.]
One week after the Japanese attack on the U.S. Naval Base at Pearl Harbor, Hawaii, Elizabeth Maybank, the wife of South Carolina's junior senator, wrote to her father-in-law to report on "the week of excitement and readjustment" in the capital.[8] *Joseph Maybank likely received this letter at his summer home in Flat Rock, North Carolina. He was in declining health and died two weeks later.*

Dearest Papa,

We have been thinking of you and realize that now more than ever you are keeping tuned in in your radio.

This has been a week of excitement and readjustment for everyone.

Now it seems almost as if we are actually "settling down" to war.

---

[8]Elizabeth deRosset Myers Maybank (1901–1947) was born in Charleston, South Carolina, where she was active in historic preservation efforts as well as the Charleston Poetry Society. Joseph Maybank (1868–1942) was born in Beaufort County and attended Charleston High School. He attended the Medical College of South Carolina before graduating from the Medical University of Maryland. In addition to operating his own private practice, Maybank was a clinical professor of medicine at the medical college and a physician for the Charleston County Dispensary.

The night that the dreadful news of Pearl Harbor broke we had dinner at Evelyn Walsh McLean's (She of the Hope Diamond).[9]

She had a handsome party with people from political, diplomatic, and newspaper circles. The various discussions were interesting.

We were late to the dinner because we had to pass the Japanese Embassy. The avenue was massed with traffic and there were groups of angry people milling about or standing in groups. The glow of the bonfires was still evident where they were burning official records and correspondence.[10]

The next day I went down to the Capitol to hear the President make his address. It was very impressive to see the house, the Senate, the Cabinet, the members of the Supreme Court and the President all gather together at the same time. The galleries were packed by special ticket permission.[11]

The war has changed our plans. We had looked forward to a long Christmas holiday—now Burnet will be lucky to get a few days. Never the less I am going with Roberta on Thursday and will stay for awhile. I am anxious to see Libby and young Burnet again. I hope to see you too. Roberta would like to spend a few days in F.R. with Betty so we may come up.[12]

Love—Elizabeth
P.S. We are dining Wednesday night with Vice President and Mrs. Wallace.[13]

Autographed Letter Signed.
Donald Frost Parker, in private hands.

---

[9] Evelyn Walsh McLean (1886–1947) was an American heiress and the last private owner of the infamous Hope Diamond, which according to its mythology brought misfortune to its owners. McLean and her husband, Edward Beale McLean, were socialites who often entertained notables at "Friendship," their Washington estate.

[10] Shortly after news of the Pearl Harbor attack became public, a large crowd watched from the street as Japanese officials burned fifteen containers of records in the embassy yard ("Burning of Records Watched by 1,000," *New York Times*, 8 December 1941).

[11] After declaring that 7 December would be "a date which will live in infamy," President Roosevelt urged Congress to declare war on Japan. Both houses did so within the hour (Frank L. Kluckhohn, "Unity in Congress," *New York Times*, 9 December 1941).

[12] Maybank referred to her children, Burnet Jr., Roberta Macon, and Elizabeth "Libby" de-Rosset Maybank. Betty Andrews Lee was a childhood friend of Roberta Maybank.

[13] Henry Wallace (1888–1965) was vice president (1941–45) after serving as Roosevelt's secretary of agriculture. He married Ilo Brown Wallace in 1914.

Memories of the Great Depression, 1996–2012

Gordan B. Stine, Interview by Dale Rosengarten

19 February 1996
Charleston, S.C.

Abe Stine was entrepreneurial, but "happened not to be one of the lucky ones," according to his son's recollection.[1] He lost several jobs and moved his family often "if he could make ten dollar more a week."

He was a forerunner of what today, is public relations, because he was very talented in making signs. Signs weren't just printed in those days. They either were handmade or you just didn't have one. And Dad did that real well. When you had an ad in the newspaper, he did the layouts on that. He also was, in those days, he trimmed the windows, you know, dressed the windows. He was very creative. Like I say, he was ahead of his time.

He went into many businesses here in Charleston during the Depression years, always undercapitalized. Had the right enthusiasm, but in those days it was tough. And he happened not to be one of the lucky ones, that's all that survived. So he always ended up working for somebody. His last real job, he was with Kerrison's Department Store.[2] Advertising and display—what they called it then. I was telling somebody today; I was laughing about it. He was what they call a floorwalker. There was four stories there. He had two stories and another man had two floors.

---

[1] Gordan Bernard Stine (1924–2012) was born in Charleston, South Carolina, and served in the U.S. Marine Corps for three years and was a naval reservist until 1984. Stine graduated from the College of Charleston (1944) and Emory University Medical School (1950). He worked as a dentist in Charleston and was active in civic affairs.

[2] Charles and Edwin L. Kerrison opened the Kerrison Dry Goods Store in 1830. The store grew rapidly just before and during World War II.

Dad would always move in those days, the Depression days, if he could make ten dollar more a week, he'd move, which I admired him for because he was always trying to better himself. Like in Asbury Park. We lived there for about a year, and he did the same kind of work, you know, window, and managed a store. Then we moved to New York again and he had another for another little bit, which he thought was better. Then he worked for a family called Siegel in Trenton, New Jersey. As a matter of fact, we rented an apartment above their store. The store had three or four apartments above the department store, and so we lived right above it. I went to Trenton Central High and so did my sister.

All economic, always trying to look for something better. What do you call it? Chasing that rainbow. Then we came back in '39 and he went to work with Kerrison's, and he worked with them most of the time. When he became sick—we really didn't realize he was sick, but he was slipping a little bit, and it was hard to tell. Then he worked a little bit with Henry Berlin's dad, trimming windows and selling.[3] I went to dental school in '46 and that was about when he finally just started to—he was working sporadically. When I graduated dental school, I guess, basically, he wasn't working anymore—in '50. Daddy died in 1966.

I had taken pre-med at the College of Charleston, and one of the businesses my dad had started during those Depression years was he had the first Cut-Rate drug store in Charleston. He loved pharmacy but it wasn't a pharmacy. I can still remember the odor, you know, the aroma of—he was not a druggist, so we didn't have a pharmacy, but just all the sundries, the soaps and the medicines.

Typed Document. Jewish Heritage Collection,
Special Collections, Addlestone Library,
College of Charleston, Charleston, S.C.

Abe Dumas, Interview by Michael Grossman

14 December 1996
Charleston, S.C.

In the 1930s, Abe Dumas and his brother carved out a niche by selling uniforms and sportswear from their 294 King Street store, M. Dumas and Sons.[4]

---

[3]Eastern European immigrant Henry Berlin founded Berlin's for Men in 1883 at the corner of King and Broad Streets.

[4]Abe Dumas (1913–1998) was born on Sullivan's Island. In the summer of 1934, Dumas served as a driver for composer George Gershwin, who was living at Folly Beach while composing the music for *Porgy and Bess*.

My brother and I, when we got to be the ages of six and eight, we loved to go down there because they had bicycles and they had shotguns. It was a very interesting business. By the time we got into high school and college, we decided that we didn't particularly like being in the pawn shop business because it had a certain aroma that you were dealing business with very poor people and then questionable people; people with all kinds of self-imposed needs for money by ruthlessly or recklessly spending it and whatnot and having to sell everything but their soul to exist. Anyway, that part of the business was finally—we got rid of—and we became one of probably the most successful enterprises of its kind on King Street and it still is.

Roosevelt came into his presidency in 1932. Charleston was in a huge depression. We were doing a thriving business then because we were one of the few stores in the city of Charleston that put in a full line of outdoor clothing—hunting wear—and we hit a very sensitive cord. Everybody in Charleston aspired to be a duck hunter and a plantation owner. Anyway, when Roosevelt opened the Civilian Conservation Corps, which was the 3C camps, they put eligible people to work—blacks as well.[5] That was the beginning, in my opinion, of a type of recognized assimilation of the blacks and whites, even though the blacks were separated even under the auspices of Roosevelt. But we started—we developed the uniform business. And that was in 1934 and 1935. And then from 1935 on—even though this country didn't go to war—the whole world was preparing for war and the defense industry started picking up and we had a uniform business—one of the early uniform retailers in this part of the country. We sold Army, Navy and Marine Corps. And that started in 1935 until 1955. But in that twenty-year period, that was a tremendous business. It wasn't limited just to Charleston, we had people from all over the country. We'd send—you know, have a mail order business.

Then we got into industrial uniforms, which went on until, oh, I guess, 1985. We always had a line of workwear that was indigenous to the needs of people who worked in this community. So that meant we had the black people and the stevedores and the white people who had outside jobs—that weren't professionals. And we had a modest amount of the beginning of what we call sportswear. And we still always had back-to-school things. And that was a nice little business. And the store kept growing. We were the L. L. Bean of Charleston. We were the Banana Republic of Charleston.

Typed Document. Jewish Heritage Collection,
Special Collections, Addlestone Library,
College of Charleston, Charleston, S.C.

---

[5]The Civilian Conservation Corps was a public relief program aimed at putting young men to work. CCC workers lived in camps, of which several were located in the Charleston area.

Shera Lee Ellison Berlin, Interview by Dale Rosengarten and Michael Grossman

16 April 1997
Charleston, S.C.

Shera Berlin's parents operated a thriving uptown Charleston clothing store during the Depression. She recalled that their success put the family "in the position to help others."[6]

Well, my mother was quite a stylish lady and very tall, slim, good-looking woman. People liked the way she looked, and so they used to buy. They sold very inexpensive clothes, but it was during the Depression. People didn't have any money. My mother could put on a $5.95 Bamberg sheer dress and look great in it. They wanted to look like she did, so they would come there. But that was the price of clothes: $5.95, $6.95. A formal dress was $10.95, $12.95. They were very successful in that business. But my father had been in business since he was about nineteen years old. He was in Ellison's Dress Shop, 581 King Street. Before Ellison's Dress Shop, he had Ellison's Dry Goods, which he owned when he got married, and it was directly across the street. It must have been 582 or 584.

I remember my mother telling me that my father did not believe in stocks—never had any stock—because during the Depression his friends went broke and he didn't. He may have had three or four hundred dollars to his name, but he had three or four hundred dollars and he was in a position to help other people. Only one bank that I knew of that any money was in that we lost—somebody had given me money at birth—and there was money in a little People's Bank or something uptown that went broke. But Daddy had done business with C&S, I think, and that bank was sound.

Other than business being bad, he didn't lose anything during the Depression. We had a car. We owned our own house and we had plenty to eat. Nobody threw money away though. You saved strength, let me put it that way. I remember I had dress shoes and school shoes, but money was never wasted. I knew that I had friends—children in the orphan house—who had parents, but the reason they were

---

[6]Shera Lee Ellison Berlin was born in 1929 and raised in Charleston. She graduated from the University of South Carolina (1950) and taught elementary school.

in the orphan home was because their parents couldn't feed them. There was that Jewish orphan society, but I didn't know of any. No, there were none when I was coming up.[7] In fact, now that I think of it, I think Jewish kids in Charleston who were orphaned got sent to Atlanta to the orphan house.

I went to school with people who didn't have skates and used to take food from the table to give them. I do remember people coming to the door—knock on the back door—to ask for something to eat, and you never turned them away. You just didn't. Now today if somebody came to your house, knocked on your door and said they were hungry, you'd be scared, you wouldn't open your door. I don't remember doing without anything.

I had really very few Jewish friends growing up. I had Jewish friends in Sunday school. I can tell you who they were. Joyce Prystowsky, Harriet Feinberg, Jean Ann Mendelson, and Rae Baker were the girls in my Sunday school class who I was friendly with. Used to go to the movies with them on Saturday. Two of them didn't handle money or ride. Harriet and Jean Ann used to walk from Race Street down to St. Philip Street to pick up Joyce. I would walk up—usually to Calhoun Street—and meet them there, and then walk around to the Gloria Theater, or the Garden, or one of those, and go to the movies on Saturday. Somebody else bought their ticket for them.

My father was a big Democrat. Oh my goodness. He was treasurer of the Democratic Party for Charleston County for about forty years. No election was to be held on any Jewish religious holiday. That's why I am such a staunch Democrat today—through and through—because Republican primaries are held on Shabbos. I wouldn't vote Republican.

I can remember wearing a blue and white polka dot sun suit with a bonnet and riding in my father's car in that NRA parade down on King Street.[8] Now, I had to be pretty young to be wearing a blue and white polka dot sun suit with a bonnet.

Typed Document. Jewish Heritage Collection,
Special Collections, Addlestone Library,
College of Charleston, Charleston, S.C.

---

[7]Hebrew Orphan Society.

[8]Organized to encourage businesses to abide by the codes established under the National Recovery Act, the Charleston NRA parade on 30 August 1933 was among the largest in the history of the city ("City Drive at 6 p.m.; Big Parade Still Thrills," *Charleston Evening Post*, 31 August 1933).

William F. Ladson, Interview by Kieran W. Taylor

13 May 2009
Charleston, S.C.

William Ladson was born in Georgia and entered the Citadel in 1932. In the following interview excerpt, he reflected on the effect the Great Depression had on his classmates and their ability to attend college.[9]

I believe the entire corps, that first year, was less than eight hundred people; as I recall there was two hundred and twenty-eight in my class, started class. Now that number sticks with me but I know there was less than a thousand students, and I believe it got even lower before it started.[10] I finished my sophomore year. My dad and I just talked about it and we discussed it. He said, "I need you." And I starting so early working with him. My brother, he was more interested in antiques and genealogy and he didn't want any part of sawmill operations, or farming either. I was somebody that Dad could trust and that was familiar enough with it that I was a big help to him. And probably would have ended up there. But I thought enough of my dad and I knew the situation, I knew what he needed and that I was able to fill that gap.

Typed Document. Citadel Oral History Program,
Citadel Archives and Museum, Charleston, S.C.

Anne Marie Gilliard, Interview by Clarissa D. Brown

2 October 2011
Mt. Pleasant, S.C.

A visit to the doctor could be an all-day affair for Anne Marie Gilliard's family and their neighbors in Mt. Pleasant. At the age of ten, she was once tasked with accompanying her

---

[9] William Francis Ladson (1915–2010) was born in Moultrie, Georgia, and graduated from the Citadel (1938). He joined the U.S. Army Reserve in 1940 as part of the Coast Artillery and served stateside in the engineering corps. He served in Korea during the Korean War and retired from the army in 1965 as a colonel. Ladson later worked as an engineer and as city manager of Cocoa Beach, Florida.

[10] According to Citadel records, Ladson's class dropped from 165 members his freshman year to 123 during his sophomore year. Only 83 returned for their third year.

younger sister on the long trip to the Cannon Street Hospital, which served the Charleston-area's African American communities from 1897 to 1959.[11]

My youngest sister, she was a sickly child and she couldn't go out as much. She would swell up like real big sometimes, like a big puffer fish, and she would be swollen all over. My parents would take her to Cannon Street so she could be seen by the black doctors. His name was Dr. [Herbert U.] Seabrook maybe. That was during the Depression before the war. I know that I was about seven or eight. They still charged tolls to cross, and during those times, they would take her in the afternoon and wouldn't make it back home until past dark. One time, I went in place of momma, I was about ten then, and there were so many people crowded around. There were sick people all over, some young, some old. I remember all that day, I didn't go to school. I only went up until about fourth grade anyway.

The hospital was right there on Cannon Street. It was a big brick building, and they set up seating outside for some people, some of the older people. There were people from Daniel Island and Mount Pleasant. There had even been another little girl all the way from Edisto. We all bring lunches and the nurses would be really nice. This young nurse, some brought food for us children. She rounded up all the children, and she brought ham and fruits to us. I remember when we finally made it in the hospital, it was already dusk, but it had a smell in there. It smelled like antiseptic. I know that sounds bad, but I hated them. The hospital was really old and run down on the outside. There had been lots of love on the inside. The people who worked there were very nice and just nice people. There were a lot of black, a lot of nurses back then, a lot. See, you waited a long time to see a doctor. My father knew one of the doctors he sold them fruit cocktails for their parties and functions. My father had the best fruit cocktail drinks. I had been glad to go to the hospital on Cannon Street; Roper been the worst ever. One time, I hurt my arm and I had to go there. Blacks had been seen separate and they'd been awful over there. They had treated poor black folk like lepers. And the doctors been just as bad. They ain't give us a chance to talk or nothing. They were just plain mean. I remember my momma saying she would give one of them a piece of her mind if she wouldn't get killed later.

Typed Document. Citadel Oral History Program,
Citadel Archives and Museum, Charleston, S.C.

---

[11] The Cannon Street Hospital, officially the Hospital and Training School for Nurses, trained African American nurses and provided a hospital where black physicians could see patients. The physicians were barred from seeing patients at other area hospitals.

Virginia Bonnette, Interview by Virginia Ellison and Kieran W. Taylor

15 March 2012
Folly Beach, S.C.

Charleston native Virginia Bonnette grew up downtown and was seven years old when the stock market crashed in October 1929.[12] Her parents struggled to raise four young children. Bonnette's father worked for the city and her mother operated a small dry-cleaning operation from a shed in their yard. In this interview excerpt Bonnette remembered the weekends of her childhood, including Sunday walks to the Battery and watching cowboy movies at the theater.

I always remember us being struggling. The City of Charleston didn't have the money to pay him, and they paid him—they printed—they called it scrip. It is pieces of paper, and I don't know how—I can't tell you how they took that piece of paper and paid the electric bill or the grocery on the corner. I don't remember how it was divided up.[13] But you know, my dad, he was doing his financial thing. He might have paid some of them bills around town with that, I don't know. I don't know.[14]

My family never got a car. Never, never. We would walk on Sundays, for entertainment, we would walk from our house way up there to the Battery, walk all around the Battery, and we would dress up.[15] I mean even when I got to be—in fact, I've got a picture in the room, that we would go use on the invitation to my party, but I had found this picture of me at the Battery, in my—I think it was a gorgeous dress, and high heel shoes. We would walk from there all the way to the Battery in high heel shoes, and back home. That's why we weren't fat. I mean we never had—my parents never had a car, never.

---

[12] Virginia Elizabeth Robinson Bonnette was born in Charleston in 1922. She attended Memminger High School before graduating from Murray Vocational School in 1939. She worked as a cashier at Edwards five-and-ten store and Read Brothers variety store on King Street. She began working as a cellophane wrapper at the American Tobacco Company's cigar factory before taking a job at the Navy Yard. She was one of five women in the pipe shop and trained as a welder. During the war she and her husband moved to housing built for war workers in North Charleston.

[13] The City of Charleston paid employees in scrip, an alternative form of currency, for two years until its finances improved.

[14] Her father, Henry C. Robinson, earned extra money by providing small loans to his employees, which they returned with interest.

[15] The Battery is a defensive seawall that lines the southern tip of the Charleston peninsula.

After school, we would go around—across from Mitchell School was the Mitchell playground, and we would go around to the playground and play basketball and softball, and table tennis, and tennis. And that's what we did for entertainment. And on Saturdays, sometimes, we had a theater called the Palace Theater.[16] It was on King Street, near Spring, and on Saturdays, they had the cowboy pictures, Tom Mix, Tim McCoy, Gene Autry and all like that.[17] And you could buy a ticket—probably was three cents. And if you wanted to stay in that theater all day long and look at that movie over and over, you could. And that's what we did on Saturday, probably about once a month.

Typed Document. Citadel Oral History Program,
Citadel Archives and Museum, Charleston, S.C.

Henry W. Fleming, Interview by Danielle Lightner

17 March 2012
Charleston, S.C.

In this interview conducted just blocks from his childhood home, ninety-year-old Henry Fleming recalled joining the Civilian Conservation Corps to assist his family following the death of his father. Fleming later served in the U.S. Army during World War II and saw combat in the Pacific.

I'm raised from Charleston, South Carolina. I was right where we are at, I was raised, and yeah, this place was a river. I used to swim in here. Right across there, there was a hump. That was the place they call a whirlpool, where the water turn around. There's a lot of fellows drown in there, I remember. All this was the river. Right here. We're sitting in the river, what they used to call the pond.

We didn't have but one street, Spring Street, to go across the old Ashley River Bridge, to go into Ashley. There was a lot of farm area over there. And right back where the stadium is at, all that was the river. I remember back in about—maybe 1940, when that was the dump, and they had a high wind and they had a lot of houses burn down Back of the Green.

That's been—must have been about—must have been around forty, here when that happened because in 1939, I was a boy seventeen years old, and my father passed

---

[16]The Palace Theater at 568 King Street opened as the Dixieland Theater in 1921 and catered to an African American audience. It featured live entertainment and motion pictures. It was remodeled in 1931 and reopened as the Palace. The Palace closed in 1957 and the building was demolished in 1968.

[17]Autry, McCoy, and Mix were among the most popular cowboy actors in the early years of the motion picture industry.

away when I was about twelve years old. The people put me in the organization they called the CC, Civilian Conservation Corps. It was like the army, and I was over there on Bull's Island, and we get all our supply at Fort Moultrie. I remember Fort Moultrie, and I remember the old wooden bridge we used to go to Fort Moultrie, and we went to Bull's Island out there, I guess off the Atlantic Ocean.

So, I didn't like going in the army, but after I got into the army, I realized I had to obey and I listened and I learned how to take care of myself to today. I lived by myself. My wife passed in September last year.[18] And I was living by myself from that day until today. I learned how to take care of myself through that army life, I learned a lot because when you hit them beach head, there ain't nobody there to help you, you got to help yourself.

Typed Document. Citadel Oral History Program, Citadel Archives and Museum, Charleston, S.C.

Herman Stramm, Interview by Luke Yoder

19 March 2012
Charleston, S.C.

Herman Stramm grew up in Charleston. In the following interview he recalled that as the son of a postal worker, his family was largely unaffected by the Great Depression.[19]

I remember the soup lines and stuff like that, the WPA, and the CCC camp that a lot of people went into.[20] They built roads, campgrounds and stuff like that. But you know, it didn't affect me really. My dad had a job, thank God. He worked at the post office. Only job he ever had—forty-four years. Retired and lived six months. That ain't for me.

---

[18]Fleming refers to his wife of sixty-nine years, Dorothy Buckingham Fleming.

[19]In the early 1930s both the Hoover and Roosevelt administrations cut wages for postal workers and instituted furloughs to balance the federal budget. Herman Stramm was born in Charleston in 1927 and served in the navy during World War II. He attended signalman school prior to being assigned to the USS *Dale* at Pearl Harbor. Returning to Charleston after the war, he attended the Citadel and worked for United States Post Office and the Atlanta airport before retiring in 1990.

[20]Various local church and civic groups undertook efforts to feed poor people during the 1930s. At one soup kitchen in Summerville, black farmers reportedly "came for miles with their small cans or jars and gratefully received their half pint of soup" (see "Needy Get Soup at Summerville," *Charleston Evening Post,* 12 January 1933).

I lived on Darlington Avenue until I was nine years old, as I remember. And Darlington Avenue wasn't even paved. We had sidewalks, but the street wasn't paved—dirt streets. But you know, that's the only life I knew. I was born and raised in Charleston. I think I left Charleston one time before I went in the service. I saw the Great Lakes when we had—on the troop train, we had to get off, and we had four or five hours and they marched us. And the only lakes I was familiar with was a few around here. And I thought, "My God, you can't even see across it."

Typed Document. Citadel Oral History Program,
Citadel Archives and Museum, Charleston, S.C.

Index

A. E. Holleman Stevedoring Company, xxvi
African Americans, xii, 1, 36–37, 69, 72, 73, 89, 90, 91, 128, 142, 143, 162; activism, xxiii, xxvi, xxxiii, xxxvi, 36–37, 58; education, xxvii, xxxiv, 48, 49; fictional portrayals, 52–58, 142; labor market, xx, xxii, xxvi, xxx, xxxiii, 39, 44, 45, 47, 48, 155; medical care, 3, 159; neighborhoods, xv, 159; performance/performers, 52, 56, 133, 161; political disenfranchisement, xxxi, xxxiii; poverty, xiv, xx, xxi, 52, 162; religion, 125; segregation, xx, xxxii–xxxiii, 33, 34, 35, 119, 143, 155; superstitions, 68; wages, xxii, xxvi, xxx–xxxi, xxxvii, 44, 45, 47; Young Women's Christian Association, 33, 34, 35. *See also* Federal Council of Negro Affairs
Aldredge, Robert C., 135
Alston, Caroline Simonton, 43, 45, 46
American Missionary Association, 48, 49
American Tobacco Company, xxv, 160
Anderson Lumber Company, 99
Anglicans, 65
aristocracy, xxxi, 44, 69
Atlantic Coast Line Railroad, 7
Autry, Gene, 161
Avery Institute, xxvii, 48–49
Azalea Festival, xv, xvii, xxxiv

Baker, Rae, 157
Ball, William Watts, xxxi, 119–20
bank failures, xiv, 33
Bankhead Cotton Control Act (1934), 59
Banov, Leon, 5, 147–50
Baptists, xxiii, 65
Barbot, Joseph C., 33

Baruch, Bernard, xvi, xxx
baseball, 142, 143, 144
Battery, 68, 70, 71, 72, 73, 74, 77, 82, 83, 127, 160
Beauregard, Pierre Gustave Toutant, 71, 81
Berkman, Herman, 11
Berlin, Henry, 154
Berlin, Shera Lee Ellison, 156, 157
boll weevil, xix
Bond, W. C., xxi
Bonnet, Stede, 83
Bonnette, Virginia Elizabeth Robinson, xxiv, 160, 161
Bonus Army, xiv, xix
Bowles, Eva D., 34, 35
Bowman, William McKinley, xxiii, 36–37
Bragg, Laura, 1, 2, 3
Branford, William, 82
Briggs v. Elliot (1952), 29, 90
Brown v. Board of Education (1954), 29
Brown, Clarissa D., 158
Brown, Henry, xxi
Brown, Isaac, 89, 90, 91, 92–98, 101, 105–11, 113–14
Bull, William, 82
Bull's Island, 162
Burbage, C. Roessler, 11
Butler, Jessie Allison, 125, 126, 129
Byrnes, James F.: relationship with Burnet Maybank, xxix, 13, 147; support for Roosevelt, xxxviii, 61, 137; as US Senator, xvi, xxxiv, 23; as US Supreme Court justice, xviii, 147

C. M. Guest and Son., xvii
Calhoun, John C., 78, 122

Campbell, William, 82
Cannon Street Hospital, 159
Carner, Thomas Joseph, xiii
Carroll, Seymour, 37, 38
Catholics, xxv, 14, 78, 82
Century Wood Preserving, xvi
Chandler, Genevieve Willcox, 140, 141, 142
Charles II, 64
Charleston Bagging Company, xxvi
Charleston City Council, xiv, xxix, 22, 29–30, 32
Charleston Community Chest, xxi
Charleston County Tuberculosis Association, xxvii, 3–7
Charleston Florists Association, xxv
Charleston Food Administration, 125
Charleston Museum, 1, 2, 79
Charleston Navy Yard, xiii, xv, xiv, xvi, xvii, 60, 148–49; economic effects of, xix–xx, 17–18, 147; and the New Deal, xxix, xxxiii–xxxiv
Charleston Oil Company, 6
Charleston Orphan Home, 79
Charleston Rebels, 142, 143, 144
Chiquola Mill (Honea Path), xv
cholera, 79
Circular Congregational Church, 80
Citadel, the, xiii, xvi, 79; Chinese transfer students, 1, 2, 3; and the New Deal, xvii, xxii–xxiii, xxix, 121; Roosevelt speech, 59, 60–61
City of Charleston, xxix, 155; employment, xiv, 22, 25–26, 29–32; financial woes, xiv, 15, 17, 18–19, 20–21, 23, 25, 26, 160; tax collection, xiv, xv, xxix, 19–20, 21, 25–26, 31; public health, 3–7, 147–50; Social Welfare Bureau, 30, 32
Civil War, xxi, xxii, 68, 87, 126
Civil Works Administration (CWA), xv, 41–46, 70
Civil Works Service (CWS), 46
Civilian Conservation Corps, xxx, xxxiv, 155, 161, 162
Clark, Septima Poinsette, 129
Clemson College, 120
Clinton, Henry, 66

College of Charleston, xxix, 21, 22, 47, 79, 154
colonial architecture, 66, 69, 70–71, 77, 81
Colonial Dames, 78
Columbus Red Birds, 142, 144
Community Facilities Bill, 149
Condon's department store, xxv
Confederate Museum, 78
Connelley, Alexander Chambliss, 32
conservatism, xxviii, xxix, xxxi, xxxiii, 61, 125
Cooper, Anthony Ashley, 64
Cornwallis, Charles, 66
Cosgrove, John I., 15, 16
cotton industry, xvi, xix, 17–18, 24, 44, 59, 67–68, 69, 77, 88. *See also* Bankhead Cotton Control Act (1934)
Cox, Benjamin F., 48
Cox, Jeannette Keeble, 48
Curry, Elijah Joseph, xxxiii, 58–59
Cypress Gardens, 71

Damewood, Evelyn, 7
Daniel, Thomas "Dick," xxii, 87
Davies, Frederick G., 4
Davis, Jefferson, 44
Defense Housing and Community Facilities and Services Act. *See* Lanham Act
Democratic Party, xiii, xiv, xxviii, xxix, xxxiii, 157
DeVeaux, John P., xiv
Dewitt, William J., 88
Disaster Loan Corporation, 137
Dock Street Theatre, xv, xvi, 66, 131
Driggers, J. C., xix
Dumas, Abe, 154, 155

Earhart, Amelia, xiv
earthquakes, 69, 81
Ellison, Louise Rhodes, 4
Ellison, Virginia, 160
Ellison's Dress Shop, 156
Ellison's Dry Goods, 156
Emancipation Day, xiii
Emanuel African Methodist Episcopal Church, xxi, 122, 124
Escoffier, Robert W., 10

evangelism, xv
Evans, Walker, 85, 86
exhibitionism, 53

Farm Security Administration (FSA), 85, 86, 138
farms/farmers, xix, 24, 26, 72, 85, 161; activism, xxii, xxvii, xxx, xxxiii; labor issues, 42, 43, 58; overproduction problems, 17, 18. *See also* Farm Security Administration
Farquhar, George, 131, 132
Federal Council of Negro Affairs, 37
Federal Emergency Relief Administration (FERA), xv, 32, 41
Federal Writers' Project, xxiii, 121–22, 125, 140
Feinberg, Harriet, 157
fertilizer industry, 18, 21, 72
Fields, Mamie Elizabeth Garvin, 34
Figg, Robert M., 90
fires, xvii, 68, 80–81
First Presbyterian Church, 82, 84
Fleming, Dorothy Buckingham, 162
Fleming, Henry W., 161, 162
Floyd, Minnie Lou Ingram, 141, 142
folklorists, xxii, 140
Footlight Players, 131, 132
Fort Moultrie, xxxiii, xxxiv, 18, 72, 74, 162
Fort Sumter, xxxiv, 68, 72
Francis Marion Hotel, xv, 72, 79, 135
Fuller, Edward N., xxiii, 122, 125, 126–27, 128
Fuller, Mary Ann Mikell, 123, 126
Fuller, William, 123

Garner, John Nance, xxxiv
Geer, Andrew Jackson, 15, 32
General Obligation Bonds, 121
Georgian architecture, 66, 69, 70, 71, 75, 76, 77, 81
Gershwin, George, xv, 52, 53, 54, 55, 56, 57
Gershwin, Ira, 55, 56
Gibbes Art Gallery, xvi, 80
Gilbreth, Frank B., xxxiv
Gilliard, Anne Marie, 158, 159
Goose Creek Church, 71
Gothic architecture, 77, 80, 83

Grace, John P., xvii, xxix, xxxi, 14, 15–17
Green, John Mercier, 148
Greene, Nathanael, 66
Grice, Edmund P., Jr., 32, 43, 44, 45
Gulf Refining Company, xiv
Gullah culture, 52, 56

Halsey, Eleanor Rose Loeb, 3–4, 8
Hamill, Jimmy, xv
Hamilton, Susan Calder, xxiii, 121–22, 123, 125–26, 129–30
Hamilton, Zara Gailliard, 34
Hampton, Wade, 78
Healy, John Joseph, 10, 11, 12, 13
Henderson, Hugh, 87
Hendrix, Leroy, 148
Heyward, Dorothy, 53
Heyward, DuBose, xv, 52–53, 57, 67, 76, 133
Hibernian Hall, 15, 77, 81
Hickok, Lorena Alice, 41, 43, 46
Hilton, Archie Smith, 30
Holiday House, 6
Holmes, Annie, 142
Holmes, Joseph, xxii
Hoover, Herbert, xiii, xiv, xix, xx, 36, 87, 162
Hopkins, Harry L., xv, xxviii, 13, 41–42, 43, 131, 137
Hoppmann, William "Walter," 30
House, Eva C., 2
Hu, Chia-Mei, 3
Huger, Alfred, 5
Huggin, Perry McKown, 4
Huguenots, 64, 65, 69, 77
Huntington, Anna Hyatt, 141
Huntington, Archer Milton, 141
Hurd, Charles W., 59, 60, 62
hurricanes, xvii, 56, 65, 72

International Longshoremen's Association (Local 1422), xxvi, 47
Irby, John Laurens McFarlane, 39–41, 119, 120, 121
Iron Workers Guild, 78
Iusti, J. A. W., 81

James II, 65
Jenkins, Charles W., 12
Jenkins, Daniel J., xvi
Jews, xxvii, 47, 69, 73, 78, 153–57
Johnson, Lyndon B., xxxiv
Johnston, A. R., xiv
Johnston, Olin D., 60, 61
Jones, Allen, Jr., xxii, 86–89
Jones, Ella Louise Smyrl, 33
Jones, J. Roy, 17
Jordan, Frederick, 7, 8

Kerrison, Charles, 153
Kerrison, Edwin L., 153
Kerrison's Department Store, 153, 154
Keyserling, Leon, xxx
Knox, Lillie Cogsdell, 141, 142
Knox, Zackie, 142
Koenig, Herman Charles, 63, 73

labor: activism, xxvi–xxvii, xxvi, 47; shortages, 41, 42, 46; wages, xx, xxv, 22, 39, 40, 41, 42, 44, 51, 58, 162. *See also* African Americans: wages; City of Charleston: pay cuts, 22
Ladson, Augustus, 121, 122, 125
Ladson, William Francis, 158
LaMotte, Bobby, 143
Lange, Dorothea, 86
Lanham Act (1940), 149
Laurens, Ray, 9
Lee, Betty Andrews, 151
Legare, William S., 23
Lewis, David Sloan, 31
Lightner, Danielle, 161
Limehouse, O. B., xiv
Lincoln, Abraham, 125
Locke, John, 64
Lockwood, Henry W., xvii, 17, 32, 101, 143
Logan, William Turner, 16
Lomax, John Avery, 122, 140, 141, 142
Lomax, Ruby, 140, 141, 142
Long, John Charles, 9, 10, 11, 13, 15, 16
Losse, J. Ernest, 135
Lovecraft, H. P., xxiv, 63–85
lynching, xiii, xxiii, xxxii, 37

M. Dumas and Sons, 154, 155
Mack, Albertha Rivers, 91
Mack, John Henry, 117
Magnolia Plantation, 71
Mamoulian, Rouben, 53, 54, 57
Manigault, Gabriel, 69, 82
Mann, Marvin M., 90
Marion, Francis, 66
Marshall, George C., xxv
Marshall, Oliver K., 89
May, A. J., xxxiv
Maybank & Company, 24
Maybank, Burnet Rhett: as Charleston mayor, xiii, xiv, xxviii, xxix–xxxi, xxxiii, xxxiv, 13–14, 15, 16, 19, 24, 39–40, 43, 44, 45, 119, 131, 137; relationship with James F. Byrnes, xxix, 13, 147; as SC governor, xvii, 13; as US Senator, xviii, 13, 147–48; support for Roosevelt, xxxviii, 61, 137
Maybank, Elizabeth deRosset Myers, 150, 151
Maybank, Joseph, 150
Mazo, Norma, 47
Mazyck, Arthur, 74
McCoy, Tim, 161
McDonald, Roberta Chauncey Blackburn, 5, 7
McDonald, William, 126
McGowan, Alonzo Russell, 15, 16
McGowan, William Oliver, Sr., 31
McLean, Edward Beale, 151
McLean, Evalyn Walsh, 151
McMillan, Thomas S., xiii
McNeill, Frank T., 10, 11, 12, 13
Memminger School, 30
Mendelson, Jean Ann, 157
Middleton Plantation, 71
Middleton, Francis "String," 93–96, 104–9, 113, 115–16
Middleton, Henry, 93
Miller, Thomas E., xvii
Miller, William C., 2
Mills, Robert, 69, 75, 81
Mix, Tom, 161
Moeller, Philip, 54
Montague Lumber Company, 4

Montgomery, Mabel, 125, 142
Moore, Benjamin Allston, 90, 91, 115
Moore, James, 65
Morton, James Ferdinand, Jr., 73
Moton, Robert R., 37, 38
Moultrie, William, 66
Murray, Chalmers S., 125

National Recovery Administration, xv, xxv
Norman, A. W. "Rock," 88

O'Neill, Eugene, 55
Old Slave Market, 77
Ortmann, Christian H., 12
Osceola, 72

Palace Theater, xxiv, 161
Parran, Thomas, 147, 148
patriotism, 87
pellagra, xxii
People's State Bank, xiv
Pete (swan), xv
Peterkin, Julia Mood, 142
Pickens, Andrew, 66
Pinckney, Lawrence M., xiii, xxix, 14
Pinehaven, 3, 5, 6, 7
Pitt, William, 71
plantations, xxx, xxxiv, 43, 66, 70, 71, 82, 88, 126
Planters Hotel, xv
Poe, Edgar Allan, 72, 77
Poinsette, Victoria, 129
Porgy and Bess, xv, 52–58, 76, 154
Port Utilities Commission, 19, 20, 23, 24, 25
Poulnot, Joseph M., 101
Prentiss, Arthur David, xxiii, 51
Presbyterians, 65
Prohibition, xiii, xiv, 9–11, 13, 22–23
prostitution, 9, 10, 13, 55, 149
Prystowsky, Joyce, 157
public schools, xxxiii, xxxiv, 7, 21, 22, 78, 90, 119, 121, 147
Public Works Administration, xv, 39, 41, 119, 120

Quakers, 65, 80

racism. *See* African Americans: segregation; white supremacy
Raisin, Jacob S., xxvii
Rankin, Watson Smith, 7
Ravenel, Harriott Horry, 74
Rayburn, Sam, xxxiv
Razor, Charles T., 88
Reconstruction, 68
Renken, Walter Albert, Sr., 31
Rhett, Blanche Salley, 5
Rhett, William, 65, 75, 78, 82, 83
Rhodes, Cecil "Dusty," 143, 145
rice industry, 65, 67, 69
Richardson, Emma B., 2
Richmond, Doc, 144, 145
Rivers, Allen, 91
Rivers, Benjamin J., xvi, xxxi–xxxii, 89–116
Rivers, Darkus, 91
Rivers, Martha, 103
Riviera theater, xvii
Robinson, Emmett E., 132
Robinson, Henry C., 160
Robinson, Ted, 93
Roosevelt, Eleanor, xvi, 41, 43
Roosevelt, Franklin D., xiv, xvi, xix, xxi, xxii, xxiii, 36, 41, 137, 147, 162; and African Americans, 36–37, 58–59, 155; criticism of, xxx, xxxii, 14, 58, 61, 87; New Deal policies, xxv, xxvii, xxxiii, 14, 50, 59–60; support for, xxviii, xxxiv, 44–45, 60; World War II, xviii, 151
Roper Hospital, 4, 21, 159
Rosengarten, Dale, 153, 156
Rothstein, Arthur, 86
Russell, Richard B., xxxiv

Sack, John W., 12
St. Andrew's Hall, 68, 81
St. Andrew's Society, 81
St. Andrews' Parish Church, 71
St. Cecelia Society, 67, 75
St. John the Divine, 81
St. John's Lutheran Church, 80
St. Mary's Catholic Church, 78
St. Michael's Episcopal Church, 21, 66, 69, 70, 71, 72, 73, 76, 77, 81

St. Paul's Episcopal Church, 79
St. Philip's Episcopal Church, 21, 70, 73, 77, 80
Sales, William, 64
Santee Cooper Project, xxx, 120
Savage, Thomas, 74
Scharloock, Theodore M., 101
Schiffley, William Archibald, 49
Schillinger, Joseph Moiseyevich, 54
Seabrook, Herbert U., 159
Second Presbyterian Church, 79
Shriver, William Henry "Mr. Live Oaks," 11
Simmons, Annie, 96, 108
Simmons, Ethel, 93, 105
Simmons, Lymus "Spark," 93, 94, 96, 106, 108, 113, 115
Simmons, Viola, 95, 104, 108, 111
Sims, Nat, 89
slavery, xxi, xxii, xxiii–xxvi, xxx, xxxiii, 14, 43, 58, 64, 68, 77, 82, 87–88, 121–30, 141
Smallens, Alexander, 57
smallpox, 79
Smith, Ellison D. "Cotton Ed," xxxiv, 23, 61
Smith, Herman "Red," 89
Smith, Lottie, xxi
Smith, Susan, 7
Smith, William Atmar, 6
Smyrl, Ella Louise, 33, 35, 36
Social Security Act (1935), xxx, xxxiii, 50, 58
Society for the Preservation of Spirituals, 133
South Carolina Power Company, xxv
South Carolina State Board of Health, 149
South Carolina State Hospital, 121
South Carolina v. Benjamin Rivers, 89–117
State of South Carolina v. Ray Laurens, 9–13
Southern Railway, xiv
Spartanburg Spartans, 142, 143
Star Painting Company, 8
Stehmeyer, Diedrich, 30
Steinert, Alexander, 57
Stewart, Mack, 144, 145
Stine, Gordan Bernard, 153, 154
Stoney, Thomas P., xiii, xvi, xxxi, 14, 16, 21
Stramm, Hermann, 162, 163
Street Bonds, 20

subsistence farming, xxii
Summerall, Charles Pelot, xxv, 59, 60, 61
Sumter, Thomas, 66

Taylor, Kieran W., 160
Texas Oil Company, 6
Thompson, Lyle, 144
Thornhill, Theodore Wilbur, 6
Timrod, Henry, 68, 71
tornadoes, xxvi, xxix, 47, 135
tourism, xxxiv, 16, 17, 18, 42, 72, 141
Tradd, Robert, 76
truck farming, 43, 45, 46
Truman, Harry S., xxxiv, 61
Tuxbury Lumber Co., 4
typhoid, 147, 148

Ugly Club, 75, 76
unemployment, xxxiii–xxxiv, 25–26, 32, 42, 48; protests, xiv, xv; relief, xiv, xv, xx, xxi, xxvi, xxx, 41, 50, 60, 121. *See also* Social Security Act
Unitarian Church, 80
United Fruit Company, 47
United Workingmen's Society, xxvi
University of South Carolina, 121

venereal disease, 147, 149
Vesey, Denmark, 68, 124
Von Dohlen, James Albert, 31, 32
von Kolnitz, Alfred H., 143

Waite, Henry Matson, 41
Wall Street crash (1929), xiii, xix
Wallace, Henry, 151
Wallace, Ilo Brown, 151
Walsh, Emmet M., xxv
Wansley, Purse A., xvi, xxxi–xxxii, 12, 13, 89, 90, 105, 116
Waring, J. Waties, xviii, 29
Washington, George, 75, 76
Washington, William, 74
Water Commission, 25
Watts, Richard C., 13
WCSC, xiii, 8, 14
Webster, Jean, 49

West Point Mills, 24
West Virginia Pulp and Paper, xvi
Whaley, Nell, 7
white supremacy, xxxi, xxxii–xxxiii, 119
White, Robert G., 19, 20
Wiggins, Mary, 94
Williams, Roy, 143
Willis, Eola, 84
Wilson, Isaac Ripon, Sr., 29, 30, 32
Wilson, Miriam Belhaugee, 64, 71
Wilson, Woodrow, xxviii, 60
Winn, Cordella Arthur, 33, 34, 35
Wister, Owen, 81
Wolcott, Marion Post, 86, 138, 139
Wolfe, Thomas, 88
Wong, Fong Lee, 1, 2, 3
Wood, Johnny, xv
Woosley, Ola M., 7
Works Progress Administration, xvi, xvii, xxiv, xxviii, 32, 39, 41, 131, 135, 140
World War II, xvii, xviii, 1
WTMA, xvii
Wyndham, Edward P., 10, 11

yellow fever, 65, 74
Yoder, Luke, 162
Young Men's Christian Association (YMCA), 72
Young Women's Christian Association (YWCA), xxvii, 33, 35

www.ingramcontent.com/pod-product-compliance
Lightning Source LLC
Chambersburg PA
CBHW070358100426
42812CB00005B/1549